HARDPRESS.NET
HOME OF HARD-TO-FIND BOOKS

Notes of Eight Year's Travels and Residence in Europe, With His North American Indian Collection
by George Catlin

Address:
HardPress
8345 NW 66TH ST #2561
MIAMI FL 33166-2626
USA
Email: info@hardpress.net

Notes of eight year's travels and residence in Europe, with his ...

George Catlin

CATLIN'S NOTES

OF

EIGHT YEARS' TRAVELS AND RESIDENCE IN EUROPE,

WITH HIS

NORTH AMERICAN INDIAN COLLECTION.

VOLUME I.

CATLIN'S NOTES

OF

EIGHT YEARS' TRAVELS AND RESIDENCE

In Europe,

WITH HIS

NORTH AMERICAN INDIAN COLLECTION:

WITH ANECDOTES AND INCIDENTS OF THE TRAVELS AND ADVENTURES OF THREE
DIFFERENT PARTIES OF AMERICAN INDIANS WHOM HE INTRODUCED
TO THE COURTS OF

ENGLAND, FRANCE AND BELGIUM.

IN TWO VOLUMES OCTAVO.

VOL. I.

WITH NUMEROUS ILLUSTRATIONS.

NEW-YORK:
BURGESS, STRINGER & CO., 222 BROADWAY.
1848.

PREFACE.

THE reader of this book, being supposed to have read my former work, in two volumes, and to have got some account from them, of the eight years of my life spent amongst the wild Indians of the "*Far West*," in the forests of America, knows enough of me by this time to begin familiarly upon the subject before us, and to accompany me through a brief summary of the scenes of eight years spent amidst the civilization and refinements of the "*Far East.*" After having made an exhibition of my Indian Collection for a short time, in the cities of New York, Boston, and Philadelphia, in the United States, I crossed the Atlantic with it—not with the fear of losing my scalp, which I sometimes entertained when entering the Indian wilderness—and entirely without the expectation of meeting with excitements or novelties enough to induce me to commit the sin of writing another book; and the thought of doing it would never have entered my head, had not another of those untoward accidents, which have directed nearly all the important moves of my life, placed in my possession the materials for the following pages, which I have thought too curious to be withheld from the world.

After I had been more than four years in England, making an exhibition of my collection, and endeavouring, by my lectures in various parts of the kingdom, to inform the English people of the true character and condition of the North American Indians, and to awaken a proper sympathy for them, three different parties of Indians made their appearance, at different dates, in England, for the purpose of exhibiting themselves and their native modes to the enlightened world, their conductors and themselves stimulated by the hope of gain by their exertions.

These parties successively, on their arrival, (knowing my history and views, which I had made known to most of the American tribes,) repaired to my Indian Collection, in which they felt themselves at home, surrounded as they were by the portraits of their own chiefs and braves, and those of their enemies, whom they easily recognised upon the walls. They at once chose the middle of my Exhibition Hall as the appropriate place for their operations, and myself as the expounder of their mysteries and amusements ; and, the public seeming so well pleased with the fitness of these mutual illustrations, I undertook the management of their exhibitions, and conducted the three different parties through the countries and scenes described in the following pages.

In justice to *me*, it should here be known to the reader, that I did not bring either of these parties to Europe ; but, meeting them in the country, where they had come avowedly for the purpose of making money, (an enterprise as lawful and as unobjectionable, for aught that I can see, at least, as that of an actor upon the boards of a foreign stage,) I considered my countenance and aid as calculated to promote their views; and I therefore justified myself in the undertaking, as some return to them for the hospitality and kindness I had received at the hands of the various tribes of Indians I had visited in the wildernesses of America.

In putting forth these notes, I sincerely hope that I may give no offence to any one, by endeavouring to afford amusement to the reader, and to impart useful instruction to those who are curious to learn the true character of the Indians, from a literal description of their interviews with the fashionable world, and their views and opinions of the modes of civilized life.

These scenes have afforded me the most happy opportunity of seeing the *rest* of Indian character (after a residence of eight years amongst them in their native countries), and of enabling me to give to the world what I was not able to do in my former work, for the want of an opportunity of witnessing the effects which the exhibition of all the ingenious works of civilized art, and the free intercourse and exchange of opinions with the most refined and enlightened society, would have upon their untutored minds. The reader will therefore see, that I am offering this as *another Indian book*, and intending it mostly for those who have read my former work, and who, I believe, will admit, that in it I have advanced much further towards the completion of a full delineation of their native character.

I shall doubtless be pardoned for the unavoidable

want of system and arrangement that sometimes appears in minuting down the incidents of these interviews—for recording many of the most trivial opinions and criticisms of the Indians upon civilized modes, and also the odd and amusing (as well as grave) notions of the civilized world, upon Indian manners and appearance, which have got into my note-book, and which I consider it would be a pity to withhold.

I have occasionally stepped a little out of the way, also, to advance my own opinion upon passing scenes and events; drawing occasional deductions, by contrasting savage with civilized life (the modes of the "Far West" with those of the "Far East"); and, as what I have written, I offer as matter of history, without intending to injure any one, I do not see why I should ask pardon for any possible offence that may be given to the reader, who can only be offended by imagining what never was meant.

During the series of lectures which I had been giving in various parts of England, and in my own country, wherein I had been contending for the moral and religious elevation of the Indian character, many of my hearers have believed that I had probably been led to over-estimate it, from the fact that I had beheld it in the wilderness, where there was nothing better to contrast it with. But I venture to say, that hundreds and thousands who read this book, and who became familiar with these wild people whilst in the enlightened world, and in the centre of fashion, where white man was shaking the poor Indian by the hand, and watching for his embarrassment while he was drawing scintillations from him, as the flint draws fire from the steel, will agree with me that the North American Indian rises highest in the estimation of his fellow-men, when he is by the side of those who have the advantage of him by their education, and nothing else.

Contemplated or seen, roaming in his native wilds, with his rude weapons, lurking after game or his enemy, he is looked upon by most of the world as a sort of wild beast; but when, with all his rudeness and wildness, he stands amongst his fellow-men to be scanned in the brilliant blaze of the Levée into which he has been suddenly thrown, the dignified, the undaunted (and even courteous) gentleman, he there gains his strongest admirers, and the most fastidious are willing to assign him a high place in the scale of human beings.

Into many such positions were these three parties of the denizens of the American forest thrown, during their visits to the capitals and provincial towns of England, Scotland, Ireland, France, and Belgium; and as I was by their side, their interpreter, at the hospitable boards, the Soirées and Levées to which they were invited by the gentry, the nobility, and crowned heads of the three kingdoms, I consider it due to them, and no injustice to the world, to record the scenes and anecdotes I have witnessed in those hospitable and friendly efforts of enlightened and religious people, to elicit the true native feelings of, and to commune with, their benighted fellow-men.

THE AUTHOR.

CONTENTS OF VOL. I.

CHAPTER VIII.

CHAPTER IX.

CHAPTER X.

CHAPTER XI.

CHAPTER XV.

CHAPTER XVI.

APPENDIX.

APPENDIX—A.

APPENDIX—B.

CATLIN'S NOTES IN EUROPE,

&c.   *&c.*

CHAPTER I.

The Author embarks at New York, with his Indian Collection, and cage
 with two grizly Bears, for England, in the fall of 1839—Packet-ship
 Roscius, Captain Collins—Gale in the middle of the ocean—A ship
 dismasted and in distress—The Captain and twenty-eight men taken off
 and saved—The shipwrecked Captain and his faithful dog—" My man
 Daniel "—Sailor's nose taken off by grizly bear—Dr. Madden—Terrible
 gale—Sea-sickness of the grizly bears—Alarm on deck—" Bears out of
 their cage"—Passengers rush below and close the hatches—A *supposed*
 Bear enters the cabin !—Great excitement—The explanation—The gale
 subsides—Amusing mistake—The Author in the steerage—Two eccentric characters—Arrival in Liverpool.

In the fall of the year 1839 I embarked at New York on
board of the packet-ship Roscius, Captain Collins, for
Liverpool, with my Indian collection; having received a
very friendly letter of advice from the Hon. C. A. Murray,
master of Her Majesty's household, who had formerly been
a fellow-traveller with me on the Mississippi and other rivers
in America; and who, on his return to London, had kindly
made a conditional arrangement for my collection in the
Egyptian Hall, in Piccadilly.

Mr. George Adlard, an Englishman, residing in the city
of New York, had also exerted a friendly influence for me
in procuring an order from the Lords of Her Majesty's
Treasury for passing my collection into the kingdom free
from the customary duties; and under these auspices I
was launched upon the wide ocean, with eight tons freight,
consisting of 600 portraits and other paintings which I had

made in my sojourn of eight years in the prairies and Rocky Mountains of America—several thousands of Indian articles, costumes, weapons, &c., with all of which I intended to convey to the English people an accurate account of the appearance and condition of the North American tribes of Indians.*

On board also, as a part of my heavy collection, and as a further illustration of the rude inhabitants of the "*Far West*," I had, in a huge iron cage, two *grizly bears*, from the Rocky Mountains; forming not only the heaviest and most awkward part of my freight, but altogether the most troublesome, as will be seen hereafter.

The wind was kind to us, and soon drove us across the Atlantic, without more than an incident or two worth recording, which I had minuted down as follows:—About the middle of the ocean, and in the midst of a four or five days' heavy gale, we came suddenly upon a ship, partly dismasted, with signals of distress flying, and water-logged, rolling about at the mercy of the merciless waves. We rounded-to with great danger to our own craft, and, during the early part of the night, succeeded, with much difficulty, in taking off the captain and crew of twenty-eight men, just before she went down. This was a common occurrence, however, and needs no further notice, other than of a feature or two which struck me as new. When the poor, jaded, and water-soaked fellows were all safely landed on the deck of our vessel, they laid down upon their faces and devoutly thanked God for their deliverance; and last of all that was lifted on board from their jolly-boat was their keg of rum, the only thing which they had brought with them when they deserted the ship. "This," good Captain Collins said, "you will not want now, my boys," and he cast it into the sea.

Captain James, a bland and good-natured Scotsman,

---

* If the reader has forgotten to read the Preface, it will take him but a moment to run his eye over it, and by turning back to it he will find it an useful key to what follows.—*Author*.

commander of the Scotia, the unfortunate vessel, was invited by Captain Collins to the cabin of the Roscius, and into his state-room, where he was soon put into a suit of dry and warm clothes, and afterwards seated at the table; where, suddenly, a sullen resistance to food, and contemplative tears rolling over his cheeks, showed his rough shell to contain a heart that was worthy of the fondest affections of a dear wife and sweet little ones—none of which was he blessed with, if I recollect aright. But when his grief found utterance, he exclaimed, " My God! I have left my poor dog tied to the mast of my old craft. There he is, poor fellow! When we took to the jolly-boat I never thought of my poor Pompey!"

The briny tears seemed to burn this veteran's hardened features as they ran over his cheeks; and hunger and fatigue, and all gave way to them and grief, until sleep had dried them up, and taken the edge from his anguished mind.

The next morning, his recital of the affectionate deeds of the life of his faithful dog, " who had made eighteen voyages across the Atlantic with him, and who would always indicate land a-head by his nose sooner than the sailors could discern it from the mast-head—whom he had, in kindness, lashed to the mast for his safety, and in carelessness abandoned to his unavoidable fate," brought tears of pity in my own eyes. Poor man! he often wept for his faithful dog—and I as often wept for him, on our way from the middle of the ocean to Liverpool. We were, at this time, still in the midst of the terrible gale, which was increasing in its fury, and had already become quite too much for the tastes and the stomachs of the *grizlies*— a few words more of whom must go into this chapter.

These two awkward voyageurs from the base of the Rocky Mountains, which I had reared from cubs, and fed for more than four years—for whose roughness in clawing and " chawing" I had paid for half a dozen cages which they had demolished and escaped from, and the prices of as many dogs " used up" in retaking them, had now grown to the enormous size of eight or ten hundred pounds each; requiring a cage of iron so large that it could not be packed amongst the ship's cargo below, but must needs occupy a considerable space on the deck, in the form and size somewhat of a small house.

The front of this cage was formed of huge iron bars, kindly indulging the bruins to amuse themselves with a peep at what was progressing on deck, whilst it afforded the sailors and steerage passengers the amusement of looking and commenting upon the physiognomy and manœuvres of these rude specimens from the wilderness of America. This huge cage, with its inmates, had ridden into and partly through the gale with us, when the bears became subjects of more violent interest and excitement than we had as yet anticipated or could have wished. What had taken (and was taking) place amongst the sick and frightened group of passengers during this roaring, whistling, thrashing, and dashing gale, was common-place, and has been a thousand times described; but the sea-sickness, and rage, and fury of these two grizly denizens of the deep ravines and rocky crags of the Rocky Mountains, were subjects as fresh as they were frightful and appalling to the terrified crew and passengers who were about them, and therefore deserve a passing comment.

The immediate guardian of these animals was a faithful man by the name of Daniel Kavanagh, who had for several years been in my employment as curator of my collection, and designed to accompany me in my tour through England. This man has occupied a conspicuous place in my affairs in Europe, and much will be said of him in the following pages, and the familiar and brief cognomen of " Daniel " or " Dan " applied to him. On embarking with this man and his troublesome pets at New York, I had fully explained to Captain Collins their ferocious, and deceitful, and intractable nature, who had consequently issued his orders to all of his crew and to the steerage passengers not to venture within their reach, or to trifle with them. Notwithstanding all this precaution, curiosity, that beautiful trait of human nature, which often becomes irresistible in long voyages, and able to turn the claws of the Devil himself into the soft and tapering fingers of a Venus or a Daphne, got the better of the idle hours of the sailors, who were amusing themselves and the passengers, in front of the iron bars, by believing that they were wearing off by a sort of charm the rough asperities of their grizly and grim passengers by shaking their paws, and squaring and fending off the awkward sweeps occasionally made at them by the huge paw of the *she* bear, which she could effectually make by lying down and running her right arm quite out between the iron bars. On one of these (now grown to be amusing) occasions, one of the sailors was "squared off" before the cage, inviting her grizly majesty to a sort of set-to, when she (seemingly aware of the nature of the challenge) gradually extended her arm and her huge paw a little and a little further out of her cage, with her eyes capriciously closed until it was out to its fullest extent, when she made a side-lick at his head, and an exceedingly awkward one for the sailor to parry. It was lucky for him, poor fellow, that he partly dodged it; though as her paw passed in front of his face, one of her claws carried away entirely his nose, leaving it fallen down and hanging over his mouth, suspended merely by a small piece of skin or gristle, by which alone he could claim it.

Here was a sudden check to the familiarity with the bears; the results of which were, a renewal of the orders of non-intercourse from Captain Collins, and a marked coolness between the sailors and steerage passengers and the grizlies during the remainder of the voyage.

The sailor was committed to the care of Dr. Madden, in the cabin, the distinguished traveller in Africa and the West Indies, and now one of our esteemed fellow-passengers, who skilfully replaced and arranged his nose with stitches and splints, and attended to it during the voyage. The poor fellow continued to swear vengeance on the bears when they should reach the land; but I believe that when they were landed in Liverpool, his nose was not sufficiently secure to favour his design.   This unlucky affair had happened some days previous to the gale which I have begun to describe; and with the unsociable and cold reserve with which they were subsequently treated by all on board (visited only at stated periods by their old, but not yet confiding friend Daniel, who brought them their daily allowance), they had, as I have mentioned, become partakers and sufferers with us in the pangs and fears of the hurricane that was sweeping over the vessel and the sea about us.

The third day of the gale became the most alarming, and the night of that day closing in upon us, seemed like the gloomy shroud amidst the hurrying winds and the cracking spars, that was to cover us in death.   Until this day, though swinging (and now and then jumping) from mountains to mountains of waves, the ship and the elements mingled our fears with amusement.   When, however, this day's light was gone, curiosity's feast was finished, and fear was no longer chained under our feet—we had reached the climax of danger, and terror seemed to have seized and reigned through every part of the ship.   The bears, in contemplative or other vein, had been mute; but at this gloomy hour, seeming to have lost all patience, added, at first their piteous howlings, and then their horrid growls, to the whistling of the winds; and next, the gnashing of their teeth, and their furious lurches, and bolts, and blows against the sides of their cage, to the cracking of spars and roaring of the tempest!   Curiosity again, in desperate minds, was resuscitated, and taking in its insatiable draughts even in the midst of this jarring and discordant medley of darkness—of dashing foam, of cracking masts, and of howlings and growlings and raging of grizzly bears; for when the lightnings flashed, men (and even women) were seen crawling and hanging about the deck, as if to see if they could discover the death that was ready with his weapons drawn to destroy them.

The captain had twenty times ordered all below, but to

no purpose, until in the indiscriminate confusion of his crew and the passengers, in the jet blackness of the gale, when his ship was in danger, and our lives, his trumpet announced that "the bears were on deck!"

"Good God!" was exclaimed and echoed from one end of the ship's deck to the other; "the grizly bears are out! down with the hatches—down the hatches!" The scrambling that here took place to reach the cabins below can only be justly known to each actor who performed his part in his own way; and of these there were many. Some descended headlong, some sidewise, and others rolled down; and every one with a ghastly glance back upon the one behind him, as a grizly bear, of course, that was to begin his "chawing" the next moment.

When the scrambling was all over, and the hatches all safe, all in the cabin were obliged to smile for a moment, even in the midst of the alarm, at the queer position and manœuvres of a plump little Irish woman who had slipped down the wrong hatchway by accident, and left her "other half" to spend a night of celibacy, and of awful forebodings, in the steerage, where she would have gone, but to which her own discretion as well as the united voices of the cabin passengers decided her not to attempt to make her way over the deck during the night.

The passengers, both fore and aft, were now all snugly housed for the rest of the night, and the captain's smothered voice through his trumpet, to his hands aloft, and the stamping of the men on deck, while handling the ropes and shifting the sails, were all caught by our open ears, and at once construed into assaults and dreadful conflicts with the grizly bears on deck.

In the midst of these conjectures some one of the passengers screamed and sprang from near the stairway entering the cabin, when it was discovered, to the thrilling amazement of all, that one of the bears had pawed open the hatchway, and was descending into the cabin! The ladies' salon, beyond the cabin, was the refuge to which the instant rush was making, when the always good and musical sound of the captain's voice was recognized. "Why! you don't think I'm a grizly bear, do you?" The good fellow! he didn't intend to frighten anybody. He had just raised the hatch and came down to get a little breath and a "drop to drink." He is as unlike to a grizly bear as any one else in the world, both in looks and in disposition; but he happened to have on for the occasion a black oil-cloth hood or cap, which was tied under the chin; and a jacket covered with long fur on the outside, making his figure (which was of goodly size, and which just filled the gangway), with a little of the lively imagination belonging to such moments, look the counterpart of a grizly bear. "Where's Catlin?" said he; "damn the bears!" "Are they out?" cried the passengers all together. "Out?—yes; they have eaten one man already, and another was knocked overboard with a handspike; he was mistaken for one of the bears. We are all in a mess on deck—it's so dark we can't see each other— the men are all aloft in the rigging. Steward! give me a glass of brandy-and-water—the ship must be managed, and I must go on deck. Keep close below here, and keep the hatches down, for the bruins are sick of the scene, and pawing about for a burrow in the ground, and will have the hatches up in a moment if you don't look to them. Where's Catlin?" "We don't know," was the reply from many mouths; "he is not in the cabin."

"Will, here, Misther Captain, yer honour, I'll till ye," said a poor fellow, who in the general fright and flight had tumbled himself by accident into the cabin, and observed sullen silence until the present moment; "I'll jist till ye—I saw Misther Cathlin (I sippose he's the jintleman that owns the bastes) and his mon Dan (for I've known Dan for these many a long year in ould Amiriky, and I now he has chargin o' the bears on board); I saw the two, God bliss them, when the bastes was about gettin their hinder parts out of the cage, stannin on the side jisth before 'em, Misther Cathlin with his double-barrel gun, and his mon Dan pointin at 'em in the face,

with a pistol in each hand ; and this was jist whin I heard
they were outh, and I jimped down here jist in the wrong
place, as I am after observin when it is too late, and I hope
there is no offence to your honour."

"Catlin's gone then," said the captain ; "he is swallowed !"

The captain was at his post again, the hatches closed,
and in the midst of dozing, and praying, and singing (and
occasionally the hideous howlings of the grizlies whenever
a wave made a breach over the deck of the vessel) was
passed away that night of alarm and despair, until the rays
of the morning's sun having chased away the mist and
assuaged the fury of the storm, had brought all hands
together on the deck, and in the midst of them the cheerful
face of our good captain ; and in their huge cage, which
had been driven from one side of the deck to the other, but
now adjusted, sitting upon their haunches, with the most
jaded and humiliating looks imaginable, as they gazed
between their iron bars, their two grizly majesties, who had
hurt nobody during the night, nor in all probability had
meditated anything worse or more sinful than an escape,
if possible, from the imprisonment and danger they considered themselves unfortunately in.

In the general alarm and scramble on deck in the fore-
part of the night, the total darkness having been such that it
was impossible to tell whether the bears were out of their
cage or not, and quite impossible to make one's way to the
quarter-deck, unaccustomed to the shapes of things to be
passed over, "Misther Cathlin" had dropped himself into
the steerage as the nearest refuge, just before the hatch
was fastened down for the night. Any place, and anything
under deck at that time, was acceptable ; and even at so peril-
ous a moment, and amidst such alarming apprehensions, I
drew a fund of amusement from the scenes and conversations around me. The circumstance of sixty passengers, men,
women, and children, being stowed into so small a compass,
and to so familiar an acquaintance, would have been alone,
and under different circumstances, a subject of curious

interest for a stranger so suddenly to be introduced to; but to be dropped into the midst of such a group in the middle of the night, in the thickest of a raging tempest, and the hour of danger, when some were in bed—some upon their knees at their prayers—others making the most of the few remaining drops of brandy they had brought with them, and others were playing at cards and enjoying their jokes, and all together just rescued from the jaws and the claws of the bears over their heads, was one of no common occurrence, and worthy at least of a few passing remarks.

The wailings of the poor fellow whose wife had got into the cabin were incessant, and not much inferior to the howlings of the grizzlies on deck. She had been put into my berth, and I had had the privilege of " turning in " with her disconsolate husband, if I had seen fit to have done so, or if his writhings and contortions had not taken up full twice the space allotted to him. It was known and told to him by some of his comrades, that they saw his wife go into the cabin, and that she was safe. " Yis," said he, " but I 'm unasy, I 'm not asy about her, d'ye see; I don't fale asy as she's there, God knows where, along with those jintlemen."

Amongst the passengers in this part of the vessel I at once found myself alongside of at least two very eccentric characters. The one, I afterwards learned, was familiarly called by the passengers " the little Irishman in black," and the other " the half-Englishman, or broken-down swell."

The first of these two eccentrics was a squatty little gentleman of about four feet nine inches elevation, and between two and three feet breadth of beam, with a wrinkled face and excessively sharp features. To be all in black he showed no signs of a shirt, though he was decently clad, but in black from head to foot, being in mourning, as he said, for "his son who had emigratin to Amiriky fifteen years sin, and livin there jist long enough to become a *native*, had died and leaven of a fortin, which he had been over to sittle up and receivin, with which he was recrossin the ocean to his native country." He said he wished to be rispectable and dacent, havin received 12,000 dollars ; and as he thought the dacent thing was in "payin," now-a-days, he had paid for a berth in the cabin, but preferred to ride in the steerage. He made and found much amusement in that part of the vessel with his congenial spirits, and seemed peculiarly happy in the close communication with the other oddity of the steerage, whom I have said the passengers called the half-Englishman, or broken-down swell, who, I learned from my man Daniel, had laid in three barrels of old English porter, in bottles, when leaving the city of New York, and the last of which they were now opening and making the whole company merry with, as a sort of thanksgiving on their lucky escape from the grizly bears, who they firmly believed held possession of everything on the vessel outside of the hatchway.

This eccentric and droll, but good-natured gentleman, with the aid of porter made much amusement in the steerage, even in the hour of alarm ; and though I did not at that time know his calibre, or exactly what to make of him, I afterwards learned that he was an English cockney who had been on a tour through the States, and was now on his way back to his fatherland. He had many amusing notions and anecdotes to relate of the Yankees, and in his good-natured mellowness told a very good one of himself, much to the amusement of the Yankees on board, and the little Irishman in black, and my man Daniel. He said that " the greatest luxury he found in New York were the hoisters, and much as he liked them he had eaten them for two years before he had learned whether they were spelled with a haitch or a ho." Much valuable time would be lost to the reader if I were to chain him down to the rest of the incidents that happened between the middle of the ocean and Liverpool : and I meet him there at the beginning of my next chapter.

CHAPTER II.

ON nearing the docks at Liverpool, not only all the passengers of the ship, but all the inhabitants of the hills and
dales about, and the shores, were apprised of our approach
to the harbour by the bellowing and howling of the grizlies,
who were undoubtedly excited to this sort of *Te Deum* for
their safe deliverance and approach to *terra firma,* which
they had got a sight (and probably a smell) of.

The arrival of the Roscius on that occasion was of course
a conspicuous one, and well announced ; and we entered the
dock amidst an unusual uproar and crowd of spectators.
After the usual manner, the passengers were soon ashore,
and our luggage examined, leaving freight and grizly bears
on board, to be removed the next morning. From the
moment of landing on the wharf to the Custom-house, and
from that to the hotel where I took lodgings, I was obliged to
" fend off," almost with foot and with fist, the ragamuffins
who beset me on every side ; and in front, in the rear, and
on the right and the left, assailed me with importunities to
be allowed to carry my luggage. In the medley of voices
and confusion I could scarcely tell myself to which of these

poor fellows I had committed my boxes; and no doubt this (to them) delightful confusion and uncertainty encouraged a number of them to keep close company with my luggage until it arrived at the Grecian Hotel. When it was all safely landed in the hall, I asked the lad who stood foremost and had brought my luggage in his cart, how much was to pay for bringing it up? "Ho, Sir, hi leaves it to your generosity, Sir, has you are a gentleman, Sir; hit's been a werry eavy load, Sir."

I was somewhat amused with the simple fellow's careless and easy manner, and handed him eighteen pence, thinking it a reasonable compensation for bringing two small trunks and a carpet-bag; but he instantly assumed a different aspect, and refused to take the money, saying that no gentleman would think of giving him less than half-a-crown for such a load as he had brought. I soon settled with and dismissed him by giving him two shillings; and as he departed, and I was about entering the coffee-room, another of his ragged fraternity touched my elbow, when I asked him what he wanted. "Wo, Sir, your luggage there—" "But I have paid for my luggage—I paid the man you see going out there." "Yes, Sir; but then you sees, hi elped im put it hon; hand I elped im along with it, hand it's werry ard, Sir, hif Ise not to be paid has well as im." I paid the poor fellow a sixpence for his ingenuity; and as he left, a third one stepped up, of whom I inquired, "What do *you* want?" "Why, Sir, your luggage, you know, there —I am very sorry, Sir, to see you pay that worthless rascal what's just going out there—I am indeed sorry, Sir—he did nothing, but was hol the time hin our way—hit urts me, Sir, to see a gentleman throw is money away upon sich vagabonds, for it's hundoubtedly ard earned, like the few shillings we poor fellows get." "Well, my good fellow, what do you want of me?" "Ho, Sir, hit's honly for the cart, Sir—you will settle with me for the cart, Sir, hif you please—that first chap you paid ad my cart, hand I'll be bound you ave paid im twice has much has you hought."

"Well, to make short," said I, " here, take this sixpence for
your cart, and be off." I was thus brief, for I saw two or
three others edging and siding up in the passage towards
me, whom I recollected to have seen escorting my luggage, and I retreated into the coffee-room as suddenly
as possible, and stated the case to one of the waiters, who
promised to manage the rest of the affair.

I was thus very comfortable for the night, having no
further annoyance or real excitement until the next morning after breakfast, when it became necessary to disembark
the grizly bears. My other heavy freight had gone to Her
Majesty's Custom-house, and all the passengers from the
cabin and steerage had gone to comfortable quarters, leaving the two deck passengers, the grizlies, in great impatience, and as yet undisposed of. My man Daniel had
been on the move at an early hour, and had fortunately
made an arrangement with a simple and unsuspecting old lady
in the absence of her " good man," to allow the cage to be
placed in a small yard adjoining her house, and within the same
inclosure, which had a substantial pavement of round stones.

This arrangement for a few days promised to be an ad-
vantageous one for each party. Daniel was to have free
access and egress for the purpose of giving them their food,
and the price proposed to the good woman was met as a
liberal reward for the reception of any living beings that
she could imagine, however large, that could come within
her idea of the dimensions of a cage. Daniel had told her
that they were two huge bears; and in his reply to inquiries, assured her that they were not harmless by any
means, but that the enormous strength of their cage prevented them from doing any mischief.

The kind old lady agreed, for so much per day, to allow
the cage to stand in her yard, by the side of her house, at
least until her husband returned. With much excitement
and some growling about the docks and the wharf, they
were swung off from the vessel, and, being placed on a
" float," were conveyed to, and quietly lodged and fed in,

the retired yard of the good woman, when the gate was shut, and they fell into a long and profound sleep.

The grizly bears being thus comfortably and safely quartered in the immediate charge of my man Daniel, who had taken an apartment near them, and my collection being lodged in the Custom-house, I started by the railway for London to effect the necessary arrangements for their next move. I had rested in and left Liverpool in the midst of rain, and fog, and mud, and seen little else of it; and on my way to London I saw little or nothing of the beautiful country I was passing through, travelling the whole distance in the night. The luxurious carriage in which I was seated, however, braced up and embraced on all sides by deep cushions; the grandeur of the immense stations I was occasionally passing under; the elegance and comfort of the cafés and restaurants I was stumbling into with half-sealed eyes, with hundreds of others in the middle of the night, with the fat, and rotund, and ruddy appearance of the night-capped fellow-travellers around me, impressed me at once with the conviction that I was in the midst of a world of comforts and luxuries that had been long studied and refined upon.

I opened my eyes at daylight at the terminus in the City of London, but could see little of it, as I was driven to Ibbotson's Hotel, in Vere-street, through one of the dense fogs peculiar to the metropolis and to the season of the year in which I had entered it. To a foreigner entering London at that season, the first striking impression is the blackness and gloom that everywhere shrouds all that is about him. It is in his hotel—in his bed-chamber—his dining-room, and if he sallies out into the street it is there even worse; and added to it dampness, and fog, and mud, all of which, together, are strong inducements for him to return to his lodgings, and adopt them as comfortable, and as a luxury.

I am speaking now of the elements which the Almighty alone can control, and which only we strangers first see, as the surface of things, when we enter a foreign land, and before our letters of introduction, or the kind invitations of strangers, have led us into the participation of the hospitable and refined comforts prepared and enjoyed by the ingenuity of enlightened man, within. These I soon found were all around me, in the midst of this gloom; and a deep sense of gratitude will often induce me to allude to them again in the future pages of this work.

My breakfast and a clean face were the first necessary things accomplished at my hotel, and next to them was my first sally into the streets of the great metropolis, to inhale the pleasure of first impressions, and in my rambles to get a glance at the outer walls and the position of the famous Egyptian Hall, which I have already said my kind friend the Hon. C. A. Murray had conditionally secured, as the locale of my future operations. It is quite unnecessary, and quite impossible also, for me to describe the route I pursued through the mud and the fog in search of the Hall. Its direction had been pointed out to me at my start, and something like the distance explained, which, to an accustomed woodsman like myself, seemed a better guarantee of success than the names of a dozen streets and turnings, &c.; and I had "leaned off" on the point of compass, as I thought, without any light of the sun to keep me to my bearings, until I thought myself near its vicinity, and at a proper position to make some inquiry for its whereabouts. I ran against a young man at the moment (or, rather, he ran against me, as he darted across the street to the pavement, with a black bag under his arm), whom I felt fully at liberty to accost; and to my inquiry for the Egyptian Hall, he very civilly and kindly directed me in the following manner, with his hand pointing down the street in the opposite direction to the one in which I was travelling :—" Go to the *bottom*, d'ye see, sir, and you are at the *top*, of Piccadilly; you then pass the third turning to the left, and you will see the hexibition of the uge hox; that hox is in the Hegyptian All, and ee *his* a wapper, sure enough!" By this kind fellow's graphic direction I was soon in the Hall, got a glance of it and "the fat ox," and then commenced my first peregrination, amidst the mazes of fog and mud, through the Strand, Fleet-street, and Cheapside; the names of which had rung in my ears from my early boyhood, and which the sort of charm they had wrought there had created an impatient desire to see.

I succeeded quite well in wending my way down the Haymarket, the Strand, and Fleet-street, slipping and sliding through the mud, until I was in front or in the rear (I could not tell which) of the noble St. Paul's, whose black and gloomy walls, at the apparent risk of breaking my neck, I could follow up with my eye, until they were lost in the murky cloud of fog that floated around them. I walked quite round it, by which I became duly impressed with its magnitude below, necessarily leaving my conjectures as to its elevation, for future observations through a clearer atmosphere.

I then commenced to retrace my steps, when a slight tap upon my shoulder brought me around to look upon a droll and quizzical-looking fellow, who very obsequiously proceeded (as he pointed to the collar of my cloak, the lining of which, it seems, had got a little exposed), "The lining of your cloak, sir; hit don't look very well for a gentleman, sir; hexcuse me, hif you please, sir." "Certainly," said I; "I am much obliged to you," as I adjusted it and passed on. In my jogging along for some distance after this rencontre, and while my eyes were intent upon the mud, where I was selecting the places for my footsteps, I observed a figure that was keeping me close company by my side, and, on taking a fairer look at him, found the same droll character still at my elbow, when I turned around and inquired of him, "What now?" "Ho, sir, your cloak, you know, sir; hit didn't look well, for a gentleman like you, sir. Your pardon, sir; ha sixpence, hif you please, sir." I stopped and gave the poor fellow a sixpence for his ingenuity, and jogged on.

The sagacity of this stratager in rags had detected the foreigner or stranger in me at first sight, as I learned in a few moments, in the following amusing way. I had proceeded but a few rods from the place where I had given him his sixpence and parted company with him, when, crossing an intersecting street, I was met by a pitiable object hobbling on one leg, and the other twisted around his hip, in an unnatural way, with a broom in one hand, and the other extended towards me in the most beseeching manner, and his face drawn into a triangular shape, as he was bitterly weeping. I saw the poor fellow's occupation was that of sweeping the crossing under my feet, and a sixpence that I slipped into his hand so relaxed the muscles of his face, by this time, that I at once recognised in him the adjuster of the lining of my cloak; but I had no remedy, and no other emotion, at the instant, than that of amusement, with some admiration of his adroitness, and again passed on.

Casting my eyes before me I observed another poor fellow, at the crossing of another street, plying his broom to the mud very nimbly (or rather passing it over, just above the top of the mud), whilst his eye was fixed intently upon me, whom he had no doubt seen patronizing the lad whom I had passed. I dodged this poor fellow by crossing the street to the right, and as I approached the opposite pavement I fell into the hands of a young woman in rags, who placed herself before me in the most beseeching attitude, holding on her arm a half-clad and sickly babe, which she was pinching on one of its legs to make it cry, whilst she supplicated me for aid. I listened to her pitiable lamentations a moment, and in reproaching her for her cruelty in exposing the life of her little infant for the purpose of extorting alms, I asked her why she did not make her husband take care of her and her child? "Oh, my kind sir," said she, "I give you my honour I've got no husband; I have no good opinion of those husbands." "Then I am glad you have informed me," said I; "you belong to a class of women whom I will not give to." "Oh, but, kind sir, you mistake me; I am not a bad woman —I am *not* a bad woman—I assure you! I am a decent woman, and God knows it : the child is not mine ; it is only one that I hires, and I's obliged to pay eighteen pence a day for it ; which is as true as God's holy writ ; that's what it is." "Then," said I, "you are a wretch, to keep that innocent little thing here in the cold ; and, instead of alms, you deserve to be handed over to the police." She gave me many hard names as I was stepping into a cab which I had beckoned up and directed to drive me to Ibbotson's Hotel, in Vere-street.

"Where, sir ?" asked the cab-driver as he mounted his seat. "Vy, sir, didn't you ear the gentleman ?" said a man with a large bronze medal hanging on his breast, who had one hand on the door; "drive im to Hibbotson's Otel, Were-street, Hoxford-street." "Who are you ?" said I, as we were moving off, and he held the door open with one hand and his hat raised with the other ; "what do you want ?"

"I'm the vaterman, sir ; you'll recollect the vaterman ?" "Yes, I'll not forget you in a long time." So I shut the door without giving the poor man his ha'penny, not knowing the usual custom yet, and too much pressed for time to learn it at that moment.

I observed, in passing several equestrian and other statues in the streets, that they were all black ; which seemed curious ; and also, in every street, I saw what was new to me, and not to be seen in the streets of the American cities—meat-shops and fishmongers indiscriminately mingled along the same side-walks with dry goods — hosiers, china, and hardware—and fancy shops ; and also performed the whole route, outward and homeward, without having seen a solitary pig ploughing the gutters, as we too familiarly meet them in many of the American cities, though the gutters, much of the way, would seem to have offered a tolerably rich field for their geological researches.

I met with evidences enough, however, that I was not out of the land of pigs, though they were not seen promenading or ploughing the streets. I passed several shops, all open in front, where poor piggies were displayed in a much less independent way—hanging by their hind legs at full length, and the blood dripping from their noses upon the sills of the shops and pavements, to amuse the eyes of the silken and dazzling throng that was squeezing and brushing along by them ; and whilst I easily decided which was the most cruel to the poor brutes, I was much at a loss to decide which mode was calculated to be the most shocking to the nerves that would be weak enough to be offended by either.

I was thus at the end of my first day's rambles in London, without at present recollecting any other occurrences worthy of note, excepting a little annoyance I had felt by discovering with my left eye, while walking in the street, something like a small black spot on the side of my nose, which, by endeavouring many times to remove by the brush of my hand across it, I had evidently greatly enlarged, and which, when I returned, I examined and found to have been at first, in all probability, a speck of soot which had alighted there, and by passing my hand over it had, as in other instances, on other parts of my face, mashed it down and given it somewhat the shape and tail of a comet, or the train of a falling star, though differing materially in brilliancy and colour.

I used the rest of this gloomy day in obtaining from the Lords of the Treasury the proper order for passing my collection through the Customs, which has been before mentioned, arranging my letters of credit, &c., and returned by the evening's train to Liverpool, to join my collection again, and Daniel and the grizly bears.

On my return to that city I found poor Daniel in a sad dilemma with the old lady about the bears, and the whole neighbourhood under a high excitement, and in great alarm for their safety. The bears had been landed in the briefest manner possible; exempted from the usual course that almost everything else takes through the Queen's warehouse ; and, though relieved from the taxes of the customs, I soon found that I had duties of a different character accumulating that required my attention in another quarter. The agreement made by the old lady with

Daniel to keep them in her yard for so much per day, and for as long a time as he required, had been based upon the express and very judicious condition that they were to do no harm. From the moment of their landing they had kept up an almost incessant howling, so Rocky-Mountain-ish and so totally unlike any attempts at music ever heard in the country before, that it attracted a crowd night and day about the old lady's door, that almost defeated all attempts at ingress and egress. A little vanity, however, which she still possessed, enabled her to put up with the inconvenience, which she was turning to good account, and counting good luck, until it was ascertained, to her great amazement as well as alarm, that the bears were passing their huge paws out of the cage, between the iron bars, and lifting up the round stones of her pavement for the pleasure of once more getting their nails into the dirt, their favourite element, and which they had for a long time lost sight of.

In their unceasing pursuit of this amusement, by night and by day, they had made a sad metamorphosis of the old lady's pavement, as, with the strength of their united paws, they had drawn the cage around to different parts of the yard, totally unpaving as they went along. At the time of the poor old lady's bitterest and most vehement complaint, they were making their move in the direction of her humble tenement, the walls of which were exceedingly slight; and her alarm became insupportable. The ignorant crowd outside of the inclosure, who could get but a partial view of their operations now and then, had formed the most marvellous ideas of these monsters, from the report current amongst them that they were eating the paving-stones; and had taken the most decided and well-founded alarm from the fact that the bears had actually hurled some of the paving-stones quite over the wall amongst their heads, which were calling back an increased shower of stones and other missiles, adding fresh rage and fears to the growling of the bears, which altogether was threatening results of a more disastrous kind.

In this state of affairs I was very justly appealed to by the old lady for redress and a remedy, for it was quite evident that the condition of her agreement with Daniel had been broken, as the bears were now decidedly doing much harm to her premises ; destroying all her rest, and (as she said) " her appetite and her right mind ;" and I agreed that it was my duty, as soon as possible, to comply with her urgent request that they should be removed.   She insisted on its being done that day, as " it was quite impossible to pass another night in her own bed, when there was such howling and groaning and grunting in her yard, by the side of her house."   Daniel took my directions and immediately went through the town in search of other quarters for them, and was to attend to their moving whilst I was to spend the day in the Custom-house, attending to the examination of my collection of 600 paintings and many thousand Indian costumes, weapons and other curiosities, which were to be closely inspected and inventoried, for duties.

Immersed in this mystery of difficulties and vexations at the customs during the day, I had lost sight of Daniel and his pets until I was free at night, when I was assailed with a more doleful tale than ever about the bears.   Troubles were gathering on all sides.   Poor Daniel had positively arranged in several places for them, but when " their characters were asked from their last places," he met defeat in every case, and was obliged to meet, at last, the increased plaints of his old landlady, whose rage and ranting were now quite beyond control.   She had made complaint to the police, of whom a *posse* had been sent to see to their removal.   Daniel in the mean time had dodged them, and was smiling amidst the crowd at the amusing idea of their laying hold of them, or of even going into the yard to them.   The police reported on the utter impossibility of removing them to any other part of the town, their " character " having been so thoroughly published already to all parts ; and it was advised, to the utter discomfiture of the old lady, that it would be best for them to remain there until they should be removed to London, and that I should pay for all damages. The poor old lady afterwards had a final interview with Daniel in the crowd, when she very judiciously resolved that if the bears did not move, *she must*—which she did that night, and placed Daniel in her bed, as the guardian of her property and of his pets, until the third or fourth day afterwards, when they were moved to the railway, and by it (night and day, catching what glimpses they could of the country they were serenading with their howls and growls as they passed through it under their tarpaulin) they were conveyed to the great metropolis.

Owing to the multiplicity of articles to be examined and inventoried in the customs, and the great embarrassment of the clerks in writing down their Indian names, my labours were protracted there to much tediousness; but when all was brought to a close by their proposing, most judiciously. to count the number of curiosities instead of wasting paper and time and paralysing my jaws by pronouncing half a dozen times over, and syllable by syllable, their Indian names, my collection of eight tons weight was all on the road and soon at the Euston station in London, where we again recognised the mournful cries of the grizlies, who had arrived the night before.

On arriving at the station, I found Daniel at a small inn in the vicinity, where he seemed highly excited by some unpleasant altercation he had had with the landlord and inmates of the house, growing out of national and political prejudices, which had most probably been too strongly advanced on both sides. Daniel had suddenly raised a great excitement in the neighbourhood by his arrival with the grizly bears, whose occasional howlings had attracted crowds of people, curious to know the nature of the strange arrival; and all inquirers about the station being referred to their keeper, who was at the inn, brought Daniel and his patience into notoriety at once.

Daniel (*Plate No.* 2) is an Irishman, who emigrated

to the United States some twenty years since, and, by dint of his industry and hard labour, had met with success in acquiring an humble independence, and had formed the most undoubted attachment to the Government and its institutions; and, from his reading, and conversation with the world, had informed himself tolerably well in political matters, which he was always ready to discuss; and being rather of a hasty and irascible temperament, he often got into debates of that nature, that led him into danger of unpleasant results. It was in the midst of one of these that I found him at the inn, surrounded by at least a hundred labouring men and idlers from the streets, who had been drawn around him at first, as I have said, to get some information of the bears, but who had changed their theme, and were now besieging him on all sides, to combat him on some political dogma he had advanced relative to his favourite and adopted country, the United States; or to taunt him with slaunts at his native country, all of which, with his native wit, he was ready to meet with ability, until, as he afterwards told me, " they were showered upon him so rapidly, and from so many quarters at once, that it became quite impossible to answer them, and that the stupid ignorance and impertinence of some of them had worn out all his patience, and irritated him to that degree, that I must excuse him for the excitement I had found him under when I arrived." With much difficulty I rescued him from the crowd that had enclosed him, and, retiring to a private room, after matters of business had been arranged, he gave me the following account of the difficulties he had just been in, and of the incidents of his journey from Liverpool to London with the bears.

At Liverpool he had had great difficulty in getting permission to travel by the luggage train, to keep company with the bears, the necessity of which he urged in vain, until he represented that, unless he was with them to feed them, their howlings and other terrific noises and ravings would frighten their hands all out of the stations, and even add probabilities to their breaking loose from the

Nº 2.

cage in which they were confined, to feed upon the human flesh around them, and of which they were peculiarly fond. Upon these representations, he was allowed the privilege of a narrow space, to stand or to sit, in the corner of one of the luggage-trains, and thus bore the bears company all the way.

When they entered the first tunnel on their way, they raised a hideous howl, which they continued until they were through it, which might have been from a feeling of pleasure, recognizing in it something of the character of the delightful gloominess of their own subterranean abodes ; or their outcries might have been from a feeling of dread or fear from those narrow and damp caverns, too much for their delicate tastes and constitutions. This, however, is matter for the bears to decide. At Birmingham, where they rested on the truck for the greater part of a day, their notification to the town had called vast crowds of spectators around them ; and though their tarpaulin prevented them from being seen, many, very many, drew marvellous accounts of them from one another, and from the flying reports which had reached them several days before from Liverpool, of " two huge monsters imported from the Rocky Mountains, that had scales like alligators, with long spears of real flint at the ends of their tails; that they made nothing of eating paving-stones when they were hungry, and that in Liverpool they had escaped, and were travelling to the north, and demolishing all the inhabitants of Lancashire as they went along," &c. Their occasional howls and growls, with, once in a while, a momentary display of one of their huge paws, exhibited from under the tarpaulin, riveted the conviction of the gaping multitude as to the terror and danger of these animals, while it put at rest all apprehensions as to their being at large and overrunning the country. Poor Daniel had to stand between the crowd and his pets, to save them from the peltings and insults of the crowd, and at the same time, to muster every talent he had at natural history, to answer the strange queries and theories that were raised about them.   He was assailed on every side with questions as to the appearance and habits of the animals, and at last, about "the other animals," as they called them, "running on two legs, in America;" for many of them, from his representations, had come fresh from the coal-pits and factories, with ideas that Americans were a sort of savages, and that savages, they had understood, were " a sort of wild beastises, and living on raw meat."   These conjectures and queries were answered amusingly for them, by Daniel; and, after he had a little enlightened them by the information he gave them, their conversation took a sort of political turn, which, I have before said, he was prone to run into;   and thus, luckily, the time was whiled away, without any *set-to* to bother the bears and himself, which he had seen evidently preparing, until the whistle announced them and him on their way again for the metropolis.

The next morning he found himself and the bears safe landed at the terminus in London, where I have already said that I found him and released him from a medley of difficulties he had worked himself into.

The keeper of the inn had himself been the first to provoke poor Daniel, but when he found it for his interest, and advised a different course, he endeavoured to turn his criticisms into good nature, and had taken sides with him. Daniel, very amusingly however, describes his remarks as so excessively ignorant, that they excited his mirth more than anger, and he repeated several of them in the following manner:—He first provoked Daniel by inquiring "who his master was, and where he was at that time."   Daniel replied to him, somewhat to his surprise, "I have no master, Sir; I live in a country, thank God, where we are our own masters.   My 'boss' (if you will have it that way) is a Mr. Catlin, who I expect here in a few hours."   Finding that Daniel and the bears were from America, of which country he had heard some vague accounts, he very innocently enquired who was the King in America at that time, apologizing, that by the treacherousness of his memory he had lost the run of them. Daniel told him that they had no king in America. He then said " he well recollected when the old fellow died, but he had equally forgotten the name of the Queen; he recollected to have read of the King of New York." Daniel soon put his recollection right, and in doing so had given umbrage to the poor man, which led to the long and excited political debate with which I found Daniel so much exasperated when I arrived.

Daniel had, in the beginning of this affair, explained to the bystanders around him the difference between a King and a President, and then had provoked his landlord by amusingly and pleasantly repeating the anecdote of " King Jefferson " (which is current in America) in reply to his questions about the " King of New York ;" and in the following manner :—

"During the presidency of Thomas Jefferson, who lived in the city of Washington, two poor emigrants from the county of Cork, in my own country, made their way to America in a vessel which landed them in Philadelphia ; they got ashore, and as they were taking their first stroll through the streets in the 'land of liberty and equality,' without a shilling in their pockets, they began to ' sing out ' ' Huzza for King George !' This of course excited too much opposition to last long in the streets of a republican city, and a gentleman very kindly stopped the poor fellows, and to their great surprise informed them that he feared they would get into difficulty if they continued to huzza for the king, as King George was not the king of the country they were now in. He informed them that Mr. Jefferson was the great man in America—that he was President of the United States, and that it would not do for them to huzza for King George. They thanked him, and as they proceeded on they increased the volume of their voices in huzzas for ' King Jefferson !—huzza for King Jefferson !' This soon excited the attention of the police, who silenced their bawling by ' putting them in the jug !' "

CHAPTER III.

Letters of introduction—Driving a friend's horse and chaise—Amusing accidents—English driving—"Turn to the *right*, as the law directs"—A turn
to the *left*—A fresh difficulty—Egyptian Hall—Lease for three years—
Arrangement of collection—Bears sold and removed to Regent's Park
Zoological Gardens—Their fates.

HAVING landed all my effects safely at the terminus in
London, the next thing was the final *locale ;* and to decide
on this, my letters of introduction, or a part of them at
least, should be delivered ; and for this and other dodgings
about through the city for a few days, the first gentleman to
whom I delivered a letter had the kindness to insist on my
using his horse and chaise during certain portions of the day,
when he did not use them himself. This was the kindest
thing that he could have done for me, and I shall never
forget the obligation he laid me under by doing so. His
footman, who accompanied me, relieved me from all anxiety
about the horse, which was a noble animal; and my long
errands through the mud were most delightfully abridged.

As the fatalities of life seem to bring us more or less
trouble in every step we take in it, I had mine, even in
this new and independent arrangement. In my first dash
through the streets with all the confidence and tact I had
acquired from my boyhood in driving a similar vehicle in
my own country, I was suddenly in the midst of fresh
misfortune by "turning to the right, as the law directs"
(the regulation and custom of the United States), which
brought my horse into the most frightful collision with a
pair that were driven by a gentleman, and who had reined

in the same direction under the English custom of "turn to the left."

This affair was not only one of imminent danger of harm, which we had all luckily escaped, but one of exceeding mortification to me from the circumstances which immediately followed.

The extreme care and skill in driving, with the fine training of horses in England (of which we have little idea in the United States), render accidents in the streets of London so exceedingly rare, that when they do occur they immediately attract an immense crowd, and into the midst of such an one was I thrown by the unfortunate accident which my ignorance rather than carelessness had just been the cause of.

By the violence of the concussion I had been landed in the street, and the gentleman, to whose harness I had done some injury, was suddenly in front of me with his whip in his hand; and in the hearing of the crowd that was hovering around, in the most excited manner, demanding of me what I meant by driving against him in that awkward manner, and threatening to hold me responsible for damages done by not turning the right way, whilst I felt every disposition to answer his questions respectfully, as I saw the injury was all on his side. I still felt that a little tenacity was allowable on my side; and I almost as peremptorily demanded of him why he did not rein to the right, as the law requires:—"Rein to the right!" said he, "who the devil ever heard of such a thing as turning to the right? Where are you from, I should like to know?" "I am from a country, sir, where the law directs all vehicles to 'turn to the right.'" "What country is that, I should like to know?" "North America, sir." "Ha! just about what I should have thought, sir:—I suppose I shall get pay for my coupling-lines about the time the States pay interest." "Most likely," said I, as we were mutually taking our seats, amidst the sullen remarks that I heard in various parts of the crowd as I was driving off—" There 's a Yankee for you!—ee's a rum-looking fellow, ha?—There 's a Repudiator for you"—" I 'll be bound—" &c., &c., &c.

I drove off from this scene with some satisfaction that I had learned so important a fact at so little expense, and steered my way very safely amidst the thousands of vehicles of various sorts that I was passing and meeting, in which time I was very pleasantly receiving a brief lecture on the subject from my good-natured and very civil footman, who was behind me; in which (having silently learned in the disaster we had just witnessed that I was from a foreign country) he took especial pains to explain to me that " in Hengland it 's holays the abit to turn to the left." Just at that moment I found myself in a fresh difficulty, and some danger also, by one wheel of my chaise grinding against the curbstone, and a huge omnibus in full press against us, and driving us on to the pavement, where it had at that moment stopped and fastened us, whilst discharging a passenger. I demanded of the driver, a sullen-looking fellow, half covered with an apron or boot which protected him from the weather in front, and something like a feather-bed and bolsters tied around his neck and chin, and half concealing his bloated face, what he meant by reining in upon me in that way, and crowding me upon the pavement? to which he grumly replied as he snapped his whip, " I should like to know what business you have in there?" "Never mind," said I, " I shall go ahead." " No you woan't—ain't you old enough to know which side of a carriage to pass?" At that moment the conductor of the omnibus cried out " All right!" which was echoed by a policeman who had taken my horse by the bit. I was somewhat relieved, though a little surprised, at the verdict given by the conductor and the policeman at the same instant, that "all" (or both), as I at that moment understood it, " were right." I sat still of course till the omnibus had left us, nearly crushed, but luckily not damaged, when I said to my footman, " Why, what does this mean ?—what do you call the 'left side' in this country, I should like to know ?" To this he very distinctly as well as amusingly explained, that the invariable custom in England is when *meeting* a vehicle, to turn to the *left*, and when *passing*, to turn to the *right*. But why did the policeman and the conductor say we were both right or " all right ?" " Why, sir, you know wen the homnibus olds up to land a gent or a lady, or to take em hin, it would be wery hawkard to drive off wen the lady ad one leg hin the bus and the other hout; so wen they are both hout or both hin, and all right, the conductor ollows out ' Holl right !' and the bus goes hon, d'ye see, sir ?" " Ah, yes, I thank you, Jerry, I understand it now." I was then growing wiser every moment amongst the incidents that were occasionally taking place in my drives with the goodnatured footman and his fine horse, which I used for several days, much to my satisfaction and amusement, without other accident or incident worth the reader's valuable time.

I called upon my kind friend the Hon. C. A. Murray, at his office in Buckingham Palace, where I was received with all that frankness and sincerity peculiar to him ; and, with his kind aid, and that of Charles D. Archibald, Esq., of York Terrace, to whom I am also much indebted, the arrangements were soon made for my collection in the Egyptian Hall, which I took on a lease, for three years, at a rent of 550*l*. per annum.

My collection was soon in it, and preparing for its exhibition, while the grizly bears were still howling at the Euston station, impatient for a more congenial place for their future residence. It was quite impossible to give them any portion of the premises I had contracted for in the Egyptian Hall, and the quarters ultimately procured for them being expensive, and the anxieties and responsibilities for them daily increasing upon me as they were growing stronger and more vicious in their dispositions, it was decided that they should be offered for sale, and disposed of as soon as possible.   For this purpose I addressed letters to the proprietors of zoological gardens in Liverpool, in Dublin, and Edinburgh, and several other towns, and received, in reply from most of them, the answer that they already had them in their gardens, and that they were so complete a drug in England that they were of little value.   One proprietor assured me that he had recently been obliged to shoot two that he had in his gardens, in consequence of mischief they were doing to people visiting the grounds, and to the animals in the gardens.

My reply to several of these gentlemen was, that since the death of the famous old grizly bear, that had died a few months before in Regent's-park, it was quite certain that there had not been one in the kingdom until the arrival of these, "and that if either of those gentlemen would produce me another living grizly bear, at that time, in the kingdom, I would freely give him my pair."   This seemed, however, to have little weight with the proprietors of wild beasts ; but I at length disposed of them for about the same price that I had given for them four years before, when they were not much larger than my foot (for the sum of 125*l.*) ; and they went to the Zoological Gardens, Regent's Park.

A word or two more of them and the reader will have done with the grizlies, who had been much obliged to me, no doubt, for four years' maintenance, and for a sight of the beauties of the ocean, and as much of the land of comforts and refinements as they were allowed to see through the bars of their cage, while they were travelling from the rude wilds of the Rocky Mountains to the great metropolis, the seat and centre of civilization and refinement.   As in their new abode they were allowed more scope and better attendance, it was reasonable to suppose that their lives would have been prolonged, and their comfort promoted ; but such did not prove to be the case.   From the continual crowds about them, to which they had the greatest repugnance, they seemed daily to pine, until one of them died of exceeding disgust (unless a better cause can be assigned), and the other with similar symptoms, added to loneliness perhaps, and despair, in a few months afterwards.

Thus ended the career of the grizly bears, and I really believe there were no tears shed for them, unless they were tears of joy, for they seemed to extend their acquaintance only to add to the list of their enemies, wherever they went.

CHAPTER IV.

Indian Collection arranged for exhibition—Description of it—The Hon. Charles Augustus Murray—Collection opened to private view—Kindness of the Hon. Mr. Murray—Distinguished visitors—Mr. Murray's explanations—Kind reception by the Public and the Press—Kind friends—Fatigue of explaining and answering questions—Curious remedy proposed by a friend—Pleasures and pains of a friendly and fashionable dinner.

My business now, and all my energies, were concentrated at the Egyptian Hall, where my collection was arranged upon the walls. The main hall was of immense length, and contained upon its walls 600 portraits and other paintings which I had made during eight years' travels amongst forty-eight of the remotest and wildest tribes of Indians in America, and also many thousands of articles of their manufacture, consisting of costumes, weapons, &c. &c., forming together a pictorial history of those tribes, which I had been ambitious to preserve as a record of them, to be perpetuated long after their extinction. In the middle of the room I had erected also a wigwam (or lodge) brought from the country of the Crows, at the base of the Rocky Mountains, made of some twenty or more buffalo skins, beautifully dressed and curiously ornamented and embroidered with porcupine quills.

My friend the Honourable C. A. Murray, with several others, had now announced my collection open to their numerous friends and such others as they chose to invite during the three first days when it was submitted to their private view, and by whom it was most of the time filled; and being kindly presented to most of them, my unsentimental and unintellectual life in the atmosphere of railroads and grizly bears was suddenly changed to a cheering flood of soul and intellect which greeted me in every part of my room, and soon showed me the way to the recessed world of luxury, refinements, and comforts of London, which not even the imagination of those who merely stroll through the streets can by any possibility reach.

During this private view I found entered in my book the names of very many of the nobility, and others of the most distinguished people of the kingdom. My friend Mr. Murray was constantly present, and introduced me to very many of them, who had the kindness to leave their addresses and invite me to their noble mansions, where I soon appreciated the elegance, the true hospitality and refinement of English life. Amongst the most conspicuous of those who visited my rooms on this occasion were H. R. H. the Duke of Cambridge, the Duke and Duchess of Sutherland, the Duke and Duchess of Buccleuch, Duke of Devonshire, Duke of Wellington, the Bishop of London, the Bishop of Norwich, Sir Robert and Lady Peel, Lord Grosvenor, Lord Lennox, Duke of Richmond, Duke of Rutland, Duke of Buckingham, Countess-Dowager of Dunmore, Countess-Dowager of Ashburnham, Earl of Falmouth, Earl of Dunmore, Lord Monteagle, Lord Ashley, Earl of Burlington, Sir James and Lady Clark, Sir Augustus d'Este, Sir Francis Head, and many others of the nobility, with most of the editors of the press, and many private literary and scientific gentlemen, of whose kindness to me while in London I shall have occasion to speak in other parts of this work.

The kindness of my friend Mr. Murray on this occasion can never be forgotten by me. He pointed out to my illustrious visitors the principal chiefs and warriors of the various tribes, with many of whom he was personally acquainted; explaining their costumes, weapons, &c., with all of which his rambles in the Indian countries beyond the Mississippi and Missouri had made him quite familiar. He led Duchesses, Countesses, and Ladies in succession upon his arm, into the wigwam of buffalo-hides, where he descanted, to the great satisfaction and amusement of his friends, upon the curious modes of Indian life into which he had been initiated, and which he had long shared with these simple people, whilst he resided with them under roofs of buffalo-hides (like the one now over their heads) on the vast plains and prairies of the wilds of America.

This was evidently an opportunity affording him great satisfaction, of illustrating to his friends the styles of primitive life which he had witnessed in America, whilst his explanations and descriptions were exceedingly entertaining and amusing to them, and at the same time the strongest corroboration of the fidelity with which I had made them, and therefore the best recommendation of them and me to the consideration of the English community.

He was fully employed, as he led alternately the Duchess of Sutherland (with her lovely daughters by her side), and the Duchess of Buccleuch on his arm, and a numerous group around him, while he commented upon the features and disposition of his old friend *Wee-ta-ra-sha-ro*, who had taken him under his immediate protection and saved his life from the designs of some young men who had laid their plans to destroy him when in the country of the Pawnees.

He explained to them and the Bishops of London and Norwich, who were following in the wake of the ladies and giving ear, the religious ceremony of the Indians, their modes of warfare, of hunting, and throwing the lasso in catching the wild horse. He showed them the Indian cradles in which the squaws carry their pappooses, slung on their backs. He took in his hands the lasso, and illustrated the mode of throwing it, with which he was familiar. He took also in his hands their war-clubs, their tomahawks and scalping knives, and then the scalps from the heads of enemies slain in battle, and ably explained them all. With these he made lasting and thrilling impressions; but with more satisfaction to himself, and to the fair and tender Graces, whose sylph-like gracefulness formed a halo of loveliness around him, he pointed to my paintings of the ever verdant and enamelled prairies—to the very copses and lawns through which, with his unerring rifle, he had stalked the timid antelope or the stately elk and shaggy bison, and, after quieting his raving stomach with their broiled delicacies, he had straightened his wearied limbs upon his spread buffalo robe, and, with the long, waving grass and bowing lilies stooping over his head, he had reflected upon London, upon Palaces and friends, as he had glided into that sweet forgetfulness that belongs peculiarly to the wearied huntsman, whose rifle has catered for his stomach, and whose quiet conscience starts him not at the rustling of the sweetened winds that are gently breezing over him.

I was also constantly engaged with surrounding groups, who were anxious to know the meaning and moral of this strange and unintelligible collection, while my man Daniel, with his rod in his hand, was enlightening another party at the end of the room, by pointing out the leading personages of the various tribes, explaining their costumes, weapons, &c., and answering the thousand questions which were put to him, and which several years of familiarity with the subject had abundantly qualified him to do.

Thus passed my first interview with the English aristocracy. I was in the midst and the best of it; and by it, on all sides, was met with the kindliest feelings and condescension, while I received compliments from all (in the most undoubted sincerity) for the successful efforts I had thus made to perpetuate the records of an abused and dying race of human beings.

The reception that myself and my works met on these days, amongst the highest critics, the most refined and elevated of the world, was beyond description pleasurable to me, as I had arrived a stranger in a foreign land, where I had risked everything upon the value that should be set upon my labours; and that, where I had been told that national prejudices would labour to defeat me. My life had been a tissue of risks and chances, and I resolved to hazard again; and I am now pleased (and bound) to acknowledge that I was frankly met with the most unprejudiced and congenial feelings ; and, even more than that, with a settled and genuine sympathy for the benighted people whom my works were representing, and a disposition to reward my labours by kind and unexpected invitations to the hospitable boards of those who fill the highest and most enviable stations in life.

To this general feeling it affords me pleasure to respond in general terms, in this place ; and I shall have occasion, in other parts of this work, to return my personal thanks for such spontaneous kindness, which my lasting gratitude will make it my duty to allude to.

The editors of the leading literary and scientific journals of London, and of the daily newspapers, were chiefly there, and with their very friendly and complimentary notices of my collection, with the usual announcements by advertisements, I opened it for the inspection of the public on the first day of February, 1840.*

Its commencement was flattering, from the numbers and high respectability of my visitors, and I was pleased, from day to day, to meet the faces and friendly greetings of those whom I had seen there at the private view.

I was pleased also with the freedom which is granted to exhibitions in London, leaving them entirely independent of tithing or taxation, as well as of licences to be obtained from the police, as is the case in France and some other countries. Under such auspices I very pleasantly commenced, with a rent of 550l. per annum, and continued it with reasonable success for the space of four years. The vicissitudes and incidents of that time it is not the object of this work to detail ; but I shall connect the links of my narrative better, and, I trust, do no injustice to my readers, by reciting a few of the incidents that transpired in that

---

* The reader, by referring to Appendix A of this volume, will see the comments of the Press on this Collection, in *England, France,* and the *United States.*

time : and, while I am doing so, endeavouring to do the justice which gratitude prompts, to those persons whose kindness has laid me under peculiar obligations.

Amongst those kind friends I must be allowed at present to mention the names of the Hon. C. A. Murray, Sir Augustus d'Este, Charles D. Archibald, Esq., Sir James Clark, Sir Thomas Phillips, Mr. Petty Vaughan, Dr. Hodgkin, Capt. Shippard, Sir Francis Head, Lord Monteagle, John Murray, A. M. Perkins, and Sir David Wilkie ; and there were many others with these who were very frequently at my rooms ; and for their friendly and constant efforts to promote my interest they have my sincerest thanks.

Several of these gentlemen, and others, whose visits were so frequent to my rooms, having formed an acquaintance with the Indians in their own country, or, from feelings of sympathy for them, taken so deep an interest in the subject, relieved me much of my time from the fatiguing task which I had adopted of explaining around the rooms such subjects as I considered most curious and instructive, and of answering the thousands of questions which were naturally put in every part of the room for information on so novel and exciting a theme.

I had entered upon this, at first, not as a task but an amusement, from which I drew great pleasure whilst I was entertaining my visitors and cultivating their pleasing acquaintance. From an over desire and effort on my part to explain the peculiar and curious modes of those wild people, and from a determination on the part of my visitors to get these explanations from my own lips (although I had my man Daniel and several others constantly in the rooms for the same purpose), I was held in my exhibition rooms almost daily from morning until night.

My men were able to explain the meaning of everything in the collection, but this did not satisfy the public whilst I was present. All inquired for me : "Where's Mr. Catlin? he's the Lion; his collection is wonderful; but I would give more to see him than all the rest." "He is yonder, Madam, at the farther end of the room, where you see a crowd of people around him."

I was generally in the midst of a crowd, who were densely packed around me; moving about the rooms whilst, with a rod in my hand to point with, I was lecturing or answering the numerous questions which were naturally put relative to these strange people and their modes. To lecture or to explain all day, following the current of one's thoughts, would have been a thing feasible, though fatiguing; but to stand upon one's feet and all day long to answer to interrogations, and many of those fifty times over, to different parties who were successively taking me in tow, I soon found was far more fatiguing than my travels and labours in the Indian wilderness; and I at length (at a much later period than my friends and my physician advised) gradually withdrew from the scene and this suicidal course, just before it might have been too late to have saved anything useful of me.

I followed the advice of my physician by going to my rooms at stated hours, but soon departed from it by failing to leave them with punctuality, and take recreation in the open air. The partial change I had adopted, however, was of advantage to me—talking part of the day and breaking off and leaving my men to do the talking for the other half.

Like most adventurers in wilderness life I was fond of describing what I had seen; and, having the works of several years around me, in their crude and unfinished condition, spread before the criticising world, and difficult to be appreciated, I was doubly stimulated to be in the collection, and with all the breath I could spare, to add to the information which the visitors to my rooms were seeking for. Under these conflicting feelings I struggled to keep away from my rooms, and did so for a part of the day, and that, as I soon found, only to meet a more numerous and impatient group when I re-entered.

All of the above-mentioned kind friends, and many others, repeatedly called to impress upon me the necessity of leaving my exhibition to my men, " to save my lungs—to save my life," as they said. Some snatched me away from the crowd, and in the purest kindness hurled me through the streets in their carriages, still *yelling* answers to their numerous questions as we were passing over the noisy pavements; and then at their kind and festive boards, to which I had been brought as places of refuge and repose, I was, for an instance, presented as—" My dear, this is Mr. Catlin! (*Plate No.* 3, *next page.*)—Mother, you have heard of Mr. Catlin?—Cousins Lucy and Fanny, here 's the celebrated Mr. Catlin you have heard me speak of so often. Poor fellow! I have dragged him away from his exhibition, where they are talking him to death—he *must* have *repose* — and here we can entertain and amuse him. Here, my little chicks—come here all of you—here 's Mr. Catlin!—here 's the man who has been so long among the wild Indians! he will tell you a great many curious stories about them. Where 's sister Ellen, and Betty?" " Oh, they are in the garden with Mr. S. and his son, who has just returned from New Zealand." " Good, good; run for them, run for them, quick! Send the carriage for aunt W——n as swift as possible, and don't let her fail to stop on the way and bring Lady R——e : you know how fond she is of the Indian character—she was three years, you know, in Canada—and the poem she is now writing on the Indians! What a treat this will be to her! Won't it be delightful to see her and Mr. Catlin come together? She told me the other day she had a thousand questions she wished to put to Mr. Catlin—how interesting! Have the dinner up at *six*—no, say at *seven;* it will give us the more time for conversation, and for Professor D., the phrenologist, to get here, and whom I have invited—he 's always behind the time—and this treat will be so rich to him—I would not miss him for anything in the world."

My lecturing lungs and stomach being under a running engagement for dinner at three o'clock, the sound of " *six* " —then, " no, *seven,*" with the words " Indian poem," " phrenologist," &c., produced a most rebellious and faltering sensation in my chest; the one entirely exhausted from its customary exertions until three o'clock, and the other, at that moment, completely in a state of collapse. The difficult trials I had lived through with the latter, however, in my wild adventures in the Indian wilderness, and the more recent proofs in the Egyptian Hall, of the elasticity of the other, inspired me with courage to enter upon the ordeal that was before me, and (even in distress) justly to appreciate what was so kindly preparing for me.

I here instantly forgot my troubles as the party entered from the gardens, when I was thus presented by my good friend:—" Ellen, my dear, and Betty, here 's Mr. Catlin ; and, Mr. S——n, I have the extreme pleasure of presenting to your acquaintance the famous Mr. Catlin, whose name and whose works are familiar to you : and now, Catlin, my dear fellow, I introduce you to Mr. J. S., the son of the gentleman with whom I have just made you acquainted. Mr. J. S. has just returned from amongst the natives of New Zealand, where he has spent three or four years ; and your descriptions of all the modes and customs of the North American Indians, compared with his accounts of the New Zealanders, will be so rich a treat to us !——But, Catlin, you look pale ! Are you not well? You look so fagged !"   " Yes, yes ; I am well."   " Oh, that plagued exhibition of yours—it will be the death of you ! You must keep away from it, or you will talk yourself to death there ! My good friends, come, take seats !   Catlin, my dear fellow, come, join us in a glass of good old sherry—it will give you an appetite for your dinner—Is it to your liking?"   " I thank you, it is very fine."   " Will you take another?" " No, I am much obliged to you."   " My dear, look at the clock—what time is it?"   " Quarter past five."   " Ah, well, I didn't think it was so late—be sure to have the dinner up at seven—do you hear?"

Oh, Time and Paper! I will not tax you with the pains of kindness I was at that moment entering upon—I, who had been for eight years eating at the simple Indians' hos-

Nº 3.

pitable boards, where eating and talking are seldom done together; or taking my solitary meals, cooked by my own hand, where I had no one to talk with—but will leave it to Imagination's exhaustless colours, which, for a harmless pastime, will paint the pleasures, perhaps, of the dragging hours of my lifetime that I sighed through from that until twelve o'clock at night (the last half-hour of which I had stood upon my feet, with my hat in my hand, taking affectionate leave, with, " My dear, charming Sir, you can't tell how happy we have all been—your accounts have been so interesting! You *must* come another evening and dine with us, and we will have Mr. G. and Mr. and Mrs. L——n; they will be so impatient to hear you tell all you have told us. Good night!—*good* night!—we shall all be in a party at your exhibition to-morrow at an early hour, at ten o'clock—mind, don't forget the hour—and it will be so delightful to hear you explain everything in your collection, which my dear husband has seen so often, and says are so curious and interesting. Poor fellow! he is quite knocked up—he has been up all day, and constantly talking; and was so completely worn out that he went off to bed an hour ago—you will know how to excuse him. We ladies can often entertain our friends long after *his* powers of conversation are fagged out. Good night—good night, my dear Sir —farewell !"

Thus and at that hour I took leave, when the busses and cabs were all still, and I had, from necessity, a solitary walk of three miles to my lodgings ; and before I laid my head on my pillow, from an equal necessity, to feed my poor stomach with some substitute for *dinner,* which had been in abundance before my eyes, but which the constant exercise of my lungs had prevented me from eating. Such a rendezvous as had been appointed for ten o'clock the next day, and by so fair and so kind a lady, even the rough politeness of a savage would have held sacred.

At twelve o'clock on the following morning, and when I had nearly finished my descriptions of Indian modes to the ladies, my kind friend who had taken me to his house the day before, and having a little overslept himself on that morning had taken a late breakfast at eleven, entered the rooms with three or four of his friends, and quite rapidly addressed his wife in the following manner :—"Come now, my dear, you and your party have kept poor Catlin talking and answering questions quite long enough; you will kill him if you don't let him rest once in a while. See how pale the poor man is. Go off and get home as quick as possible. See all this crowd waiting around to talk him to death when you are done with him. I have brought Mr. C., the famous mineralogist, and the two Mr. N.'s, the geologists, to whom I want him to explain the mineralogy and geology of those boundless regions, of the Missouri and Rocky Mountains, and I was to have had the famous botanist, Mr. D. S—, but he may come by and by; and after we have done here, I am going to take him, that he may have a little relaxation and repose, to the British Museum, which he has not seen yet, and to the Geological Society's rooms; and after that, I have got for him an invitation to dine with the Reverend Mr. O., who will have several reverend gentlemen, and the famous Miss E. and Mrs. W., who you know are all so anxious to learn about the Indians' religion and modes of worship." I was then introduced to my friend's three or four companions, but a few moments after was reminded, by one of my men, of an engagement which took me off for the remainder of that day.

CHAPTER V.

In this manner passed the time from day to day, from week to week, and from month to month; and as I was daily growing richer, I was daily growing poorer—*i. e.* I was day by day losing my flesh, not from the usual cause, the want of enough to eat, but from derangement of the lungs and the stomach, both often overworked, with a constant excitement and anxiety of the mind, the seat of which was not far distant.

I endeavoured, however, and gradually succeeded in dividing my time and my thoughts, giving a proper proportion to the public in my rooms, a portion to my friends, and (as it was then becoming a matter of necessity for the preparation of my notes of eight years' travel, which were soon to be published) decidedly the greater part to myself, leaving my exhibition mostly to the management of my men, of whom I had several, and all familiar enough with the meaning of everything in the collection to give a lucid description of its contents.

As I was gradually receding from the exhibition, the arduous duties began to thicken more strongly upon my man Daniel, of whom I have before often spoken. He had been longest associated with me and my collection, and having it more by heart than the rest, was the foremost man in illustrating it, of which he had been curator for seven or eight years. I have before mentioned that he was of a quick and irascible disposition, exceedingly tenacious of national feelings, and those national prejudices mostly in favour of the country I said he had some twenty years since adopted—the United States. Though he was quick-tempered and violent in his prejudices, there was always the redeeming trait at the end, that his anger was soon over, and there was good nature and civility at the bottom.

Though I had often complaints made to me of the want of politeness or of the rudeness of my man Daniel, I generally found that they were instances where he had been provoked to it by some unnecessary allusions to the vices of his own country, or by some objections to his political opinions relative to the institutions of the United States, upon which subjects he holds himself exceedingly punc-tilious and very well prepared for debate. With whatever foibles he has, I have found him invariably and strictly an honest man ; and many of his highest offences alleged to have been given to the public in my rooms, were given strictly in obedience to my orders for the support of the regulations of my exhibition, or for the protection of my property and the advancement of my interest. To those who entered my rooms respectfully for information, he was civil and communicative, and all such drew valuable infor-mation from him, and many became attached to him. His lungs were now labouring for me, while mine were getting a little rest ; and from morning to night of every day he was conducting individuals and parties around the rooms, pointing out and explaining the leading peculiarities of the museum, and answering the thousand questions that were asked by all classes of society relative to the looks, the modes, and habits of the Indians—the countries they lived in—and also of Mr. Catlin, the proprietor and collector of the museum, whom all were anxious to see, and many of whom had been led to believe was himself an Indian.

In my own answering of these questions, many of which

were natural to be raised on so new and exciting a subject, I was often amused, and as often surprised at the novelty and ignorance of many of them, even amongst a polite and well-clad and apparently well-educated class of people. Many of the questions, which only excited a smile with me, elicited broad laughter from Daniel, which he could not help, and having laughed, could not well avoid expressing his surprise at, and his detection of, which gave umbrage, and sometimes was another cause of difficulties that he occasionally though seldom got into.

I observed, after a while, that the same causes which had affected me were emaciating him, and he finally told me that he was talking his lungs out—and that he could not bear it much longer at the rate he was going on. The questions which were constantly put to him in the room were so much of a sort, or class, that there was little variety or novelty in them to please or excite him ; almost every person putting the same ; much the greater part of them being general, and therefore irksome to him, as they were often asked a hundred or more times in the day and as often answered. He came to me one evening, seemingly much relieved from the painful prospect he had been suffering under, and which was still before him, by the hope that I would adopt a plan he had hit upon for obviating much of the difficulty, and of saving his lungs for the explanations of questions which might be casual, and not exactly reduced to rule. He said he had ascertained that there were about 100 questions which were commonplace—were put (and in the same way precisely) by the greater part of people who came in, and had time to ask them ; and that 50 of those, at least, were asked 100 times per day, the answering of which took the greater part of his time and the best part of his strength, which he thought might be reserved for giving more useful information, while these 100 questions, the most of which were extremely simple or silly, and of little importance to be known, might be disposed of by a printed table of answers placed around the rooms for every one to read as they walked, without the loss of time and fatigue consequent upon the usual mode of asking and answering questions. Though I could not consent to adopt his mode, yet I was amused at its ingenuity; and I give here but a small part of his list, which commenced and ran thus:—

" The Indians have *no beards at all*, only may be one in twenty or so."

" The Indians *don't* shave—they pull it out, when they have any beard."

" Virtuous ?—Yes. I should say they are quite as much so as the whites, if the whites would keep away from them and let them alone."

" Ah, as amorous ?—No. Mr. Catlin says they have not the spices of life and the imaginations to set them on, or I'll venture they would be quite as bad as the whites."

" The Indians in *America are not* cannibals. Mr. Catlin says there is no such thing."

" No, there are no tribes that go entirely naked ; they are all very decent."

" The Indians *don't* eat raw meat, they cook it more than the whites do."

" Mr. Catlin was amongst the Indians eight years, and was never killed during that time."

" The scalp is a patch of the skin and hair taken from the top of the head by a warrior when he kills his enemy in battle."

" No, they don't scalp the living—it is not a scalp to count if the man is alive."

" They *sometimes* eat a great deal, to be sure, but generally not so much as white people."

" They *do* get drunk sometimes, but white people sell them rum and make them so, therefore I don't think we ought to call them drunkards exactly."

" The Indians all get married—some have a number of wives."

" Yes, they seem as fond of their wives as any people I ever saw."

" The Indians never injured Mr. Catlin in any way."

" Mr. Catlin *didn't* live on ' raw meat ;' he was one time eighteen months with nothing but meat to eat, but it was well cooked."

" The Indians know *nothing about salt*—they don't use it at all."

" Reason ! yes ; why, do you think they are wild beasts ? to be sure they reason as well as we do."

" They *are* thieves, sometimes ; but I don't think they thieve so often as white people do."

" The Indians *do* lend their wives sometimes to white men, but it is only their old superannuated ones, who are put aside to hard labour, so it is a sort of kindness all around, and I don't see that there is much harm in it."

" The Indians all have their religion, they all worship the Great Spirit."

" They are *treacherous*, to be sure, towards their enemies only, and I'll be whipped if the white people an't just as bad."

" The Indians *are cruel*, there's no mistake about that ; but it is only to their enemies."

" Sale ? there *won't be* any sale ; Mr. Catlin don't intend to sell his collection in this country."

" Mr. Catlin *is not* an Indian."

" No, he has *no* Indian blood in him."

" Mr. Catlin speaks the English language very well."

" The Indians *don't raise* tea."

" They *never eat* the scalps."

" The Indians that Mr. Catlin saw are not *near* Chusan, they are 3,000 miles from there, they are in America."

" You *can't come overland* from America."

" A scalping-knife is *any* large knife that an Indian takes a scalp with."

" A prairie is a meadow."

" The Indians speak *their own* language."

" A pappoose is an Indian baby while it is carried in the cradle."

" A prairie bluff is a hill that is covered with grass."

" The Rocky Mountains are in *America*, between New York and the Pacific Ocean, and *not* in the *Indies* at all."

" A snag is a large tree that is lying in the river, its roots fast in the mud at the bottom, and its trunk at the top, pointing down the stream."

" Sawyers *are not* alligators."

" An alligator is a sort of crocodile."

" The Chesapeake didn't take the Shannon, it was the Shannon that took the Chesapeake."

" The Americans are *white*, the same colour exactly as the English, and speak the same language, only they speak it a great deal better, in general."

" A stump is the but-end and roots of a tree standing in the ground after the tree is chopped down."

" It *is* true that all Indian women stay away from their husbands the seven days of their illness, and I think they are the decentest people of the two for doing it."

" A squaw is an *Indian woman* who is married."

" The *Calumet* is a pipe of peace."

" Horns on a chief's head-dress have *no bad* meaning."

" Mr. Catlin *is not* a repudiator," &c., &c.

And thus went on poor Daniel's list to the number of about 100 commonplace questions which he had hoped to have disposed of by a sort of steam operation ; but finding that they must all continue to be "done by hand," as before, he returned to his post, which, from his disappointment in his unrealized hopes, seemed to drag more heavily than ever upon him, and so rapidly to wear him down that he was obliged to plan a tour to his own native land of Erin, where he went for some weeks, to restore his lungs and his strength. His labour-saving suggestion might have been a very convenient one for me in his absence, but it was dispensed with, and he was soon back at his post, recruited and assuming the command again, whilst I was busy in advancing the material for my forthcoming work.

The Notes of my Eight Years' Travels amongst Forty-eight different Tribes of Indians in America, to be illustrated with more than 300 steel plate illustrations, were nearly ready to be put to press; and I called on my good friend John Murray, in Albemarle Street, believing that he would be glad to publish them for me. To my surprise he objected to them (but without seeing my manuscript), for two reasons which he at once alleged : first, because he was afraid of the great number of illustrations to be embodied in the work, and secondly for (certainly) the most unfashionable reason, that "he loved me too much !" I had brought a letter of introduction to him from his old friend Washington Irving ; and from the deep interest Mr. Murray had taken in my collection and the history and prospects of the poor Indians, my rooms (which were near his dwelling-house) were his almost daily resort, and I a weekly guest at his hospitable board, where I always met gentlemen of eminence connected with literature and art. Good and generous old man ! he therefore "loved me too much " to share with me the profits of a work which he said should all belong to me for my hard labour and the risks of my life I had run in procuring it ; and as the means of enlarging those profits he advised me to publish it myself. " I would advise you," said he, " as one of your best friends, to publish your own book ; and I am sure you will make a handsome profit by it. Being an artist yourself, and able to make the drawings for your 300 illustrations, which for me would require a very great outlay to artists to produce them, and having in your exhibition-room the opportunity of receiving subscriptions for your work, which I could not do, it will be quite an easy thing for you to take names enough to cover all the expenses of getting it up, which at once will place you on safe ground ; and if the work should be well received by Mr. Dilke and others of the critical world, it will insure you a handsome reward for your labours, and exceedingly please your sincere friend, John Murray."

This disinterested frankness endeared me to that good man to his last days, and his advice, which I followed, resulted, as he had predicted, to my benefit. My subscription list my kind friend the Hon. C. A. Murray had in a few days commenced, with the subscriptions of

Her most gracious MAJESTY the QUEEN,
H. R. H. Prince Albert,
Her Majesty the Queen Dowager,
H. R. H. the Duchess of Kent,
His Majesty the King of the Belgians,
H. M. the Queen of the Belgians,
His Royal Highness the Duke of Sussex,
H. R. H. Leopold Duc de Brabant,

After which soon followed a complimentary list of the nobility and gentry, together with the leading institutions of the kingdom.

My work was published by myself, at the Egyptian Hall, and the only fears which my good friend John Murray had expressed for me were all dispersed by the favourable announcements by Mr. Dilke, of the Athenæum, and the editors of other literary journals, from which it will be seen that the subjoined notices are but very brief extracts.

It may not be improper also here to remark, that for all the Royal copies subscribed for above, the Hon. C. A. Murray was ordered to remit me double the amount of the price of the work ; and that, on a subsequent occasion, when my dear wife and myself were guests at the dinner table of John Murray, he said to his old friend Thomas Moore, who was by our side, " That wild man by the side of you there, Mr. Catlin, who has spent enough of his life amongst the wild Indians (sleeping on the ground and eating raw buffalo meat) to make you and I as grey as badgers, and who has not yet a grey hair in his head, applied to me about a year ago to publish his Notes. I was then—for the first time in my life—too honest for my own interest, as well as that of an author ; and I advised him to publish it himself, as the surest way of making something out of it. My wife here will tell you that I have read every word of it through, heavy as it is, and she knows it is the only book that I have read quite through in the last five years. And I tell Mr. Catlin now, in your presence, that I shall regret as long as I live that I did not publish that work for him ; for as sincerely as I advised him, I could have promoted his interest by so doing, and would have done so, had I known what was in the work when he proposed it to me."

The reader will pardon me for inserting here the critical notices which follow :—

EDINBURGH REVIEW. *Fifteen pages.*

" Living with them as one of themselves ; having no trading purposes to serve ; exciting no enmity by the well-meant but suspicious preaching of a new religion, Mr. Catlin went on with his rifle and his pencil, sketching and noting whatever he saw worthy of record ; and wisely abandoning all search for the ancient history of a people who knew no writing, he confined his labours to the depicting exactly what he saw, and that only. Notes and sketches were transmitted, as occasion served, to New York, and the collected results now appear, partly in a gallery which has been for some time exhibited in London, containing some five hundred pictures of Indian personages and scenes, drawn upon the spot, with specimens of their dress and manufactures, their arts and arms ; and partly, as just stated, of the volumes under our hands, which display engravings of most of those specimens and pictures, accompanied by a narrative, written in a very pleasant, homely style, of his walks and wanderings in the ' *Far West.*'

" The reader will find a compensation in the vigour of the narrative, which, like a diary, conveys the vivid impressions of the moment, instead of being chilled and tamed down into a more studied composition. Such as the work is, we strongly recommend it to the perusal of all who wish to make themselves acquainted with a singular race of men and system of manners, fast disappearing from the face of the earth; and which have nowhere else been so fully, curiously, and graphically described." ,

WESTMINSTER REVIEW. *Twelve pages.*

" This is a remarkable book, written by an extraordinary man. A work valuable in the highest degree for its novel and curious information about one of the most neglected and least understood branches of the human family. Mr. Catlin, without any pretension to talent in authorship, has yet produced a book which will live as a record when the efforts of men of much higher genius have been forgotten. Every one in London has seen Mr. Catlin's unique gallery, and his attractive exhibition of living models at the Egyptian Hall; we cannot too strongly recommend them to our country friends. And here we take our leave of a work over which we have lingered with much pleasure, strongly recommending it to the reader, and hoping its extensive sale will amply repay Mr. Catlin for the great outlay he must have incurred."

DUBLIN UNIVERSITY MAGAZINE. *Fifteen pages.*

" Mr. Catlin's book is one of the most interesting which we have perused on the subject of the Indians. His pencil has preserved the features of races which in a few years will have disappeared; and his faithful and accurate observations may be considered as the storehouse from whence future writers on such topics will extract their most authentic statements."

TAIT'S EDINBURGH MAGAZINE. *Two Notices, Twenty-two pages.*

" This is altogether an *unique* work. It may be considered as a *Catalogue Raisonnée* of the numerous objects of art and curiosity which Mr. Catlin has collected in the course of his wanderings, and arranged in his Indian Gallery. The narrative of Mr. Catlin's personal adventures during the wandering years in which he was thus engaged, forms a work as unique in literature, as his collection of original portraits and curiosities is rare in art.

" Many curious traits of character and pictures of manners are exhibited in these large and closely-printed volumes, which will remain an interesting record of the Homeric age and race of North America, when, save a few wild traditions and scattered relics, and a few of the musical and sonorous Indian names of lakes, rivers, and hunting grounds, every other trace of the red man will have perished on that vast continent."

LITERARY GAZETTE, *London. Three Notices, Twenty-five Columns.*

" *Catlin's Book on the North American Indians.*—An *unique* work ! A work of extraordinary interest and value. Mr. Catlin is *the* Historian of the Red Races of mankind ; of a past world, or at least of a world fast passing away, and leaving hardly a trace or wreck behind. We need not recommend it to the world, for it recommends itself, beyond our praise."

ATHENÆUM, *London.   Four Notices, Thirty-one Columns.*

" The public have fully confirmed the opinion we formerly pronounced on Catlin's Indian gallery, as the most interesting exhibition which, in our recollection, had been opened in London.   The production of the *work* will, therefore, be most acceptable to those who have seen the exhibition, as serving to refresh their memories ; to those who have not, as helping to explain that of which they have heard so much ; to all as a pleasant narrative of adventure, and a circumstantial and detailed history of the manners and customs of an interesting people, whose fate is sealed, whose days are numbered, whose extinction is certain.   The Americans should make much of Mr. Catlin for the sake of by-gone days, which his books, portraits, and collections will present to their grandchildren."

ART UNION, *London.*

" We have rarely examined a work at once so interesting and so useful as this ; the publication of which is, in truth, a benefit conferred upon the world ; for it is a record of things rapidly passing away, and the accurate traces of which are likely to be lost within a brief time after they have been discovered.   As a contribution to the history of mankind, these volumes will be of rare value long after the last of the persecuted races are with ' the Great Spirit,' and they may even have some *present* effect ; for they cannot fail to enlist the best sympathies of humanity on the side of a most singular people.   The book is exceedingly simple in its style ; it is the production of a man of benevolent mind, kindly affections, and sensitive heart, as well as of keen perceptions and sound judgment.   If we attempted to do justice to its merits, we should fill a *number* of our work instead of a *column* of it ; we must content ourselves with recommending its perusal to all who covet knowledge or desire amusement ;—no library in the kingdom should be without a copy.".

TIMES, *London.   One Notice, Three Columns.*

" The reflection is almost insupportable to a humane mind, that the indigenous races of America, comprising numerous distinct nations, the original proprietors of that vast continent, are probably doomed to entire extermination—a fate which has already befallen a large portion of the red tribes.   It is still more painful to think that this should be the effect of the spread of the civilized races, who thus become the agents of a wholesale destruction of their fellow-men.   If these melancholy truths were capable of aggravation, it may be found in the dreadful fact that the process of destruction is not left to the slow operation of invisible and insensible causes, but is hastened by expedients devised for that express end by civilized men, the tribes being stimulated or compelled to the destruction of each other, or provided with the means of destroying themselves.

" Mr. Catlin, the author of the work which has suggested these observations, has had better opportunities for studying the character of the North American Indians than most travellers since the early French writers.

" Mr. Catlin is an American, a native of Wyoming, and the publisher of his own work, at the Egyptian Hall."

MORNING CHRONICLE, *London.*

" As a work intended merely for general amusement, and independently of the higher object to which it is devoted, Mr. Catlin's book will be found exceedingly interesting. The salient or rugged points of its style have not been smoothed down by any literary journeyman. Mr. Catlin ventures alone and unaided before the public. What he has seen in the prairie, and noted down in its solitude, he sends forth, with all the wildness and freshness of nature about it. This, together with his free and easy conversational style, plentifully sprinkled with Americanisms, gives a peculiar charm to his descriptions, which are not merely animated or life-like, but *life* itself. The reader is made to believe himself in the desert, or lying among friendly Indians in the wigwam, or hurried along in the excitement of the chase. He is constantly surrounded by the figures of the red man, and hears the rustle of their feathers, or the dash of their half-tamed steeds as they bound by him.

" The work is ornamented with hundreds of engravings, taken from original pictures drawn by Mr. Catlin, of the persons, manners, customs, and scenes that he met with in his wanderings. They give an additional value to those volumes which are published, as the title-page informs us, by Mr. Catlin himself, at the Egyptian Hall. We wish him all the success to which his candour no less than his talents fully entitle him."

MORNING HERALD, *London.*

" In the two ample volumes just published, and illustrated with more than 300 plates, Mr. Catlin has given to the world a lasting and invaluable memorial of the doomed race of the Red Man, which, after having from immemorial time held the unmolested tenancy of an entire continent, is now but too obviously hurried on to utter extinction. Mr. Catlin's literary matter resembles his drawings; it has all the freshness of the sketch from nature. Through both he brings us into companionship with the red man, as if careering with him over the boundless plains, the primeval forests of his hunting grounds in the far West, or in the vicinity of his temporary village settlements, witnessing his athletic games, his strange, fantastic dances, and his spontaneous endurance of those revolting tortures by which he evinces his unflinching stoicism."

Morning Post, *London.*

" Upwards of three hundred very well executed etchings from the paintings, drawn by Mr. Catlin, adorn these volumes, and offer to the eye one of the most complete museums of an almost unknown people that ever was given to the public. The style of the narrative is diffuse, inartificial, and abounding in Yankeeisms ; but it is earnest, honest, and unpretending ; and contains most undoubted and varied information relative to the red savage of America, fresh from the wilds, and unembittered by border hostility or unfounded prejudice. These volumes are handsomely printed, and ' brought out,' in all respects, with much care and taste."

Spectator, *London. Five Columns.*

" The illustrative plates of these volumes are numbering upwards of three hundred subjects—landscapes, hunting scenes, Indian ceremonies, and portraits form a remarkable feature, and possess a permanent interest as graphic records. They are outline etchings from the author's paintings, and are admirable for the distinct and lively manner in which the characteristics of the scenes and persons are portrayed : what is called a *style of art* would have been impertinent, and might have tended to falsify. Mr. Catlin, in his homely, but spirited manner, seizes upon the most distinguishing points of his subjects by dint of understanding their value, and every touch has significance and force : hence the number of details and the extent of view embraced in these small and slight sketches, hence their animation and reality."

Atlas, *London. Three Notices, Twelve Columns.*

" This publication may be regarded as the most valuable accession to the history of the fast perishing races of the aboriginal world that has ever been collected by a single individual. The descriptions it contains are minute and full, and possess the advantage of being wonderfully tested by the long experience of the writer, and verified by the concurrent testimonials of many individuals intimately acquainted with the scenes and races delineated. The engravings, which are liberal to an unprecedented extent, cannot be too highly praised for their utility as illustrations. To the readers who have never had an opportunity of visiting Mr. Catlin's gallery, these engravings will form for them quite a museum of Indian curiosities in themselves ; while to those already familiar with the actual specimens, they will serve as useful and agreeable souvenirs. But we chiefly approve and recommend this work to universal circulation for the sake of the pure and noble philanthropy by which it is everywhere inspired. As the advocate of the oppressed Indian, now vanishing before the white man on the soil of his fathers, Mr. Catlin deserves the unmixed thanks of the Christian world. His volumes are full of stimulants to benevolent exertion, and bear the strongest testimony to the character of the races for whose preservation he pleads."

UNITED SERVICE GAZETTE, *London.*

" Mr. Catlin is one of the most remarkable men of the age. Every one who has visited his singularly interesting gallery at the Egyptian Hall, must have been struck by his remarkable intelligence on every subject connected with the North American Indians ; but of its extent, as well as of his extraordinary enthusiasm and thirst for adventure, we had formed no idea until we had perused these volumes. In the present *blazé* condition of English literature, in which hardly any work is published that is not founded more or less on other volumes which have preceded it, until authorship has dwindled to little more than the art of emptying one vessel into another, it is refreshing to come across a book which, like the one before us, is equally novel in subject, manner, and execution, and which may be pronounced, without hyperbole, one of the most original productions which have issued from the press for many years. It is wholly impossible, in the compass of a newspaper notice, either to analyze or afford even a tolerable idea of the contents of such a book ; and for the present, at least, we must limit ourselves altogether to the first volume."

CALEDONIAN MERCURY, *Edinburgh.*

"*Mr. Catlin's Lectures on the North-American Indians.*—We have much pleasure in publishing the following testimonial from a gentleman well qualified to pronounce an opinion, on the remarkable fidelity and effect of Mr. Catlin's interesting and instructive exhibition :—

'Cottage, Haddington, 15th April, 1843.
' Dear Sir,—I have enjoyed much pleasure in attending your lectures at the Waterloo-rooms in Edinburgh. Your delineations of the Indian character, the display of beautiful costumes, and the native Indian manners, true to the life, realised to my mind and view scenes I had so often witnessed in the parts of the Indian countries where I had been ; and for twenty years' peregrinations in those parts, from Montreal to the Great Slave River, north, and from the shores of the Atlantic, crossing the Rocky Mountains, to the mouth of the Columbia River, on the Pacific Ocean, west, I had opportunities of seeing much. Your lectures and exhibition have afforded me great pleasure and satisfaction, and I shall wish you all that success which you so eminently deserve, for the rich treat which you have afforded in our enlightened, literary, and scientific metropolis.
'I remain, dear Sir, yours very truly,
' *To George Catlin, Esq.*' 'JOHN HALDANE.

" The following is an extract of a letter received some days since by a gentleman in Edinburgh, from Mr. James Hargrave, of the Hudson's Bay Company, dated York Factory, Hudson's Bay, 10th December, 1842 :—

'Should you happen to fall in with Catlin's Letters on the North American Indians, I would strongly recommend a perusal of them for the purpose of acquiring a knowledge of the habits and customs of those tribes among whom he was placed. Catlin's sketches are true to life, and are powerfully descriptive of their appearance and character.' "

THE WORLD OF FASHION, *London.*

" We venture to affirm of Mr. Catlin's book, which can be said of very few others, that it is impossible to open it at any page, and not continue its perusal with unmingled satisfaction. It has too the rare quality of being written by a man who says nothing but that which he knows, who describes nothing but that which he has seen. We feel while reading the book as in the society of a man of extraordinary observation, of great talent, of wonderful accomplishments; and most cordially and earnestly do we recommend this invaluable book to the patronage of the public generally, and to the perusal of our readers in particular."

WEEKLY DISPATCH, *London.*

" A person might well be startled and frightened at the appearance of two such large volumes as these on only the manners, customs, and condition of the North American Indians, a race of savages now almost extinct. With all this complaint against the immense bulk of a book, moreover, on such a subject, we are bound to confess that not only is it the least wearisome of large books that we have for a long time seen, but that it is at least one of the most amusing and animating amongst even the condensed publications that for a considerable period have been submitted to our perusal and judgment, and we can confidently recommend it to our readers."

CHAMBERS'S EDINBURGH JOURNAL. *Two Notices, Four Columns.*

" Of all the works yet published on the subject of the aboriginal inhabitants of North America, no one, it seems to us, can be compared in point of accuracy and extent of research with that of Mr. Catlin. In the course of eight years he traversed North America almost from end to end, saw and mixed with forty-eight Indian tribes, composing a large portion of the two millions of red people yet in existence, examined personally into all their peculiarities, and, finally, accumulated a noble gallery of portraits, and a rich museum of curiosities, calculated to form at once a lasting monument to himself and an invaluable record of Indian persons, manners, and habiliments.

" Mr. Catlin, combining all the qualities of the traveller, artist, and historian, merits no sparing notice. His two volumes, large octavo, and closely printed, are full of most interesting matter, and contain, besides, upwards of three hundred beautiful illustrations, engraved from the original paintings."

"Légation des Etats-Unis, Paris, Dec. 8th, 1841.

" Dear Sir,—No man can appreciate better than myself the admirable fidelity of your drawings and book, which I have lately received. They are equally spirited and accurate; they are true to nature. Things that *are*, are not sacrificed, as they too often are by the painter, to things as in his judgment they should be.

" During eighteen years of my life I was superintendent of Indian affairs in the north-western territory of the United States; and during more than five I was Secretary of War, to which department belongs the general control of Indian concerns. I know the Indians thoroughly; I have spent many a month in their camps, council-houses, villages, and hunting grounds; I have fought with them and against them; and I have negotiated seventeen treaties of peace or of cession with them. I mention these circumstances to show you that I have a good right to speak confidently upon the subject of your drawings; among them I recognize many of my old acquaintances, and everywhere I am struck with the vivid representations of them and their customs, of their peculiar features and of their costumes. Unfortunately they are receding before the advancing tide of our population, and are probably destined, at no distant day, wholly to disappear; but your collection will preserve them, as far as human art can do, and will form the most perfect monument of an extinguished race that the world has ever seen.

" *To Geo. Catlin.*"   " LEWIS CASS.

CHAPTER VI.

The Author's wife and two children arrive in the British Queen, from New York—First appreciation of London—Sight-seeing—Author lectures in the Royal Institution—Suggests a *Museum of Mankind*—Great applause—Vote of thanks by members of the Royal Institution—The "*Museum of History*"—Author lectures in the other literary and scientific institutions of London—Author dines with the Royal Geographical Society, and with the Royal Geological Society—Mrs. Catlin's travels in the "Far West"—Her welcome, and kind friends in London.

MY work being published under the flattering auspices explained in the foregoing pages, and now in the hands of the reading public, attracted additional numbers of visitors to my Rooms, greatly increasing the labours of poor Daniel, and calling also for more of my time and attention, which I could now better devote to it. My old friends were calling to congratulate me on the success of my book, and strangers to form an acquaintance with me and offer me the civilities of their houses.

Though every part of these calls upon my time, either in the labours of my exhibition or in the society of friends, was pleasing and gratifying to me, yet it became necessary for my health to evade a part of these excitements on either hand, and I subsequently endeavoured, by a limited indulgence in the pleasures of society, and a moderate endurance of the excitements and fatigue of my Rooms, to save my life; throwing the cares and labours of the exhibition, as much as possible, upon the broader shoulders and stronger lungs of Daniel and his assistants.

I felt now as if I had a sort of citizenship in London, and began to think of seeing its "sights;" and from this time may date the commencement of my real appreciation of the elegances and comforts of London, its hospitalities, and the genuine English character.

It was an opportune moment, also, for the arrival of my dear wife and her two infant children, for whom I had written to New York, and who were just landing from the British Queen, in London, to share the kind attentions and compliments that were being paid to me, and also for seeing with me the sights and curiosities of the metropolis.

About this time I was highly complimented by an invitation to deliver a lecture in the Royal Institution, Albemarle-street. The venerable members of that institution were nearly all present, and every seat was filled. I had, on the occasion, several living figures, dressed in Indian costumes, with weapons in hand, as well as many of my paintings exhibited on my easel, as illustrations; and I was highly gratified with the attention and repeated applause, convincing me that the subject and myself were kindly received.

I endeavoured, in the compass of an evening's lecture, to give as comprehensive a view as I could of the motives which had led me into the Indian countries—of the time I had spent in them—of the extent and nature of the collection I had made—of the condition and numbers of the various tribes, and of their personal appearance and habits of life, which I illustrated by my numerous paintings, and by the curious manufactures of their own hands. I endeavoured also to delineate their true native character, as I had found it in its most primitive condition—and to explain the principal causes that have been, and still are, leading to their rapid declension.

I took advantage of this occasion likewise to introduce a subject which had been for many years my favourite theme, which had constantly stimulated me through my toils in the Indian country, and which, as I was the first to propose in my own country, I believe I was the first to suggest on this side of the Atlantic—a MUSEUM of MANKIND. A shout of enthusiastic applause burst from every part of the Hall when the subject was named, and rounds of applause followed every sentence when I proceeded to say, that in the toils and dangers of my remotest travels in the wilderness I had been strengthened and nerved by the hope and the belief, that if I lived to finish my studies and to return with my collection, I should be able to show to the world the plan upon which a Museum could be formed, to contain and perpetuate the looks and manners and history of all the declining and vanishing races of man, and that my collection would ultimately form the basis of such an institution.

I agreed with all the world as to the great interest and value of their noble collections of beasts, and birds, and reptiles, of fossils, of minerals, of fishes, of insects, and of plants, all of which can be gathered hundreds of years hence as well as at the present time; and I believed that all of the reasoning world who would give the subject a moment's thought, would agree with *me*, that there was one museum yet to be made, far transcending in interest and value all others yet designed, and which must needs be made soon, or it will be for ever lost—a museum containing the familiar looks, the manufactures, history, and records of all the remnants of the declining races of our fellow-men.

It occurred to me, and I said it then, that Great Britain has more than thirty colonies in different quarters of the globe, in which the numbers of civilized men are increasing, and the native tribes are wasting away—that the march of civilization is everywhere, as it is in America, a war of extermination, and that of our own species. For the occupation of a new country, the first enemy that must fall is *man*, and his like cannot be transplanted from any other quarter of the globe. Our war is not with beasts or with birds: the grizly bear, the lion, and the tiger are allowed to live. Our weapons are not employed against them : we do not give them whiskey, and rum, and the small pox, nor the bayonet; they are allowed to live and thrive upon our soil, and yet their skins are of great value in our museums ; but to complete a title, man, our fellow-man, the noblest work of God, with thoughts, with sentiments and sympathies like our own, must be extinguished ; and he dies on his own soil, unchronicled and unknown (save to the ruthless hands that have slain him, and would bury his history with his body in oblivion), when not even his *skin* has a place assigned it amongst those of the beasts and birds of his country.

From England, from France, and the United States, government vessels, in this age of colonization, are floating to every part of the globe, and in them, artists and men of science could easily be conveyed to every race, and their collections returned free of expense, were there an institution formed and ready to receive and perpetuate the results of their labours.

I believed that the time had arrived for the creation of such an institution, and that well-directed efforts to bring it into existence would have the admiration and countenance of all the philanthropic world.

There was but one expression of feeling from every part of the hall at the close of these remarks, and every voice seemed to say " Yes—the noble philanthropy of this Christian and enlightened and enlightening age calls for it, and it must be done before it is too late."*

A few days after my lecture was delivered, I received with much satisfaction from the secretary of the institution the following communication, which the reader will allow me the vanity of inserting here :—

" Sir,—I have the honour to return you the thanks of the members of the *Royal Institution of Great Britain* for your interesting account of your residence and adventures among the native tribes of North American

---

* The noble and unaided efforts of my best of friends, Captain Shippard, to bring into existence such an institution, are, I believe, too well known and appreciated by the English public to require more of me here, than barely to refer to his beautifully illustrated lectures on the " *Arabians* " and the " *Ruined Cities of America ;*" and whilst wishing all success to his noble enterprise, I beg to refer the reader to Appendix B for a synopsis of his design.

Indians, with notices of their social condition, customs, mysteries, and modes of warfare—communicated at the weekly meeting of the members on Friday, the 14th February.

"I am, Sir, your very obedient Servant,

"EDWARD R. DANIELL, *Secretary*.

"*To Geo. Catlin, Esq.*"

Invitations from the other literary and scientific institutions of London afforded me the opportunity of repeating my lectures in most of their halls, where I was uniformly received with applause, which was also a source of much gratification to me. These interviews suddenly and delightfully led me into the society of literary and scientific men, and also into the noble collections and libraries under their superintendence. I was here at once ushered, as it were, into a new world—a new atmosphere—and in it was met and welcomed every where with the utmost cordiality and kindness; libraries, museums, laboratories, and lectures were free to me; and not only the private tables of the advocates of science, but their public tables in their banqueting halls, prepared a seat for me.

Thus were my labours being requited; and I was happy in the conviction that the claims of the poor Indians were being heard in the right tribunal, and that I was their advocate at the true source from which emanated most of the great and moral influences that govern and improve the world.

I was invited to the annual dinners of the Royal Geographical, Geological, and Historical Societies; and in responding to the compliments paid me at all of them, in proposing my health and the prosperity of my country, I was delighted to find that my advocacy of the rights of the poor Indian, and my scheme for a *Museum* of *Mankind*, were met and sanctioned with rounds of enthusiastic applause.

I have mentioned that my dear wife with her two children had arrived from New York, and the pleasures and endearments of my own little fireside, now transplanted into a foreign land, were stealing away their part of my time, which, with the necessary attention to the kind civilities being paid us, our sight-seeing, our dinings-out, our drives, and my attendance in my rooms and lectures at night, was curiously divided and engrossed.

The advent of my dear Clara, with her two babes, was like the coming of the warm and gentle breezes of spring—she who, though delicate and tender, had been, during the three last years of my rambles in the Indian wilds, my indefatigable companion—She who had traced and retraced with me the winding mazes of the mighty Mississippi, the Missouri, the Ohio, and the Arkansas—and with the lightness of the bounding antelopes that dwell upon their shores, had darted over their grassy banks and their green carpeted and enamelled slopes, and plucked their loveliest flowers — she who had also traced with me the shores of the great lakes of the north, and inhaled the glowing sweetness of Florida's lovely coast—and had kept her journal of thirteen thousand miles of wild rambles with her husband, and since her return to the land of her birth had blessed him in the richness of gift with two children, was now by his side (as I have said, like the coming of spring), to cheer him with the familiar sweet smiles and sounds in which he never knew guile.*

Thanks to the kind friends who took her fair hand and bade her welcome—for they were many, and ready to contribute to her happiness, which filled (at that moment at least) the cup of our mutual enjoyment.

---

* The reader will pardon these expressions, and others of a similar nature that may occasionally occur, for they apply to one who now rests with the silent dead, as will be explained in future pages of this work.

CHAPTER VII.

The Author dines with the Royal Highland Society—The Duke of Richmond presides—His Grace's compliment to the Author and his country—
Sir David Wilkie—His compliment to the Author—Charles Augustus
Murray and the Author at the Caledonian Ball (Almack's) in Indian costumes—Their rehearsal—Dressing and painting—Entering the ball—
Alarm of ladies—Mr. Murray's infinite amusement (*incognito*) amongst
his friends—War-dance and war-whoops—Great applause—Bouquets
of flowers—Scalp-dance—Brooches and bracelets presented to the chiefs—
Trinkets returned—Perspiration carries off the paint, and Mr. Murray
recognised—Amusement of his friends—The " Indians " return to Egyptian Hall at seven in the morning—Their amusing appearance.

AMONG the many very friendly invitations extended to me
about this time, there was one which I cannot omit to notice
in this place.—I was invited to take a seat at the *Royal
Highland Society's* annual dinner, at which his Grace the
Duke of Richmond presided. The name of this society
explains its character, and most of the guests at the table
were in full highland dress, with their kilts, and with the
badges and plaids of their peculiar clans. The scene was
altogether a very picturesque one, and I observed that their
chiefs wore the eagle's quills for the same purpose and in
the same manner that the Indians do ; but I did not see any
of them painted red, as the Indians paint them, to adorn
their heads as symbols of war when they are going to battle.

The banqueting hall was beautifully arranged, and two
of Her Majesty's pipers from the Palace, in the most gorgeous Highland dress, were perambulating the table " in
full blast " whilst we were eating.

The Duke of Richmond, who is an easy, affable, and entirely unostentatious man, and the best president at a con-
vivial table that I ever saw, offered the customary healths, of

—the Queen—the Prince—the Duke, &c., which were drunk with the usual enthusiasm, and after that proceeded to pay his ingenious and judicious compliments to individuals at the table, by alluding, in the most concise and amusing manner, to their exploits or other merits, and then proposed their healths.

After we had all joined in the uproar of—Hip, hip, hips,— with one foot on our chairs and the other on the table, in a number of such cases, he arose and said—

"Gentlemen, I now rise quite confident of your approbation of the sentiment I am to propose, and the sentiments I am to offer. The nations of the earth, like the individuals in the different branches of a great family, stand in certain degrees of relationship towards each other; and as those degrees of consanguinity are more or less remote, so are the friendships and attachments of those nations for each other. Now, gentlemen, as an individual component part of one of the great nations of that great national family, I feel proud to say, that there are two of that family so closely related, not only in commercial interests, but by blood, as almost to identify them in an unity of existence.—The relationship that I speak of, gentlemen (and which I believe will be familiar to many of you, as married men), is that of parent and child."

At this period commenced a tremendous cheering, and all eyes seemed to be in a rotary motion, endeavouring to fix upon the representative of that nearly related country on whom the next responsibility was to fall. His Grace proceeded :—

"Gentlemen, the term parent and child I have used to express the endearments of one stage of domestic relations; but there is another which lessens not the tie, but carries with it the respect that children do not win —I would call it father and son (*immense cheering*). I perceive, gentlemen, that you all understand me, and are preparing for the sentiment I am to offer; but I would remark, that when a distinguished individual from one of those nearly related countries pays a visit to the other, common courtesy demands that he should be treated with kindness and respect. If that individual, gentlemen, be one who, by the force and energy of his own mind, has struck out and accomplished any great undertaking for the advancement of science, or the benefit of mankind, he is a philanthropist, a public benefactor, and entitled to our highest admiration (*cheering*).

"Gentlemen, I have the satisfaction of informing you that there is at our table an individual whose name when I mention it will be familiar to most of you; who, contemplating several millions of human beings in his own country sinking into oblivion before the destructive influences of civilization, had the energy of character, the courage and philanthropy, to throw himself, unprotected and unaided, into the midst of them, with his brushes and his pen, endeavouring to preserve for future ages their familiar looks, and all that appertained to their native modes and history.   In this noble enterprise, gentlemen, this individual laboured eight years of his life; and having with incessant toil and hazard visited most of the native tribes of North America, he has brought home and to our city a collection (which I trust you have all seen) of vast interest and value, which does great honour to his name, and entitles him to our highest admiration and esteem.   I now propose, gentlemen, the health of Mr. Catlin, and success to the great country that gave him birth!"

Whilst these compliments were applying to my country only, I was fully confident there was some one of my countrymen present better able than myself to respond to them; but when they became personal, and all eyes were fixed upon me, I saw there was no alternative, and that I must reply, as well as I could, to the unexpected compliment thus paid me and answered to with a bumper and many rounds of applause, every guest at the table, as before, with one foot on his chair and the other on the edge of the table.   An awful pause for a moment, while my name was echoed from every part of the room, brought me upon my feet, and I replied: but I never shall recollect exactly how.   I believe, however, that I explained the views with which I had visited the Indian tribes, and what I had done; and put in a few words, as well as I could, for my country.

His Grace next rose, and, after the most chaste and eloquent eulogium upon his works and his character, proposed the health of Sir David Wilkie, who, to my great surprise and unspeakable satisfaction, I found was sitting by my side and the next to my elbow. His health was drunk with great enthusiasm, and after he had responded to the compliment he begged to be allowed to express to his Grace and the gentlemen present the very great satisfaction he had felt in being able to join in the expression of thanks to so distinguished a gentleman as Mr. Catlin, and whom it afforded him great pleasure to find was by his side. He stated that he had been many times in my exhibition rooms, but without the good luck to have met me there.   He commented at great length upon the importance and value of the collection ; and, while he was according to me great credit for the boldness and originality of the design, he took especial pains to compliment me for the execution of my paintings, many of which, he said, as works of art, justly entitled me to the hands of artists in this country, and he was proud to begin by offering me his, in good fellowship, which he did, and raised me from my seat as he said it.

This was sanctioned by a round of applause, and as he resumed his seat I was left upon my feet, and bound again to reply, which I did as well as I could.

The reader can more easily imagine than I can describe, how gratifying to me was such a mode of acquaintance with so distinguished and so worthy a man as Sir David Wilkie, at whose elbow I was now placed, and, for the most part of the evening, in familiar conversation.

The pipers played, the wine flowed, many good songs were sung ; a Highland dance was spiritedly flung by M'Ian, M'Donald, and several others, in Highland costume.   An Indian song and the war-whoop were called for, and given—and with other good fellowship and fun this splendid affair was finished.

I was at this time devoting certain hours of the day to visitors in my Rooms, and I found my kind friend C. A. Murray almost daily bringing ladies of rank and fashion upon his arm, to take a peep into the mysteries of savage life, which he was so well prepared to explain to them, and to illustrate by my numerous paintings and works of Indian manufacture.

I met him here one day, however, on my entering, where he had been for some time waiting without acting the beau for any one, which was quite an unusual thing.   He called me aside, and told me there was a chance for us to make *a sensation* if I felt disposed to join him in it, and to make a great deal of amusement for others as well as a dish of fun for ourselves—this was, to assume the Indian costume, and throw ourselves into the Caledonian ball, which was to be given at Almack's that evening, and for which he had procured the tickets. For the information of those who never have seen one of those annual balls, I will briefly say that they are decidedly the most brilliant and splendid affairs that can be seen in London—presenting the most gorgeous display of costumes and diamonds that the world can exhibit, short of royalty itself. It was but for Mr. Murray to propose—the finest costumes were taken from the walls of my Room—weapons, head-dresses, scalping-knives, scalps, &c.—and placed in one of the chambers of the Egyptian Hall: and three o'clock was the hour appointed for Mr. Murray to meet me again, to fit us with our respective dresses, and go through a sort of rehearsal in our songs, dances, &c., which we might be called upon to enact during the evening, and in which it would be a great pity for us Indian knowing ones to make any mistake.

Mr. Murray was punctual at the hour of three; and having proposed that my nephew, Burr Catlin, a young man of 21 years and then living with me, should be of the party, we entered the dressing-room, and were soon suited with our respective dresses and took our weapons in hand. My nephew, Burr, being six feet two inches, with a bold and Indian outline of face, was arrayed in a Sioux dress; and it was instantly agreed that he should be put forward as the Big Sioux—the Great Chief Wan-ne-ton. He happened to wear the identical head-dress of that distinguished chief, which was made of war-eagle's quills and ermine skins. He was to hold himself entirely mute upon his dignity, according to the customs of the country. I was dressed as a warrior of the *Sac* tribe, with head ornaments of red and white quills of the war-eagle, denoting, according to the custom of the country, my readiness for war or for peace. Mr. Murray had chosen a dress less rich, and more light and easy to act in, and a head-dress that was made much like a wig of long black hair spreading over his shoulders and falling down nearly to the calves of his legs, surmounted by a solitary eagle's quill—giving himself more the appearance of a "Bois Brûlé," as they are termed on the Indian frontiers of America—a race of half-castes, who are generally used as interpreters, speaking a little French and some "Americaine" (as they call the English language). These curious personages are generally the spokesmen for all parties of Indians travelling abroad or delegations to neighbouring tribes. This character exactly suited Mr. Murray, as he spoke the French and the German, and also a little of two or three Indian tongues; and, in the position of an interpreter for the party, he would be the vehicle of communication between the two chiefs and his numerous friends and relations, both ladies and gentlemen, whom he was to meet in every part of the Rooms.

The least discerning will easily see that he was most ingeniously laying his plans for a great deal of amusement; and if my readers could have seen the manner in which he was dressed out and metamorphosed for the occasion, they would have insured him, at a low premium, fun enough on that evening to have lasted him for a week. Having arrayed our persons in the respective costumes we had agreed upon, and arranged the different characters which we were to sustain, I took the Indian drum or tambour in my hand, and to the music of that and the chief's rattle, and our combined voices in concert in an Indian song, we practised the war-dance and scalp-dance of the Sioux, until we agreed that we could "do them" beyond (at least) the reach of civilized criticisms, in case we should be called upon to dance, which it was agreed should be at first met as a condescension that the chiefs could not submit to, but which it was understood we should yield to if the measure was to be very strenuously urged. Matters being thus arranged, we adjourned until nine o'clock, when we were to meet again, and make our final preparations for our début in the ball-room.

At nine we were drawing on our buckskin leggings, and mocassins fringed with scalp-locks and ornamented with

porcupine quills of various dyes; our shirts or tuniques were
also of deerskins richly ornamented, and their sleeves fringed,
like the leggings, with locks of the hair of Indian victims
slain in battle. We painted our faces and hands of a copper
colour, in close imitation of the colour of the Indian, and
over and across that, to make the illusion more complete,
gave occasional bold daubs of vermilion and green or
black paint, so that, with our heavy and richly garnished
robes of the buffalo, thrown over our shoulders and trailing
on the floor as we walked, with tomahawks and scalping
knives in our belts, our shields of buffalo hides on our arms,
with our quivers slung and our bows and arrows clenched
in our hands, we were prepared for the sensation we were
in a few minutes to make. We stood and smiled at each
others' faces a few moments in curious anticipation, prac-
tising over each other's names, which we had almost forgotten to take. And having decided that the great chief
was *Wan-ne-ton*, that the warrior's name was *Na-see-us-kuk*,
and that of the interpreter *Pah-ti-coo-chee*, we seated ourselves in a carriage, and in three minutes were being ushered
through the crowded halls leading to the splendid and brilliant array, into the midst of which a long Indian step or
two more placed us!

There was a little cruelty in the suddenness of our approach,
and a simultaneous yell which we gave, innocently mis-
taking the effect it might have upon the nerves of ladies
standing near us, several of whom, on catching the sound and
then the sight of us, gave sudden shrieks far more piercing
and startling than the savage war-whoop that had been
sounded over their shoulders. By this time we formed the
centre of attraction in the room, and we stood in so dense a
crowd to be gazed at, that nothing could be scanned of us
lower down than our chins and shoulders. The big Sioux
chief, however, who was a head taller than the crowd around
him, flourishing his enormous head-dress of eagle's quills,
was quietly rolling his eagle eyes around over the multitude,
who were getting so satisfactory a view of him that it eased

us a little from the rush that otherwise would have been upon us.

We had made our entry into this world of fashion and splendour entirely unexpected by any one, and of course unknown to all. Here was truly a splendid field for my friend Mr. Murray, and the time for his operations had now arrived. All questions (and there were many, and in various languages) put to the big chief or the warrior were, by the understanding, answered only by frowns; and the interrogations referred to *Pah-ti-coo-chee*, the interpreter. This brought him at once into great demand, and he replied at first in Indian, and then strained a few distorted words of French and German into his replies, by which he made himself partially understood. Lords and ladies, dukes and duchesses, and princes and princesses of his acquaintance were in the room, and now gazing at his copper colour, bedaubed with red and black paint, and patiently listening to and endeavouring to translate his garbled French and German and Indian for some description of the grand personages he had in tow, without dreaming of the honourable gentleman upon whose visage they were actually looking. From a custom of the Prairie country, which he had wisely thought of, he carried a rifle-bullet in his mouth whilst he was talking, and his voice was thus as much a stranger as his face.

Amongst the gazers on, and those who questioned him, were many of his most familiar friends; and even his own brother, the Earl of Dunmore, drew some marvellous tales from him before he made himself known, which he did at last to him and a few others of his friends, that he might the better crack the good jokes he had come to enjoy.

The crowd, by this time, had completely wedged us in, so that there was no apparent possibility of moving from our position, yet it was not a crowd that was insupportable: it was, at least for a while, a pleasure to be thus invested, as we were, by silks and satins, by necklaces of diamonds and necks as fair as alabaster, by gold lace, and golden epaulettes, chapeaux and small swords; but the weight of our bison robes at length brought us to the expedient that our ingenious interpreter put forth, which gained us temporary relief, and gave us locomotive powers by which we could show ourselves at full length, and occasionally escape investigations when they became too close for our good friend or ourselves.

It was a lucky thought of our interpreter, which he divulged to some of his confidential friends much to our advantage, that the paints which the Indians used were indelible colours, and he regretted to learn that some of the ladies had injured their costly dresses by being in too close contact with us. And again he feared that some of the scalp-locks on the dresses of the chief and the warrior were not quite dry, as they were fresh from the country where they had just been at war with the Sacs and Foxes. This had a delightful effect, and we were not again in danger of suffocation, though the space we had to move in was limited enough during the rest of the night for our warm dresses and our enormous buffalo robes.

The introductions I had on that night, to lords and ladies, and to dukes and duchesses, as *Na-see-us-kuk*, a famous warrior of the Sacs, and my nephew, as *Wun-ne-ton*, the great Sioux Chief, were honours certainly that he or I could never have aspired to under any other names; and our misfortune was, that their duration was necessarily as brief as the names and titles we had assumed.

In the midst of this truly magnificent scene, where our interpreter was introducing us as two dignified personages from the base of the Rocky Mountains, and enjoying his own fun with his friends as he moved around, and after a set of quadrilles had finished, it was announced through the rooms that the Indians were going to give the War Dance!

This of course raised a new excitement, and the crowd thickened, until at length a red rope or cord was passed around us three about as high as our waists. The bystanders were desired to take hold of this and walk back, which they did in all directions until a large space was opened for us, and we were left standing in the centre. We found ourselves there in full display in front of the ladies patronesses of the ball, who were seated upon a platform, elevated several feet above the level of the floor, and who, it was stated to us, had expressed a desire to see the Indians dance.

Alas! poor Murray, he had then an off-hand use to make of his mongrel dialect, which seemed to embarrass him very much, and which he had found he got along with much better in the crowd. We were also pledged to hesitate about our dignity in case we were asked to dance, which here made a dialogue in Indian language indispensable, giving our interpreter fresh alarm; nevertheless, with enough of the same determination and firmness left that used to decide him to dash through the turbid rivers of the prairie, or to face the menacing savages that he met in the wilderness, he resolved to go through with it, and the Indian dialogue that he opened with me was never doubted, I believe, for it was never criticised. The objections raised by the chief and his warrior were translated in tolerable French (with the bullet accent), to their ladyships and the audience around us. The dignity of a Sioux Chief could not be lowered by such a condescension, and the dance could not be made without him. "Good Mr. *Pah-ti-coo-chee*," said her Grace the Duchess of —— (who was the presiding patroness on the occasion), in excellent French, "do, I beg of you, do prevail on that fine old fellow to gratify us with a dance—don't let him look so distressed about it—tell him that he has just been looking on to see some of the greatest chiefs in our country dance, and he must not think it degrading to show us the mode in which the Indians dance; I dare say it is very fine. Oh, dear, what shall we do? they are fine-looking men—I wish I could speak to them— I dare say they know Charles A. Murray,—he was in their country—I have read his book. Where's Murray? he ought to be here to-night; I am sure he knows them. Do

you know Murray, my good fellows? Ah, no, they don't
understand French, though."

Our interpreter smiled, and the Sioux chief and the Sac
warrior came very near the misfortune also. The arguments
of the duchess were translated to the chief and the warrior
with great difficulty, when, after a few moments of silence,
they began to put off their robes, which were very deliberately folded up and laid aside, to the great gratification of
the ladies patronesses and the rest of the crowd.

By three dancers the war dance of the Sioux is given with
considerable effect, and we were now ready to "go into it."
The drum, which until this moment had been slung on Mr.
Murray's back, was taken into my hands, the chief took his
rattle in one hand and his war-club in the other, while the
interpreter's shield skilfully manœuvred over his left
shoulder and his tomahawk brandished in his right hand,
which, with the shrill sounds of the war-song and the war-
whoop, altogether suddenly opened a new era in the musical
and dancing sphere of Almack's.

When it was done, the whole house rung with applause;
bouquets of flowers were showered upon us, and many
compliments were paid us by the most bewitching young
ladies, but which, unfortunately for us, we could not understand. The crowd now thickened around us to shake
hands with us and lavish their praises upon us; and
among them a lovely little creature, whose neck seemed
forged from a bouquet of white lilies, who was supported on
the arm of an officer, with her languishing soft blue eyes,
and breath sweeter than that of the antelope that jostles
the first dew-drops of the morning from the violets of the
prairie, was beseeching me to allow her to adjust on my
wrist a magnificent bracelet which she had taken from
her own lovely arm, and for which she wished only, as she
made me understand by signs, a small scalp-lock from the
seams of my leggings. To play our parts well it was necessary, for the time being, to do as an Indian warrior would
do—I tore off the scalp-lock and gave it to her, and when her

fair hands had adjusted the precious trinket on my wrist, I raised the leathern shirt a little higher on my arm and showed her the colour of my skin. This unfolded a secret to her which compelled me to speak, and I said to her and her guardian, "Pray don't expose us; let us have our fun. Your precious trinket I will restore to you in a little time." This was answered with the sweetest of smiles, and, as my joke was thus ended, I turned round and found the ring prepared again for another dance. Fair hands had been lavish upon the other two Indians, who were already decorated with several keepsakes of beautiful and precious workmanship. The scalp-dance now commenced, and as I had brought with me a real scalp, according to the custom of a warrior, we gave it the full effect and fury of such scenes as they are acted in the wilderness. We entered upon this unfortunate affair with our prizes displayed in the fullest exultation, and no doubt might have gained many more but for the unforeseen misfortune which our over exertions to please and astonish had innocently brought upon us. The warmth of the rooms at this hour had become almost insupportable, and, in the midst of it, our violent exertions, under the heat of our Indian dresses, had produced a flow of perspiration which had carried away the paint in streaks from our foreheads to our chins, making us simple studies for the ethnologist, if any there were present, and easy of solution. Poor Murray! he had supplied himself with a red handkerchief, which he had often pressed upon his face, the consequence of which was—and it was funny enough—that his nose and his chin, and the other prominent points of his face, had all become white, long before he had finished his fun or been willing to acknowledge our true character and caste.

However, he had much merriment in receiving the cheerful congratulations of his friends (who now recognised him once more as the Honourable C. A. Murray), and in introducing my nephew and myself in our real names to many of his friends, we distributed scalp-locks and feathers

to all the fair hands whose trinkets we held and restored;
and after partaking of the good things that were in store
for us, and looking and laughing at our white-washed faces
in the mirrors, we made our way to the front door as the
first step towards a retreat to the Egyptian Hall. We waited
in vain full half an hour for a vehicle, such was the rush
of carriages at the door.   The only alternative seemed to be
to take to our legs, and once resolved, we dashed out into
the street, and made our way in the best manner we could.
It was now past sunrise and raining in torrents, as it
had been during the whole night.   We wended our way
as fast as possible through the mud, with our white and
beautiful mocassins, and painted robes; and the reader
must excuse me here, and imagine, if he can, how we three
looked when we arrived at the door of the Egyptian Hall,
with the gang of boys and ragamuffins assembled around
us, which the cry of " Indians, Indians!" had collected as
we passed through the streets.   The poor porter, who had
waited up for us all night, happened *luckily to be* ready for
our ring; and thus, fortunately, we were soon safely withdrawn from the crowd assembling, to gaze and grin at each
other, and deliberately and leisurely to scour ourselves back
again to our original characters.

CHAPTER VIII.

Their Royal Highnesses the Duke of Coburg and Prince Ernest visit the Collection—His Royal Highness the (little) Duc de Brabant visits the Collection with the Hon. Mr. Murray—The Author presents him an Indian pipe and pair of mocassins—Visit of His Royal Highness the Duke of Sussex to the Collection—His noble sympathy for the Indians—He smokes an Indian pipe under the wigwam—The Author takes breakfast with the Duke of Sussex in Kensington Palace—The Duke's dress and appearance—John Hunter, the Indian traveller—The Duke's inquiries about him—Monsieur Duponceau—Visit to the Bank of England—To Buckingham Palace—To Windsor Castle—Author visits the Polish Ball with several friends in Indian costumes.

AMONG the distinguished visitors to my rooms about this time were their Royal Highnesses the Duke of Coburg, and Prince Ernest, the father and brother of Prince Albert, at that time on a visit to the Queen and the Prince. They were accompanied by Mr. Murray, who took great pains to explain the collection to the Duke, who took me by the hand when he left the room, and told me I deserved the friendship of all countries for what I had done, and pronounced it " a noble collection." His second visit was made to it a few days after, when he was also accompanied by Mr. Murray, and remained in the rooms until it was quite dark.

His Royal Highness the Duc de Brabant, the infant son of the King of the Belgians, on a visit to the Queen, was also brought in by Mr. Murray. He was an intelligent lad, nine or ten years of age, and was pleased with a miniature Indian pipe which I presented to him, and also a small pair of Indian mocassins suitable for his age.

His Royal Highness the Duke of Sussex, though in feeble

health, paid my collection his first visit. It was his wish, from the state that he was in, to meet me alone "in an Indian Council," as he called it. My first interview with him lasted for an hour or more, when he told me that if his strength would have permitted it, he could have been amused the whole day. To this fine old venerable man my highest admiration clung: he expressed the deepest sympathy for the Indians, and seemed to have formed a more general and correct idea of them and their condition than any person I had met in the kingdom. When he left my rooms he took me by both hands and thanked me for the rich treat I had afforded him, and assured me that for the benefits I was rendering to society, and the justice I was doing to the poor Indians, I should be sure to meet my reward in the world to come, and that he hoped I would also be recompensed in this.

The Duke of Sussex was a great amateur of pipes and good smoking, and took much interest in the hundreds of different designs and shapes of the carved pipes in my exhibition. He was curious to know what the Indians smoked, and I showed him their tobacco, a quantity of which I had brought with me. The Indians prepare it from the inner bark of the red willow, and when dried and ready for smoking, call it "k'nick-k'neck." I prepared and lit a pipe of it for His Royal Highness to smoke, with which he took a seat under the middle of the Indian wigwam, where our conversation was held at the moment; and as he drew the delicious fumes through the long and garnished stem which passed between his knees, with its polished bowl, carved in the red pipe stone, resting on the floor, he presented for a few moments the finished personification of beatitude and enjoyment. He pronounced the flavour delicious, wanting only a little more strength, which he thought the addition of tobacco would give it.

I told him that the Indians were always in the habit of mingling tobacco with it when they could afford to buy it:

"Good fellows (said he), they know what is good—their tastes are as good as ours are." After he had finished his pipe, and we were moving towards the front door, the moment before taking leave of me as I have mentioned above, he asked me if I ever knew *John Hunter*, who wrote a work on the Indians of America, to which I replied in the affirmative. He seemed much pleased in learning this fact, and said to me, "You see what a feeble wreck I am at present; my strength is gone, and I must leave you; but you will take your breakfast with me at Kensington Palace to-morrow morning: I am all alone. I am too ill to see the world; they cannot find the way to me: but I will see *you*, and take great pleasure in your society. Your name will be made known to the servants at the back entrance to the palace."

The next morning, at the hour named, found me at the door of the palace, where my name was recognised, and I at once was ushered into the apartment of the Duke, where I found him in his arm-chair, wrapped in his morning gown of white flannel, and his head covered with a cap of black velvet richly embroidered with gold. He rose and took me by the hand in the most cordial manner, and instantly led me to another part of the room, in front of a portrait hanging on the wall.—"There," said he, "do you know that face?" "Very well," said I; "that is the portrait of John Hunter; it is an admirable likeness, and looks to me like a picture by one of our American artists. If I had met it anywhere else but in this country I should have said it was by Harding, one of our most valued portrait painters." "Well," said he, "you know *that* portrait too, do you?" "Very well—that is his Royal Highness the Duke of Sussex." "Well," said the Duke, "now I will tell you, they were both painted by Mr. Harding. Harding is a great favourite of mine, and a very clever artist."

I at this moment presented to the Duke the Indian pipe, through which he had smoked the day before, and also an

Indian tobacco-pouch, filled with the k'nick-k'neck (or Indian tobacco) with which he had been so much pleased.

He thanked me for the present, which he assured me delighted him very much ; and, after showing me a great variety of curious and most ingenious pipes from various countries, we took our seats alone at the breakfast table. In the course of our conversation, which ran upon pipes— upon Indians and Indian countries, his Royal Highness said he had reasons for asking me if I had known Hunter, and should feel most happy if he found in me a person who had been acquainted with his history. He said he had known Hunter familiarly while he was in London, and had entertained him in his palace, and thought a great deal of him. He had thought his life a most extraordinary one, well entitling him to the attentions that were paid to him here—that he had been entertained and amused by his narrations of Indian life, and that he had made him several presents, amongst which was a very valuable watch, and had had his portrait painted, which he highly valued. He said he had learned, with deep regret, since Hunter had left here, that a learned French gentleman in Philadelphia, M. Duponceau, and some others, had held him up to the public, through the journals, as an impostor, and his narrations as fabulous. " This to me," said the Duke, " you can easily see, has been a subject of much pain (as I took more pains to introduce him and his works in this country than any one else), and it explains to you the cause of my anxiety to learn something more of his true history."

I replied to his Royal Highness that I had been equally pained by hearing such reports in circulation in my own country, and that my acquaintance with Hunter had not been familiar enough to enable me wholly to refute them. I stated that I had been introduced to Mr. Hunter in New Orleans, where he was well known to many, and that I had met him in two or three other parts of the United States, and since reading his work I had visited many of the Indian villages, in which he lived, and had conversed with chiefs and others named in his work, who spoke familiarly of him. I felt assured, therefore, that he had spent the Indian life that he describes in his work ; and yet that he might have had the indiscretion to have made some misrepresentations attributed to him, I was not able positively to deny. His work, as far as it treats on the manners and customs of the American Indians, and which could not have been written or dictated by any other than a person who had lived that familiar life with them, is decidedly the most descriptive and best work yet published on their every-day domestic habits and superstitions ; and, of itself, goes a great way, in my opinion, to establish the fact that his early life was identified with that of the Indians.

I stated that I believed his character had been cruelly and unjustly libelled, and that I had the peculiar satisfaction of believing that I had justly defended it, and given the merited rebuke at the fountain of all his misfortunes, which I described as follows :—

"On my return from an eight years' residence amongst the remotest tribes of Indians in America, and paying a visit to my old friends in the city of Philadelphia, M. Duponceau, of whom your Royal Highness has spoken, an old and very learned gentleman, and deeply skilled in the various languages of America, and who was then preparing a very elaborate work on the subject, invited me to meet several of his friends at his table to breakfast ; which I did. He was at this time nearly blind and very deaf, and still eagerly grasping at every traveller and trapper from the Indian country, for some new leaf to his book, or some new word to his vocabularies, instead of going himself to the Indian fireside, the true (and in fact the only) school in which to learn and write their language.

" After our breakfast was finished and our coffee-cups removed, this learned M. Duponceau opened his note-book upon the table and began in this way,—' My dear Sir (addressing himself to me), I am so delighted with such an opportunity—I am told that you have visited some forty or fifty tribes of Indians, and many of them speaking different languages. You have undoubtedly in eight years learned to speak fluently; and I shall draw from you such a valuable addition to my great work—what a treat this will be, gentlemen, ha? Now you see I have written out some two or three hundred words, for which you will give me the Blackfoot, the Mandan, the Pawnee Pict, &c. You have been amongst all these tribes?' 'Yes.' The old gentleman here took a pinch of snuff and then said, 'In this identical place, and on this very table, it was, gentlemen, that I detected the imposture of that rascal Hunter! Do you know that fellow, Mr. Catlin?' 'Yes, I have seen him.' 'Well,' said he, 'I was the first to detect him;—I published him to the world and put a stop to his impostures. I invited him to take breakfast with me as I have invited you, and in this same book wrote down the Indian translation of a list of words and sentences that I had prepared, as he gave them to me; and the next day when I invited him again, he gave me for one-third at least of those words a different translation. I asked for the translation of a number of words in languages that were familiar to me, and which he told me he understood, and he gave them in words of other tribes. I now discovered his ignorance, and at once pronounced him an impostor, and closed my book.'

"'And now,' said I, 'M. Duponceau, lest you should make yourself and me a great deal of trouble, and call *me* an impostor also, I will feel much obliged if you will close your book again; for I am quite sure I should prove myself under your examination just as ignorant as Mr. Hunter, and subject myself to the same reproach which is following him through the world, emanating from so high an authority. Mr. Hunter and myself did not go into the Indian countries to study the Indian languages, nor do we come into the civilized world to publish them, and to be made responsible for errors in writing them. I can well understand how Mr. Hunter gave you, to a certain extent, a different version on different days ; he, like myself, having learned a little of fifteen or twenty different languages, would necessarily be at a loss, with many of his Indian words, to know what tribe they belong to ; and our partial knowledge of so many tongues involves us at once in a difficulty not unlike the confusion at Babel, and disqualifies his responses or mine, as authority for such works as I hope you are preparing for the world. With these views (though I profess to be the property of the world, and ready and pleased to communicate anything that I have distinctly learned of the Indians and their modes), I must beg to decline giving you the translation of a single word ; and at the same time to express a hope that you may verbally, or in the valuable works which you are soon to bequeath to posterity, leave a repentant word at least, to remove the censure which you say you were the first to cast upon Hunter, and which is calculated to follow him to the grave.'"

His Royal Highness was much interested and somewhat amused by this narrative, and agreed with me, that such men as M. Duponceau, and others, to whom the world is to look for a full and correct account of the Indian languages of America, should go themselves to the wigwams of the Indians, and there, in their respective tribes, open the books in which to record their various vocabularies, rather than sit at home and trust to the ignorant jargon that can be caught from the trapper and the trader and the casual tourists who make flying visits through the Indian countries. He related to me many curious anecdotes of poor Hunter, and as I left him enjoying his k'nick-k'neck through his Indian pipe, he said to me, " Your name, sir, will be familiar at my door, and I shall be delighted to see you again at the same hour, whenever you feel disposed to come."

Amidst the many avocations that were now demanding and engrossing the most of my time, I was still able, by an effort, to allot certain portions of the day to the pleasures that are found in the domestic circles of wives and little ones, and nowhere else ; and with them spent the happiest moments of my life, notwithstanding the attentions of the world and the efforts to make my enjoyment complete. With my dear Clara I took my strolls and my rides to see what was amusing or instructive in the great metropolis, and we saw much that amused and still more that astonished us. Through the kindness of our untiring friend Mr. Murray, we got access to the palaces of St. James and Buckingham, and to the public and private rooms of Windsor Castle ; we saw the " five tons' weight of gold plate " that are said to enrich that noble palace, and which but few eyes are allowed to gaze upon.

We visited the Royal Mint, the Tower, the noble mansions of the Dukes of Sutherland and Devonshire, and the Bank of England. I was surprised that we were allowed to pass through every part of this wonderful sanctuary of gold and silver, and still more so that a guide should stand ready to conduct us through all its numerous ramifications, and as he passed along from room to room, from office to office, and from vault to vault, to hear him lecture upon everything we passed, as if they feared we might not appreciate it in all its parts. It has been many times described and needs no further comment here, except an occurrence in one of the vaults which deserves a current notice. The Honourable Charles Fenton Mercer, of Virginia, was among our companions on the occasion, and as we were shown into this apartment, which I think was called a vault, though it was a large square room with the light of a dome over it, the gentleman having charge of it within received us in the most courteous manner, and as if it were a public exhibition which we had paid our shilling to see, he led us around the room and with his keys opened the iron safes which were all sunk in the walls, with double doors of iron, and showed us the amount of gold and notes contained in them, and on opening one that was filled with packages of Bank of England notes, he took a bundle of them some ten or twelve inches in diameter, and smilingly placing it in the hands of my wife, asked her if she had any idea how much money she was holding. Her rough guess was a very moderate one : she was so much excited and so recently from New York, that she had forgotten pounds sterling, and replied " Perhaps a thousand *dollars;*" when he turned it the other side up and referred us to the label upon it—" two millions of pounds !" He then took out another parcel of equal size, and placing that on the top of it said to her, " Now, madam, you have four millions." Poor thing ! she looked pale as she handed it back, saying, " Ah, well, I am glad it is not mine." The kind and gentlemanly attention shown to us, and the pains taken to explain everything as we passed along, were unexpected, and even a mystery in politeness which was beyond my comprehension. We were conducted from this room to the arched vaults, where we traced for a long distance the narrow aisles to the right and the left and to the north and the south, through phalanxes of wheelbarrows loaded with bars of silver and of gold, and all with their heads one way, seemed ready for a subterraneous crusade in case of necessity.

We returned from this half-day's work, fatigued, and almost sorry that we had seen so much of the " shining dust " which our hands are labouring so hard through life to earn a pittance of.

There were several Americans with us on this day's expedition, and all agreed that we drew more pleasure from the gentlemanly politeness we met in the Bank of England than we did from its wonderful system (which was all explained to us), and from its golden riches which were all laid open to our view.

Our fatigue, when we got home, seemed enough for one day ; but as it happened on that day, our sight-seeing was only begun ; for it had been arranged that we were to go to the Polish ball at the Mansion House on that evening, and what was to make it a double task, it was arranged that we should all go, some five or six of us, in Indian costumes.

My Indian wardrobe was therefore laid under heavy contributions for that night.   My nephew Burr and myself
were dressed as chiefs, and two or three more of my friends
were arrayed as warriors.   My dear little *Christian* Clara,
whose sphere it was not, and who never wore an Indian
dress or painted her fair face before, becoming inspired with
a wish to see the splendour of the scene, proposed to assume
the dress of an Indian woman and follow me through
the mazes of that night as an Indian squaw follows her lord
on such occasions.   I selected for her one of the prettiest and
most beautifully ornamented women's dresses, which was made
of the fine white skin of the mountain sheep ; and with her hair
spread over her back, and her face and her arms painted to the
colour of a squaw, and her neck and ears loaded with the
usual profusion of beads and other ornaments, and her fan of
the eagle's tail in her hand, she sidled along with us amidst the
glare and splendour, and buzz and din of the happy throng
we were soon in the midst of, and dragging our awkward
shields and quivers and heavy buffalo robes through, as
well as we could.   We took good care not to dance on
that occasion, so we kept the paint on our faces, and by
understanding no questions, answered none, and passed off
with everybody as *real Indians*.   We went resolved to
gratify our eyes, but to give no gratification to others besides what they could take to themselves by looking at us.
Our interpreter was true to his promise : he made out his
own descriptions for us, and assured all who inquired, that
we could not speak a word of English.   French, German,
Russian, and Italian were all tried in vain upon us ; and
as they turned away, one after another, from us, they exclaimed, " What a pity ! how unfortunate the poor things
can't speak English ! how interesting it would be to talk
with them ! that's a noble-looking fellow, that big chief ;
egad, he is six feet and a half.   I'll be bound that fellow
has taken many a scalp.   That's a nice-looking little squaw :
upon my word, if she had a white skin she would be rather
pretty ! " and a thousand such remarks, as the reader can

imagine, while we were wending our tedious way through the bewildering mazes of this endless throng. The task for my poor Clara soon became more than she had anticipated before entering the room, and was growing too much for her delicate frame to bear : she had not thought of the constant gaze of thousands she was to stand in every moment of the evening; and another discipline (which she knew must be strictly adhered to, to act out the character she was supporting, and which had not occurred to her before she had commenced upon the toils of the evening) made her part a difficult one to act—that was the necessity of following in the wake of all the party of men when we were in motion, the place assigned to Indian women on the march, rather than by the side or on the arms of their husbands. This, in the street or in the wilderness or anywhere else would have been tolerable, she said, but in her present condition was insupportable. The idea was so ridiculous to her, to be the last of a party of Indians (who always walk in single file) so far behind her husband, and then the crowd closing in upon her and in danger of crushing her to death. We soon however were so lucky as to find a flight of several broad steps which led to a side room, but now closed, which furnished us comfortable seats above the crowd, which we took good care to hold until our curiosity was all gratified, and we were ready to return home. Our interpreter, in answer to all inquiries as to the locale of these strange foreigners, mentioned the Egyptian Hall ; and for weeks after, Daniel testified to the increase of our receipts, and bore sad evidence too of the trouble he had in explaining the difficulty of showing to his visiters the " real Indians." After having satiated our curiosity, and several of the youngest of the party having received some very pretty trinkets and other presents that had been forced upon them, we made our way home in good season to enjoy the joke, and part of a good night's rest.

CHAPTER IX.

POOR Daniel in the exhibition-rooms! I mentioned in the preceding chapter that our appearance at the Polish ball had greatly increased the number of shillings, but, at the same time, it was, as he said, doing great injury to the Collection, as people paid their shillings expecting to see the real Indians, and then, finding their error, revenged themselves upon poor Daniel by calling him and the whole concern hard names, and in various ways provoking him. Politics—Caste—Slavery—Truck-system—Poor-houses—Repeal—Oregon—and Repudiation were the exciting topics—all of which he was able and ready to discuss; and the kind of visitors I just now mentioned, under their disappointment at the rooms, were prepared to annoy him on these topics, and irritate him to such a degree that it made his duties doubly hard to him and their visits less pleasant to themselves than they would otherwise have been.

He had other things that annoyed him, amongst which were the constant efforts by artists and amateurs to make copies in the room for paintings and designs, which they somehow seemed to fancy. After having risked my life and spent my little fortune in the wilderness to procure such exciting and such original studies, and bring them to England, I did not consider it fair that these gentlemen should step into my rooms just when they had an hour of leisure, and industry enough to use it, and copy whatever they could most easily convert into cash.

So many of these attempts had been made, that I was obliged to post a printed notice around the walls, that " *No copying was allowed in the rooms.*"

This had the desired effect with many, but there were some to whom the temptation was so great, that Daniel was obliged to refer them to the printed regulations; and one or two others for whom this was not enough, and who seemed to think that, in my absence, Daniel's authority was rather in imagination than any thing else; and when he had requested them to desist, they had given him the finish to their provocations by replying to him, that he was of no account—that if his *master* ordered them to stop they would do so, but not for him. One of these customers had troubled him very much for several days, and it was evidently affecting his spirits, and even his health, for he was growing pale and ghastly under the excitement. He said he had repeatedly taken the printed regulation and placed it before him, and he was at last told to " Go to the devil with it." He told me this man had some object in view, for he came every night, and sketched very rapidly, and made very exact copies; and he said to me, " If you don't see fit to come in and turn him out of the room to-night, I shall lay hold of him, for your own interest. I hate to do it, for he looks like a gentleman, though he don't act like one, and that's enough; and if you don't stop him, Mr. Catlin, I will." " That's right," said I, " Daniel. You have charge of the rooms, and your regulations, and of course it is your duty to stop him; and I am responsible for any damage you may do in putting an end to it." I was at that time occupying apartments opposite to the Egyptian Hall in Piccadilly, and on that night observing the lamps burning at a much later hour than usual, was induced to step in to learn the cause. As I was passing through the Hall, and about to enter the exhibition-room, I heard a few half-stifled and hasty words, and then something like a struggle; and next, I heard distinctly Daniel's voice, in rather a stifled mood :—"No you won't. If you get that leg through, the deil a bit o' good will it do ye; for I 'll be shot if you ever pass your neck any farther through this door until you give it up!"

"Let go of my collar, then!"

"No, I 'll be blathered if I do that! I 've got a good hold now, and I might not get it again. Lay down the book and I 'll let you go, and not before."

"What business is it of yours? come, I should like to know; you are only a door-keeper." "That's what I am, you've got it right; and I'll show you, my boy, that I can *keep* a door, too."

I stood back during this conversation, easily understanding what the difficulty was, as I had a partial view of them, but was unobserved, as I was standing in the dark.

It seems that Daniel's friend the copyist had been as usual at work most of the evening, making sketches, and Daniel had allowed him to work, resolving to appropriate all his sketches at a haul, as he should be leaving the room. The gentleman had been intensely engaged, and not having been interrupted as usual, had kept at his work for half an hour or so after all visitors had left the room, and a full blaze of gas was burning at my expense and for his benefit. All these circumstances ripened Daniel's taste for laying an embargo on him; and when he had closed his book, and was about to take leave, he found Daniel standing with his back towards the door, which was open. On endeavouring to pass, Daniel civilly stopped him, and told him he should expect him on that evening to leave his sketch-book with him before he passed out. The gentleman seemed dreadfully insulted by such a suggestion, saying that he had paid for his admission and had the same

right to be in the room or to go out that *he* had; to which
Daniel at once assented, saying he had not the slightest
objection to his going out; "but," said he, "if that book goes
out, it will be because you are a stronger man than I am."

At this crisis the artist had made a rush for the door,
and Daniel had fastened his left hand into his cravat and
shirt collar, whilst he had a similar grip upon Daniel with
one hand, and his sketch-book in the other, when I discovered
them on my approach to the rooms. How long they had
been in this amusing predicament I was not yet able to
ascertain; but as Daniel, who is of a quick and rather violent
temper, was speaking quite cool and deliberate, I presumed
they must have stood there at least long enough for his first
excitement to have cooled off, which could not possibly have
been effected in a few moments.

Immediately after their last dialogue that I had heard
when approaching them, there commenced another scene
of grunting, and sighing, and shoving about, that lasted for
some minutes, when all was still again. The gentleman,
however, broke silence at length, but in a very low and
placid voice: "Why, you are a very curious fellow; I
don't see why this thing should make you so wrathy.
The pictures are not yours—come, don't clinch me so
tight there, if you please." "I don't hurt you—I told
you I didn't wish to hurt you; if you talk about my bein
'wrathy,' you don't know what you are talkin about—and
the pictures I know are not mine; but my employer
expects me to guard his property, and you may be sure
I'll do it. If you had taken my advice two or three days
ago it would have saved you all this fuss, and half an hour's
time that we have been standing in the door." Another
scuffle and struggle ensued here, and after much grunting,
the gentleman exclaimed, "You have the advantage of me,
for you have both hands to work with and I have only one!
If it were not for the book I could upset you, damned quick!"
Upon which Daniel made a grand lunge at the book, which
he snatched from his hand, and exultingly exclaimed,

"There! I'll take the book, and let you try with both hands —and now, if you touch a finger to me again, I'll lather you within an inch of your life. If your cloth be ever so much better than mine, you have behaved like anything but a gentleman; and as I told you in the beginning, if ever you carry this book out at that door you will do it over my dead body." At that instant he turned off the gas, giving the gentleman a good opportunity to depart in total silence, and for me to dodge him, as he passed by, and to withdraw myself, to enjoy Daniel's account of the affair, which was amusingly given, as he handed me the sketch-book the next morning.

Daniel's health and spirits improved very sensibly after this affair, and his duties were somewhat lightened about this time, though I added much to my own labours, by closing the exhibition at night, and giving my lectures on three evenings of the week in an adjoining hall, illustrating them with *tableaux vivans*, produced by twenty living figures in Indian costumes, forming groups of their ceremonies, domestic scenes, and warfare. These were got up and presented with much labour to myself, and gave great satisfaction; as by them I furnished so vivid and lifelike an illustration of Indian life as I had seen it in the wilderness.

For these tableaux I had chosen my men for some striking Indian character in their faces or figures, or action, and my women were personated by round-faced boys, who, when the women's dresses were on them, and long wigs of horses' hair spreading over their shoulders, and the faces and hands of all painted to the Indian colour, made the most complete illusion that could be conceived. I had furnished each with his little toilet of colours, &c., and instructions how to paint the face before a mirror, and how to arrange their dresses; and then, with almost infinite labour, had drilled them through the Indian mode of walking with their "toes in," of using their weapons of war and the chase, and of giving their various dances, songs, and the war-whoop;

and I have no hesitation in saying, that when I had brought this difficult mode to its greatest perfection, I had succeeded in presenting the most faithful and general representation of Indian life that was ever brought before the civilized world.   Many of these scenes were enlivened by action, and by the various instruments of music used by the Indians, added to their songs, and the war-whoop, giving a thrilling spirit to them, whilst they furnished scenes for the painter, of the most picturesque character, as will be easily imagined from the subjoined programme of them as announced at the time.

CATLIN'S LECTURES

WITH

TABLEAUX VIVANS ON THE NORTH AMERICAN INDIANS,

AT

THE EGYPTIAN HALL, PICCADILLY, LONDON.

PROGRAMME FOR THE FIRST EVENING.

WAR SCENES.

No. 1.—*Group of Warriors and Braves, in Full Dress*, reclining around a fire, regaling themselves with the pipe and a dish of *pemican*.   In the midst of their banquet the chief enters in full dress ; the pipe is lighted for him—he smokes it in sadness, and breaks up the party by announcing that an enemy is at hand—that a number of their men have been scalped whilst hunting the buffalo, and they must prepare for war.

No. 2.—*Warriors Enlisting*, by " smoking through the reddened stem." The chief sends " *runners* " (or *criers*) through the tribe with a pipe, the stem of which is painted red ; the crier solicits for recruits, and every young man who consents to smoke through the reddened stem which is extended to him, is considered a volunteer to go to war.

No. 3.—*War Dance*.   The ceremony of " *swearing in* " the warriors, who take the most solemn oath by dancing to, and striking the " reddened post " with their war-clubs.

No. 4.—*Foot War-Party on the March*, (" Indian file,") armed with shields, bows, quivers, and lances—the chief of the party, as is generally the case, going to war in full dress.

No. 5.—*War-Party encamped at Night*, asleep under their buffalo robes, with sentinels on the watch.   The *alarm in camp* is given, and the warriors roused to arms.

No. 6.— *War-Party in Council*, consulting with their chief as to the best and most effective way of attacking their enemies, who are close at hand.

No. 7.—*Skulking*, or advancing cautiously upon the enemy to take them by surprise—a common mode and merit in war among the North American Indians.

No. 8.—*Battle and Scalping ;* showing the frightful appearance of Indian warfare, and the mode of taking the scalp.

No. 9.— *Scalp Dance*, in celebration of a victory ; the women, in the centre of the group, holding up the scalps on little sticks, and the warriors dancing around them, brandishing their weapons, and yelling in the most frightful manner.

No. 10.— *Treaty of Peace.*   The chiefs and warriors of the two hostile tribes in the act of solemnizing the treaty of peace, by smoking mutually through the calumet, or pipe of peace, which is ornamented with eagles' quills ; the calumet resting in front of the group.

No. 11.—*Pipe-of-Peace Dance*, by the warriors, with the pipes of peace, or calumets, in their hands, after the treaty has been concluded.   This picturesque scene will be represented by the warriors all joining in the dance, uniting their voices with the beat of the Indian drum, and sounding the frightful war-whoop.

PROGRAMME FOR THE SECOND EVENING.

DOMESTIC SCENES.

No. 1.— *The Blackfoot Doctor, or Mystery-man*, endeavouring to cure his dying patient by the operation of his mysteries and songs of incantation.

No. 2.— *Mr. Catlin at his Easel, in the Mandan Village*, painting the portrait of *Mah-to-toh-pa*, a celebrated Mandan chief. The costumes of the chief and the painter the same that were worn on the occasion.

No. 3.—*An Indian Wedding.*   The chief, who is father of the girl, is seated in the middle of the group, receiving the presents which are laid at his feet by the young man, who (when the presents accumulate to what the father deems an equivalent) receives the consent of the parent, and the hand of the girl, whom he leads off ; and as she is the daughter of a chief, and admired by the young men, they are bestowing on her many presents.

No. 4.—*Pocahontas rescuing Captain John Smith, an English Officer.*
" It had been decided in council, over which *Pow-ha-tan* presided, that Captain John Smith should be put to death, by having his head placed on a large stone, and his brains beaten out by two warriors armed with huge painted clubs.   His executioners were standing with their clubs raised over him, and in the very instant for giving the fatal blow, when *Pocahontas*,

the chief's favourite daughter, then about thirteen years old, threw herself with folded arms over the head of the captain, who was instantly ordered by the chief to be released."

No. 5.— *Wrestling.* A favourite amusement among many of the tribes. For these scenes, several distinguished young men are selected on each side, and the goods bet being placed in the care of the stakeholders, the wrestling commences at a signal given, and the stakes go to the party who count the greatest number of men remaining on their feet.

No. 6.—*Ball Play.* The most beautiful and exciting of all Indian games. This game is often played by several hundreds on a side. The group represents the players leaping into the air, and struggling to catch the ball as it is descending, in their ball-sticks.

No. 7.— *Game of Tchung-kee.* The favourite play of the Mandans, and used by them as their principal gambling game.

No. 8.—*The Night Dance of the Seminolees.* A ceremony peculiar to this tribe, in which the young men assemble and dance round the fire after the chiefs have retired to rest, gradually stamping it out with their feet, and singing a song of thanksgiving to the Great Spirit ; after which they wrap themselves in their robes and retire to rest.

One will easily see that this opened a new field of amusement and excitement for my old friends, who were now nightly present, with their companions, and approving with rounds of applause. Amongst these was my untiring friend Mr. Murray, who, among the distinguished personages whom he introduced, made a second visit with the little Leopold, Duc de Brabant, whom he brought in his arms from his carriage. His Royal Highness, as the curtain rose and I stepped forward to give a brief lecture, seemed not a little disappointed, by the speech that he suddenly made—" Why, that is not an Indian, that is Mr. Catlin, who gave me the Indian pipe and the mocassins." However, a few moments more brought forth red faces, and songs and yelps that seemed more sensibly to affect his Royal Highness's nerves, and at which Mr. Murray removed with him to a more distant part of the room, from which point he looked on with apparent delight.

About this time an incident of my Transatlantic life occurred, to which I shall ever recur with great satisfaction :—there was, standing in my exhibition-room, an elaborate model of the *Falls of Niagara,* which I had made from an accurate survey of that grand scene some thirteen years before; and, in compliment for the accuracy and execution of which, a handsome silver medal had been struck, and presented to me by the American Institute in New York, at one of its annual exhibitions, where it had been exposed to public view. The Hon. Mr. Murray, whose familiarity with that sublime scene had enabled him to judge of the fidelity of the model, upon which he was often looking, with his friends, with intense interest, by his representations to Her Majesty and the Prince had excited in them a desire to see it; and he called upon me one morning to inform me that Her Majesty would be pleased to have me bring it to Windsor Castle the next day at one o'clock, at which hour I should be received.

The reader may imagine what pleasure this unexpected and unmerited honour gave me, and also to my dear Clara, who was in the habit of sharing with me the pleasures of many compliments, in the forms of which she could not join me.

I was at Windsor the next morning, with the model, and having placed and arranged it in Her Majesty's drawing-room, I took Mr. Murray's arm at the appointed hour of one o'clock, and, as we entered the drawing-room, we observed Her Majesty and His Royal Highness entering at the opposite door. We met by the side of the model—where I was presented, and received in the most gracious and kind manner. Her Majesty expressed a wish that I should point out and explain the principal features of the scene; which, with the vivid descriptions which Mr. Murray also gave, of going under the Horse-Shoe Fall, &c., seemed to convey a very satisfactory idea to Her Majesty and the Prince; they asked many questions about the characters and effects of this sublime scene, and also of the Indians, for whose rights they said they well knew I was the advocate, and retired, thanking me for the amusement and instruction I had afforded them.

Several months after this passed on in the usual routine of my business and amusements (my collection open during the days and my lectures and tableaux given at night) without incidents worth reciting, when I received an invitation from the Mechanics' Institute at Liverpool to unite my Indian collection to their biennial fair or exhibition, which was to be on a scale of great magnificence. They very liberally proposed to extend the dimensions of their buildings for the occasion, and I consented to join them with my whole collection for two months. My lease had expired at the Egyptian Hall, and my collection was soon on its way to Liverpool.

I was received with great kindness in that town, and my collection for the two months gained me great applause and some pecuniary benefit. During its stay there I kept several men in Indian costumes constantly in it, and twice a day gave a short lecture in the room, explaining the costumes and many of the leading traits of the Indian character, sung an Indian song, and gave the frightful war-whoop.

There were here, as in London, many pleasing incidents and events for which I cannot venture a leaf in this book, with the exception of one, which I cannot forbear to mention. During the last week of their noble exhibition, the children from all the charitable and other schools were admitted free, and in battalions and phalanxes they were passed through my room, as many hundreds at a time as could stand upon the floor, to hear the lectures (shaped to suit their infant minds), and then the deafening war-whoop raised by my men in Indian paint and Indian arms, which drove many of the little creatures with alarm under the tables and benches, from which they were pulled out by their feet; and the list that we kept showed us the number of 22,000 of these little urchins, who, free of expense, saw my collection, and having heard me lecture, went home, sounding the war-whoop in various parts of the town.

At the close of this exhibition I selected the necessary

H 2

collection of costumes, weapons, &c. for my lectures and tableaux, and calling together my old disciplined troop from the City of London, I commenced a tour to the provincial towns of the kingdom, leaving my collection of paintings behind. My career was then rapid, and its changes sudden, and all my industry and energies were called into action—with twenty men on my hands, and an average expense of twelve pounds per day. This scheme I pushed with all the energy I could, and in the space of six months visited, with varied success, the towns of *Chester, Manchester, Leamington, Rugby, Stratford-on-Avon, Cheltenham, Sheffield, Leeds, York, Hull, Edinburgh, Glasgow, Paisley, Greenock, Belfast*, and *Dublin*. In all these towns I was received with kindness, and formed many attachments which I shall endeavour to cherish all my days. The incidents of such a tour can easily be imagined to have been varied and curious, and very many of them were exceedingly entertaining, but must be omitted in this place. On my return I was strongly urged by several friends in Manchester to open my whole collection of paintings, &c. in that town a while before leaving for the United States, for which I was then on the eve of embarking. I consented to this invitation, and, a hall being prepared for its reception, I removed it and my family there for a stay of two or three months.

The collection was soon arranged and on exhibition, and I found myself and my dear wife in the atmosphere (though of smoke) of kind friends who used their best endeavours to make our stay comfortable and pleasant. The strangers who sought our acquaintance and offered us their genuine hospitality were many, and will have our grateful thanks while we live.

My exhibition had been tolerably successful, and, strange and unexpected, like most of the turning points in my life, during the very week that I had advertised it as " positively the last in the kingdom, previous to embarking for New York," an event suddenly occurred which brought me back to the metropolis, to the chief towns of the kingdom, to

France and to Belgium ; and eventually led me through the accidents and incidents which are to form the rest and the most curious part of this work, upon which the reader will now enter with me.

The first intimation of the cause which was to change the shape of my affairs was suggested to me in the following letter :—

"Sir,—Though a stranger to you, I take the liberty of addressing this letter to you, believing that its contents will show you a way of promoting your own interest, or at least be the means of my obtaining some useful advice from you.

"I have a party of nine Ojibbeway Indians, on the way, and about at this time to be landed at Liverpool, that I am bringing over on speculation ; and, having been in London some weeks without having made any suitable arrangements for them, I have thought best to propose some arrangement with you that may promote our mutual interests. If you think of anything you could do in that way, or any advice you can give me, I shall be most happy to hear from you by return of post.

"Several persons in London conducting exhibitions have told me that they will do nothing unless they are under your management.

"I remain, yours, very truly,

" *To Geo. Catlin, Esq.*" " ARTHUR RANKIN.

To this letter I answered as follows :—

"Sir,—I received your letter of the 4th, this morning, and hasten to reply. It will be directly opposite to my present arrangements if I enter into any new engagements such as you propose, as all my preparations are now made to embark for New York in the course of a fortnight from this time. I have always been opposed to the plan of bringing Indians abroad on speculation ; but as they are in the country, I shall, as the friend of the Indians under all circumstances, feel an anxiety to promote their views and success in any way I can. I could not, at all events, undertake to make any arrangement with you until I see what kind of a party they are ; and at all events, as you will have to meet them at Liverpool, you had better call on me in Manchester, when we can better understand each other's views.

"I remain, yours, &c.

" *To A. Rankin, Esq.*" " GEO. CATLIN.

On the third day after the posting of this letter Mr. Rankin arrived in Manchester, and called upon me in my exhibition-rooms. After a little conversation with him, and without entering into any agreement, I advised him to lose no time in proceeding to Liverpool to receive them when they landed ; and he took leave with the understanding that he would bring them to Manchester as soon as they arrived. The next evening, just after it was dark, my door-keeper, who was not yet in the secret, came running in and announced that there was a "homnibus at the door quite full of orrible looking folks, and ee really believed they were hindians!" At that moment Daniel whispered to me — "The Ojibbeways are here, and they are a pretty black-look-ing set of fellows: I think they will do." I saw them a moment in the bus, and sent Daniel with them to aid Mr. Rankin in procuring them suitable lodgings. A crowd fol-lowed the bus as it passed off, and the cry of—" Indians! real Indians!" was started in Manchester, which soon rung through the kingdom, as will be related.

CHAPTER X.

Difficulty of procuring lodgings for the Indians—The Author pays them a
visit—Is recognised by them—Arrangement with Mr. Rankin—Crowds
around their hotel—First visit of the Ojibbeways to the Author's Collection—Their surprise—Council held under the wigwam—Indians agree
to drink no spirituous liquors—The old Chief's speech to the Author—
Names of the Indians—Their portraits—Description of each—Cadotte,
the interpreter.

AT the beginning of this chapter the reader turns a new
leaf, or, opens a new book. He learns here the causes
that begat this book, and I hope will find fresh excitement
enough, just at the right time, to encourage him to go
through it with me. He finds me turning here upon a pivot
—my character changed and my occupation; travelling
over old ground, and looking up old friends, of whom I
had taken final leave, and who had thought me, ere this,
safely landed on my own native shores.

The Ojibbeways were here; a party of nine wild Indians,
from the back-woods of America. "Real Indians!" the
"Ob-jub-be-ways," or "Hob-jub-be-ways," as the name was
first echoed through Manchester—and had gone into lodgings for the night, which Daniel had procured with some
difficulty. He drove to the door of an hotel, and inquired
of the landlord if he could entertain a party of nine Indians
for the night and perhaps for a few days. "O yes, certainly; bring them in. Porter, see to their luggage."
They were in his hall in a moment, having thoughtlessly
sounded a yell of exultation as they landed on the pavement, and being wrapped in their robes, with their bows
and arrows and tomahawks in their hands—as Indians are
sure to be seen when entering a strange place—the landlord,

taking a glance at them as he passed out, called out to
Daniel, " What the devil is all this? I can't take in these
folks; you must load them up again. You told me they
were Indians." " Well! they are," said Daniel. " No,
they're not; they're wild men, and they look more like the
devil than anything else. Every lodger would leave my
house before morning. They've frightened the cook and
my women folks already into fits. —Load them up as quick
as you please." Daniel got them " on board " again, and
drove to another hotel, which was just being opened to the
public, and with a new landlord, with whom he had a
slight acquaintance. Here he was more successful, and,
advising the Indians to keep quiet, had got them in comfortably and without much excitement. This very good and
accommodating man, whose name I am sorry I have forgotten, being anxious to get his house and his name a little
notoriety, seemed delighted at the thought of his house
being the rendezvous of the Indians; and, upon Daniel's
representations that they were a civil and harmless set of
people, his family and himself all did the most they could
to accommodate and entertain them.

Daniel told him that they would make a great noise in
Manchester, and as they would be the " lions " of the day,
and visited by the greatest people in town, the clergy and
all, it would be a feather in his cap, and make his hotel
more known in three days than it would otherwise be in
three years. This had pleased the new landlord exceedingly, and he made Daniel agree that Mr. Catlin, in
announcing their arrival in the papers, should say that they
had taken lodgings at his house, which he thought would
do him great service. The good man's wish was complied
with the next morning, but there was scarcely any need of
it, for the crowd that was already gathered and gathering
around his new hotel, were certain to publish it to every
part of the town in a very little time.

After they had been landed a while, and just when they
were all seated around a long table and devouring the beef-

steaks prepared for them, I made my way with great difficulty through the crowds that were jammed about the door
and climbing to look into the windows, and entered the
room, to take the first look at them.

As I stepped into the room I uttered their customary
ejaculation of " *How! how! how!* "—to which they all responded ; and rising from their seats, shook hands with me,
knowing from my manner of addressing them who I was, or
at least that I was familiar with Indians. I requested them to
finish their suppers : and whilst conversing with Mr. Rankin
I learned, from giving ear to their conversation, that one of
the young men of the party had seen me whilst I was
painting the portraits of chiefs at a Grand Council held at
Mackinaw a few years before, and was coming forward to
claim acquaintance with me. He finished his meal a little
sooner than the rest, and made a dart across the room and
offered me his hand, with a *" How! how! how! ketch-e-wah !"*
and then telling me, with the aid of the interpreter, that he
knew me—that he was at Mackinaw at the Great Council,
when I painted the portraits of Gitch-e-gaw-ga-osh, and
On-daig, and Ga-zaw-que-dung, and others ; and I recollected his face very well, which seemed excessively pleasing
to him.

The poor fellows were exceedingly fatigued and jaded ;
and after a few minutes' conversation I left them, advising them to lie quiet for two or three days until they
were rested and recruited after the fatigues of their long
and boisterous voyage. Mr. Rankin, with the aid of my
man Daniel, settled all the arrangements for this, and
the next morning I met Mr. Rankin with a view to some
arrangement for their exhibition in my collection, which
was then open in the Exchange Rooms. He seemed alarmed
about the prospects of their exhibition, from what had been
told him in London, and proposed that I should take them
off his hands by paying him 100*l.* per month.

I instantly stated my objections to such an arrangement,
that by doing so I should be assuming all the responsibilities

for them while abroad; and as I had always been opposed
to bringing Indians abroad on that account, as well as from
other reasons, I should be unwilling to use them in any way
that should release him from the responsibilities he had
assumed in bringing them to this country. And I then said,
" I will propose what I feel quite sure will be more for your
pecuniary interest, and more satisfactory to my own feelings,
and it is the only way in which I will be interested in
their exhibition; for under such an arrangement both the
Indians and the exhibition will be sure of having our
mutual and united efforts, which they will stand in need of
to ensure the success that I hope they may meet. I will
agree to make my Indian collection the place for their
exhibition (the appropriateness of which will do away all
the objections that would in many places be raised to their
dancing), and to conduct their exhibition in the best way I
can, giving my lectures on them and their modes, sharing
equally with you all expenses and all receipts from this day
to the time they shall leave the kingdom, expecting you to
give your whole attention to the travelling and care of the
Indians while they are not in the exhibition-rooms."

To this proposition, which never was more than a verbal
one, he at once agreed, and our arrangements were accordingly being made for the commencement of their dances, &c.,
in my exhibition-rooms. During the few days of interval
between their arrival and the commencement of their exhibition, several editors of the leading journals, with other
distinguished visitors to them, had examined them, and,
being much pleased with their appearance, excited the
public curiosity to see them, to an impatient degree; and
the streets in the vicinity of their hotel became so completely besieged, that a strong party of police was necessary
to keep back the crowds, who could only now and then get
a glimpse of an eye and a nose of the Indians peeping out
between the curtains of their windows.

Their first airing in Manchester was a drive in an omnibus,
to my exhibition-rooms, which they had long wished to see.

The mayor of the city, with the editors of the *Guardian* and several other gentlemen, had been invited there to see the first effect it would have upon them. It proved to be a very curious scene. As they entered the hall, the portraits of several hundreds of the chiefs and warriors of their own tribe and of their enemies were hanging on the walls and staring at them from all directions, and wigwams, and costumes and weapons of all constructions around them : they set up the most frightful yells and made the whole neighbourhood ring with their howlings ; they advanced to the portraits of their friends and offered them their hands ; and at their enemies, whom they occasionally recognised, they brandished their tomahawks or drew their bows as they sounded the war-whoop.

This scene was truly exciting, and after our distinguished visitors had left the rooms, I spread some robes upon the floor, upon which we sat, and lighting an Indian pipe, opened our first council by saying :—

" My Friends, I am glad to see you, and to offer you my hand in friendship. You see by the paintings around you, of your friends and of your enemies, that I am no stranger to Indians—and that I am their friend. I am very happy to see you in my room, and all well after crossing the great ocean. Your friend here, Mr. Rankin, tells me you have come to this country to give your dances, &c. ; and he has proposed that I should manage your exhibition, and have your dances all given in my rooms. This I have agreed to do, provided it meets your approbation."

To which they all instantly ejaculated " *How, how, how !* " which is always an affirmative, literally meaning yes. When meeting a friend, it is the first salutation, meaning " How goes it ? " or " How do you do ? " and pronounced at the ends of sentences, when any one is speaking, implies assent, or approbation, as " hear, hear ! " is used in the English language.

" My good Friends, I have agreed to this on two conditions : the first, that it shall please you ; and the second, that you will pledge your words to me that you will keep yourselves all the time sober, and drink no spirituous liquors while you are in the country. I make this condition because I know that the Indians are generally fond of strong drink, which wicked white men carry into their country and teach them to use. I know that the Indians often drink it to excess, not knowing in their country the sin of doing so. I know that the people in England detest drunkards, and they have an idea that all Indians are drunkards ; and that if you drink and get drunk in this country, it will ruin all your prospects, and you will go home poor and despised. (' *How, how, how !*') You are a good-looking and well-behaved set of men, and I have no fears of any difficulties if you will keep sober. The English people are the friends of the Indians, and you will make many friends if you take and keep my advice.

" I will ask but one solemn promise of you, and that is, that you will drink no spirituous liquors while you are in this country, and your friend Mr. Rankin will perfectly justify me in this. (' *How, how, how !*')

" If you will keep sober, you shall have plenty of good tobacco to smoke and roast beef to eat, and there is no doubt that I will get you permission to see the Queen."

To this the old chief (Ah-quee-we-zaints, the boy chief) arose and replied :—

" My Friend, I give you my hand. The Great Spirit has been kind to us in keeping his eye upon us all in crossing the salt lake, and we are thanking Him that we are all here safe and in good health. We had heard much of you when in our own country, where all the Indians know you, and we are now happy to meet you (' *How, how !*')

" My Friend, we are here like children in this strange country, and we shall feel happy and not afraid if you will be our father—the Great Spirit has put good counsel into your mouth, and we will follow it. (' *How, how, how !*')

" We all know the dangers of fire-water ; we have all been fond of it, and have been taught to drink it. We have been told that the Great Spirit sent it to us because he loved us—but we have learned that this is not true.

" We have learned that the English people do not drink it—they are wise ; and we will all pledge our words to you in this council that we will not drink it while we are in this country, and we are ready to put our names on a paper. (' *How, how, how !*') "

" My Friends," said I, " I don't require your names on a paper ; I am satisfied ; if you were white men, perhaps I might—but no Indian who ever gave me his word has deceived me. I will take your names on paper, however, for another purpose, that I may know how to call you, how to introduce you, and to have your arrival properly announced in the newspapers." (' *How, how, how !*')

Their names were then taken as follows, and the business of our first council being finished, it broke up. (*See Plate No. 4.*)

1. Ah-quee-we-zaints (the Boy Chief).
2. Pat-au-a-quot-a-wee-be (the Driving Cloud), war-chief.

No. 1

3. Wee-nish-ka-wee-be (the Flying Gull).
4. Sah-mah (Tobacco).
5. Gish-ee-gosh-e-gee (Moonlight Night).
6. Not-een-a-akm (Strong Wind), interpreter.
7. Wos-see-ab-e-neuh-qua, woman.
8. Nib-nab-ee-qua, girl.
9. Ne-bet-neuh-qua, woman.

After a stroll of an hour or so about my rooms, where they were inexpressibly amused with my numerous paintings, &c., they were driven awhile about the town, and landed at their hotel, where the crowd had become so general and so dense, that it was almost impossible to approach it. The partial glance that the public got of their red faces and wild dresses on this day, as they were moving through the streets, and passing to and from the carriage, increased the cry of " Ob-jubbeways !" in every part of the city, and established the fact as certain, that "*real Indians*" had made their appearance in Manchester.

It should be known to the reader by this time that this party were from the northern shore of Lake Huron, in Canada ; therefore her Majesty's subjects, and part of one of the most numerous tribes in North America, inhabiting the shores of Lake Superior, Lake of the Woods, and Lake Huron, numbering some 15,000 or 20,000, and usually (in civilized parlance) called Chippeways, a mere *refinement* upon their native name, O-jib-be-way. The appearance of these wild folks so suddenly in the streets of Manchester was well calculated to raise an excitement and the most intense curiosity. They were all clad in skins of their own dressing, their head-dresses of eagles' quills and wild turkeys' feathers ; their faces daubed and streaked with vermilion and black and green paint. They were armed with their war-clubs, bows and quivers, and tomahawks and scalping knives, just as they roam through the woods in their country ; and their yells and war-whoops, which were occasionally sounded in the streets at some sudden occurrence that attracted their attention, gave a new excitement amid the smoke and din of Manchester. The leading man of this party, *Ah-quee-we-zaints* (the boy chief), was an excellent old man, of seventy-five years, with an intelligent and benignant countenance, and had been somewhat distinguished as a warrior in his younger days.

The next of consequence (*Pat-au-a-quot-a-wee-be*, the driving cloud), and called the war-chief (though I believe not a chief), was a remarkably fine man of thirty-five years of age, and had distinguished himself as a warrior in several battles in the war of 1812, having been engaged in the British lines, and in those engagements had been several times severely wounded, and of which he still carried and exhibited the most frightful scars.

Sah-mah (tobacco) and *Gish-ee-gosh-e-gee* (moonlight night) were two fine young men, denoted warriors, having their wives with them ; *Wee-nish-ka-wee-be* (the flying gull) was a sort of doctor or necromancer to the party, and a young fellow of much drollery and wit. The Strong Wind, the interpreter, whose familiar name was *Cadotte*, was a half-caste, a young man of fine personal appearance and address, and the son of a Frenchman of that name who had long been an interpreter for the English factories in those regions.

By the patient and accommodating disposition of this young man, any conversation was easily held with these people ; and through him, the interchange of feelings between the civilized world and these rude and curious people, which will appear in the subsequent chapters of this book, was principally effected.

CHAPTER XI.

Ojibbeways visit the Mayor in Town-hall—They refuse wine—Distress of the kind and accommodating landlord—Indians' first *drive* about the town of Manchester—Their curious remarks—Saw some white people drunk—Many women holding on to men's arms and apparently not sick—Saw much smoke—Vast many poor people—Indians commence dancing in the Author's Collection—Effects of the war-dance and war-whoop upon the audience—Various amusements of the evening—A rich present to the old Boy-Chief—And his speech—Numerous presents made—Immense crowd and excitement—Indians visit a great woollen-factory—Casts made from their heads by a phrenologist—Visit to Orrell's cotton-mill at Stockport—Their opinions of it—The party kindly entertained by Mr. Hollins and lady.

THE Indians having had a few days' rest, having made their first visit to my rooms, and settled all the preliminaries for their future operations, were now ready to step forth amongst the strange sights that were open and ready for their inspection in the new world that they had entered, all of which was yet before them.

The world's civilities towards them commenced in an invitation from the Mayor of Manchester to visit the Town-Hall, and they dressed and painted and armed for the occasion, not asking who the mayor was, or how near he might be in rank to the Queen herself, whom it was their greatest ambition to see; but upon the supposition, of course, that they were going to see a "great chief," as they called him.

They were moved through the streets in an omnibus, accompanied by Mr. Rankin, and I met them at the door of the hall, and conducted them to the presence of the mayor, whom they recognised, and were not a little surprised to find was one of the gentlemen to whom they had been introduced the day before. They were then presented by the mayor to his lady, and a select party of ladies and gentlemen who had been invited to see them. By these they were received with much kindness, and after having been shown the various rooms, &c., were led into the mayor's court, then in session, where they stood a few minutes, and finding that all proceedings were stopped, and all eyes upon them while there, I beckoned to them to retire.

Various refreshments were prepared for them, to which they returned, and whilst the lady mayoress and ladies and gentlemen were proposing their health in wine which was poured out for them, they were surprised to receive smiles and thanks from the Indians as they refused to partake of it. To the inquiries raised for the cause of their refusing to drink, Mr. Rankin explained that they were under a solemn pledge not to drink spirituous liquors while in England, which was applauded by all present, and they received many presents in consequence of this informa- tion, which was the beginning of encouragement to keep their promise of sobriety and total abstinence.

After leaving the town-hall, Mr. Rankin got into the omnibus with them, and during a drive of half an hour or so, giving them a passing glance at the principal streets of Manchester and its suburbs, they returned to their hotel.

This excursion was calculated, of course, to bring around their hotel its thousands and even tens of thousands of the excitable and excited idlers that an extraordinary "turn out" had at that time thrown into the streets ; and in en- deavouring to pay them my customary visit that night, I was obliged to follow in the wake of a number of police, who had the greatest difficulty in making their way through the mass.

The object of my visit to them was to talk, as usual, upon the events of the day, and of our future operations. The first "talk" I had, however, was with the kind and good-natured landlord, who said that he had now got notoriety enough—he didn't think his house would be forgotten ; and was exceedingly obliged to me, and was pleased with the Indians, who gave him no trouble; alleging that they were ten times more civil and well-behaved than the people night and day crowded around his house. " It seemed to him as if the *savages* were all outside of his house and the gentlemen inside. His house, which was fresh painted but a few days, and not dry, was ' all done up,' as high as they could reach and climb, and must be done over again; and his windows were broken and window-shutters torn from their hinges; and it was impossible for him to keep them any longer without great damage to his interest, and he hoped I would provide some other place for them as soon as possible." It happened much to my satisfaction that I had already prepared an apartment for them in the Exchange Buildings, adjoining to the exhibition-rooms, which were elevated high above the gaze of the crowd, and to which they were to be removed the next morning. This gave the good man much relief, and he said he could manage to live through that night.

The conversation of the Indians that evening, while they were passing their pipe round and making their comments upon what they had seen, was exceedingly curious, and deserves to be recorded. They expressed great satisfaction at the kind manner in which they had been entertained by the mayor, understanding that he was the head man of the town of Manchester—" chief of that village," as they called him; "they saw him and his squaw, and many other beautiful squaws, all drinking; and they saw many people through the windows, and in the doors, as they passed along the streets, who were drinking; and they saw several persons in the streets who were quite drunk, and two or three lying down in the streets, like pigs; and they thought the people of Manchester loved much to drink liquor. They saw a great deal of smoke, and thought the prairies were on fire; they saw many fine-looking squaws walking in the streets, and some of them holding on to men's arms, and didn't look sick neither. They saw a great many large houses, which it seemed as if nobody lived in. They saw a great many people in the streets, who appeared very poor, and looked as if they had nothing to eat.   They had seen many thousands, and almost all looked so poor that they thought it would do no good for us to stay in Manchester."

I explained to them the extraordinary cause that had recently thrown so many thousands of poor people into the streets; that Manchester was one of the richest towns in the world; that the immense houses they had seen, and apparently shut up, were the great factories in which these thousands of poor people worked, but were now stopped, and their working people were running about the streets in vast numbers; that the immense crowd gathered around their hotel, from day to day, were of that class; that the wealthy people were very many, but that their dwellings were mostly a little out of town; and that their business men were principally shut up in their offices and factories, attending to their business whilst the idle people were running about the streets.

Such was a little of the gossip after their first visit and drive about the town—and the next morning, at an early hour, they were removed to their new lodgings in the Exchange Buildings, and the kind landlord effectually, though very gradually, relieved from the nuisance he had had around his house for some days past.

On the same evening, by our announcements, they were to make their first appearance in my exhibition, and at an early hour the Rooms were filled, and we were obliged to close the doors. I had erected a strong platform in the middle of my room, on which the Indians were to give their dances, and having removed all seats from the room, every part of the floor was covered as densely as it was possible for men and women to be grouped together. Into the midst of this mass the party dashed in Indian file, with shield and bow and quiver slung—with war-clubs and tomahawks in hand, as they sounded the frightful war-whoop and were endeavouring to reach the platform. The frightened crowd, with screams and yells as frightful nearly as those of the

Indians, gave way, and they soon had a free passage to the platform, upon which they leaped, without looking for the flight of steps prepared for them, and were at full length before the staring, gaping multitude. Mr. Rankin was by their side, and in a moment I was there also, to commence upon the new duties devolving on me under our recent arrangement. They were in a moment seated, and were. passing their pipe around, while I was, by a brief lecture, introducing them, and the modes they were to illustrate, to the audience.

I described the country and the tribe they belonged to, and the objects for which they had crossed the Atlantic; and also expressed to the audience the happy opportunity it was affording me of corroborating the many assertions I had been heretofore making relative to the looks and modes of those people, many of which I was fully aware were difficult of comprehension. Having done this, I should leave the Indians to entertain the audience with such of their dances and other amusements as they might decide upon, and endeavour to stand by and explain each amusement as they gave it, feeling abundantly able to do so from a residence of eight years amongst the various tribes in America.

There was a shout of applause at the close of my remarks, and the most impatient anxiety evinced on all sides to see the commencement of the curious tricks which were just ready to be introduced. At this moment, with a sudden yell, the men all sprung upon their feet; their weapons brandished and their buffalo robes thrown back, while the women and children seated themselves at the end of the platform. Another shrill yell of the war-whoop, with the flourish of their weapons, and the Medicine-man or Doctor commenced with tambour (or drum), and his voice, upon the war-song; and they were all off in the dance.* At the first rest, when they suddenly stopped,

---

* All American Indians are poor in musical instruments, the principal of which, and the "heel inspiring" one, is the drum or tambour. This is

there was but one mingled roar of applause, which showed
to the poor fellows that they had made "a hit," and were
to be received with great kindness and interest. This
stimulated them to finish it with spirit; and when it was
done, and they were seated a few moments to rest, hundreds
were ambitious to crowd up to them and offer them their
hands. It was with great difficulty that I could get the
audience quiet enough to hear my explanations of the war-
dance—its meaning, and the objects and character of the
war-whoop which they had just heard. I gained the
patience of the crowd by promising them a number of
dances and other amusements, all of which I would render
instructive by my explanations, and afford all, in the remotest
parts of the room, an opportunity to shake hands with the
Indians when their amusements were finished.

After my explanations and their pipe were finished, they
arose and gave the *Wa-be-no* dance, as they call it. *Wa-be-no*,
in the Ojibbeway language, means mystery, and their
mystery-dance is one of their choicest dances, only given
at some occasion of their mystery-feasts, or for the accomplishment of some mysterious design. This dance is
amusing and grotesque, and made much merriment amongst
the audience. I explained the meaning of this also, and
they afterwards gave some surprising illustrations of the
mode of catching and throwing the ball in their favourite
game of ball-play, with their ball-sticks in their hands.
The astonishing quickness and certainty with which they
throw and catch the ball in their rackets elicited immense
applause; and after this they gave the "*scalp-dance*,"
which is given when a party returns from war, having

---

rudely, but ingeniously made, by straining a piece of raw hide over a
hoop or over the head of a sort of keg, generally made by excavating the
inner part of a log of wood, leaving a thin rim around its side. In the
bottom of this they always have a quantity of water, which sends out a remarkably rich and liquid tone. Besides this, they use several kinds of
rattles and whistles—some of which are for mystery purposes, and others
merely for the pleasing and exciting effects they produce in their dances.

brought home scalps taken from their enemies' heads, and preserved as trophies by the victors. In this dance the women, occupying the centre, hold up the scalps, attached to the tops of little poles, while men who have come from war dance around in a circle, brandishing their weapons, gnashing their teeth, and yelling the war-whoop at the highest key of their voices. At the close of this terrifying dance, which seemed to come just up to the anxiety of the excited audience, there was a tremendous roar of applause, and, in the midst of the uproar, an old gentleman took from his pocket a beautifully chased silver tobacco-box, and handing it to me, desired me to give it to the old chief, and tell him to carry his tobacco in it. I handed it to the old man, and, as he had seen the hand that gave it, he sprang upon his feet, as if he were but a boy, and reaching out his hand, grasped, over the heads of the audience, the hand of the venerable old gentleman, who told him "he was happy to see him, and to make him a little present to recollect him by." The old chief straightened up and squared himself upon the platform, throwing his buffalo robe over his left shoulder and passing it forward under his right arm and into his left hand; and with the most benignant smile (as he turned his box a moment under his eye, and passed it into his left hand) commenced—"My friends, though I am old I thank the Great Spirit for giving me strength to say a few words to you. He has allowed me to live many years, and I believe it is because I thank him for all his gifts. His eye was upon us when we were on the great salt lake, and he has brought us here safe, for which we all are thankful. He has directed you all to come here this night and to be so kind to us, for we had done nothing to make you come. We have long heard of the *Sag-a-noshes*,* and we have been anxious to come and see them. We have fought for them and with them, and our fathers and brothers have bled for

---

* **Englishmen.**

them. There are many of the *Sag-a-noshes* amongst us, and
we love them. The Great Spirit has smiled upon our undertaking, and he has guided the hand of my brother to make
me this present. My friends, my heart is warm and I am
thankful. We have now done our dancing and singing, and
we offer you our hands in friendship." At this there was a
rush towards the platform from every part of the room to
shake the hands of the Indians, who had seated themselves
on the front of the platform for the purpose.

These greetings for half an hour or so were exceedingly
warm ; and to make them more impressive, several persons
deposited in their hands valuable trinkets and money, which
they received with thanks. Thus ended the first night's exhibition of the amusements of the Ojibbeways ; and it was
quite impossible to bring it entirely to a close (such was the
avidity with which the visitors were seeking to handle and
examine every part of their costumes, their tomahawks, and
scalping-knives, &c.) until the Indians took leave and retired to their private room. And even then there was almost
an equal difficulty while I was in the exhibition-room, for
crowds were gathering around me to know what they ate—
whether they ate their meat raw—whether they were cannibals—what I brought them over for—whether they were
easy to manage, &c.—until I gradually edged along towards
the door, through which I suddenly slipped, when I had got
completely out of breath, leaving the group to fall upon
poor Daniel, who was lecturing in another part of the room.

Our first night's labour had taken us until eleven o'clock ;
and as I was wending my way home to my lodgings, I could
hear the war-whoop squeaking and echoing in the streets
in every part of the town.

On the following morning, at the very friendly invitation
of the proprietor of an extensive woollen-factory in the
vicinity of Bury, and who had sent a carriage with four
horses for them, the whole party paid a visit to his extensive
mills and to his mansion, where they partook of breakfast
with him, and returned in great glee and spirits, each

one bearing a magnificent blanket of various colours, presented to them by his generous hand.

The second night of their exhibition went off much like the first : the room was filled long before they made their appearance ; and in the roar and confusion of applause at the end of their amusements, there was a cry from the end of the room, " Let some of them come this way—we can't get near them—we can't tell whether they are in their own skins or in fleshings." And another hallooed out " Let that handsome little fellow come here (alluding to *Samah*, who was a very fine-looking young man) ; here is a lady who wants to kiss him !"

This being interpreted to him, he leaped into and through the crowd (as he would dash into the river that he was to ford), and had his naked arms around her neck and kissed her before there was any time for an explanation. The excitement and screaming and laughing amongst the women in that part of the room made kissing fashionable, and every one who laid her hand upon his arm or his naked shoulders (and those not a few) got a kiss, gave a scream, and presented him a brooch, a ring, or some other keepsake, and went home with a streak of red paint on her face, and perhaps with one or two of black or green upon her dress. The gallant little fellow squeezed himself through this dense crowd, kissing old and young as he went, and returned to the platform, from which he held up and displayed his trophies with much satisfaction.

I felt it my duty to reprimand him for his rudeness, and told him it was not fashionable in such crowds to kiss the ladies ; to which he replied, that " he knew what he was about—the white ladies are very pretty and very sweet, and I gave my kisses only where they were asked for." The response all over the house was that " he had done right ; good little fellow, he has done no harm."—A voice, " No, no harm, indeed ; I 'll kiss him again if he will come down, charming little fellow !"—He was in the act of leaping off, when Cadotte, the interpreter, seized him by the arm and turned him back. The hour was come for closing, and the Indians moved off to their lodgings. The events of that day and evening furnished the Indians with rich materials for gossip, and I retired to their chambers to smoke a pipe of k'nick-k'neck with them, and join in the pleasures of their conversation. They had many fine presents to display, and some of these valuable, being taken from arms and necks and fingers, in the moments of enthusiasm, and given to the Indians. The little gallant *Samah* had been the most successful in this way, and also had received all the kisses of the pretty women. I have already mentioned that he had his wife with him. They were joking her about this affair, and she coolly said she did not care about it; "for the more kisses he gets from pretty women, the more presents I get, for he loves me enough to give them all to me." There was much commenting also on the great factory they had been to see in the morning, and on the gentleman's kindness in presenting the blankets, which they had now paraded and were examining and showing.

They were exulting much in their happiness and success, and were still expressing fears that, by jumping and yelling, and making so much noise in Manchester, they might give dissatisfaction to the Queen, who would not feel so well disposed to see them. They asked for my opinion on the subject; I told them to have no fears, the Queen would certainly be glad to see them.

I was waited on about this time by Mr. Bally, a gentleman of great eminence and skill in the science of phrenology, and who has one of the richest collections of casts from nature, in the world. Mr. Bally is one of the most rapid and skilful men in the operation of casting from the living face, and was extremely anxious to procure casts from the Ojibbeways; and, to a gentleman of so much worth to science, as well as for his amiable and gentle disposition, I felt bound to lend my best efforts in gaining for him the privilege. I had much difficulty to overcome their superstitions; but, by assuring them that they were to be done as a present to me, and by their seeing the operation performed on one of my men, I succeeded in gaining their consent, and they were all taken with great success. They were a present to my collection; and a copy of them in the noble collection of Mr. Bally will, I hope, continue to be subjects of interest and value.

Kindnesses and attentions were now showering upon the Ojibbeways from all directions in Manchester; and amongst them many kind invitations, which it was impossible for them to comply with. They were invited to visit the mills of various kinds; and, amongst those that they went to, I must record a few words of the one they were most pleased with, and which they will talk the longest about.

I had received an invitation to bring them to Stockport, to examine the cotton-mill of Mr. Orrell, which is probably one of the finest in the kingdom, and availed myself of his kindness, by making a visit to it with them. With his customary politeness, he showed us through it, and explained it in all its parts, so that the Indians, as well as myself, were able to appreciate its magnitude and its ingenious construction.

Upon this giant machine the Indians looked in perfect amazement; though it is a studied part of their earliest education not to exhibit surprise or emotion at anything, however mysterious or incomprehensible it may be. There was enough, however, in the symmetry of this wonderful construction, when in full operation, to overcome the rules of any education that would subdue the natural impulses of astonishment and admiration. They made no remarks, nor did they ask any questions, but listened closely to all the explanations; and, in their conversations for weeks afterwards, admitted their bewildering astonishment at so wonderful a work of human invention.

After viewing, in all its parts, this stupendous work, we were shown through the not less ingenious bleaching-mills of Mr. Hollins; and then, in the kindest manner, conducted under his hospitable roof, where his charming lady and lovely little ones united in their efforts to make us welcome and happy.   The cloth was spread, and the luxuries of their house all heaped upon the table,—the substantials of life, and then its spices.   It seemed cruel to see these poor fellows devouring the one, and rejecting the other—denying and denied the luxuries that *we* could not refuse, when our friends proposed to drink to our healths and our happiness. They were happy, however, and, good fellows, enjoyed what they partook, and we returned, wishing our kind-hearted friends, Mr. Hollins and his lady, many, many happy days.

CHAPTER XII.

Indians on the housetops—Great alarm—Curious excitement—People proposing to " take them " with ropes—Railway to London—The " Iron-
horse"—"The Iron-horse (locomotive) stops to drink"—Arrive in London
—Alarm of the landlady—Visit from the Hon. Mr. Murray—Interview
with His Royal Highness the Duke of Cambridge—Old Chief's speech
—War-dance—The Duke gives them ten sovereigns and ten pounds of
tobacco—Indians ride about the city in an " omnibus and four "—
Remarks on what they saw—The smoke—" Prairies on fire "—Lascars
sweeping the streets—Visit from the Reverend Mr. S.—Impatience to
see the Queen—Great medicine-feast to gain Her Majesty's consent—
Curious ceremony—Hon. Mr. Murray's letter comes in—The Queen's
appointment to see them—Great rejoicing.

ON our return from Stockport we found two reverend
gentlemen, who had been waiting nearly all day for an
interview with the Indians (which had been appointed,
but forgotten), to talk upon the subject of religion. They
had come several miles, and seemed somewhat vexed, as
night was near approaching, and the old chief told them
that they were going to London in a few days, and
should be very busy in the meantime; and again, that
they were expecting to see the Queen, and would rather
wait until after they had seen her Majesty. They had
learned, also, that London was the *great city* of England,
and thought that anything of that kind had better be de-
ferred until they were in London, and the subject was
therefore postponed.

The exhibitions at night were progressing much as I have
above described—the hall invariably full, and the Indians,
as well as the public, had their own amusement in the room,
and also amusing themes for conversation after retiring to
their own quarters.

In the midst of our success and of their amusement and enjoyment, an occurrence took place that was near getting us into difficulty, as it raised a great excitement in the neighbourhood and no little alarm to many old women and little children.

As I was leaving my exhibition-rooms one morning, I met, to my great surprise, an immense crowd of people assembled in front, and the streets almost completely barricaded with the numbers that were rapidly gathering, and all eyes elevated towards the roof of my building. I asked the first person I met what was the matter?—supposing that the house was on fire—to which he replied, " I believes, sir, that the Hob-jib-be-ways has got loose; I knows that some on em is hout, for I seed one on em runnin hover the tops of the ouses, and they'l ave a ard matter to catch em, hin my hopinion, sir."

It seems that the poor fellows had found a passage leading from their rooms out upon the roof of the house, and that, while several of them had been strolling out there for fresh air, and taking a look over the town, a crowd had gathered in the street to look at them, and amongst the most ignorant of that crowd the rumour had become current that they " had broke loose, and people were engaged in endeavouring to take them."

I started back to my room as fast as I could, and to the top of the house, to call them down, and stop the gathering that was in rapid progress in the streets. When I got on the roof, I was as much surprised at the numbers of people assembled on the tops of the adjoining houses, as I had been at the numbers assembled in the streets. The report was there also current, and general, that they had " broke out," and great preparations were being made on the adjoining roofs, with ropes and poles, &c., to " take them," if possible, before any harm could be done. About the time I had got amongst them, and was inviting them down, several of the police made their appearance by my side, and ordered them immediately into their room, and told me that in the excited state of the town, with their mills all out, such a thing was endangering the peace; for it brought a mob of many thousands together, which would be sure not to disperse without doing some mischief. I was ordered by the police to keep them thereafter in the rooms, and not to allow them to show themselves at the windows, so great were their fears of a riot in the streets, if there was the least thing to set it in motion. As an evidence of the necessity of such rigour, this affair of about fifteen minutes' standing had already brought ten or fifteen thousand people together, and a large body of the police had been ordered on to the ground, having the greatest difficulty during the day to get rid of the crowd.

Mr. Rankin, about this time, was getting alarming apprehensions that our delay in Manchester was calculated to affect our prospect of going before the Queen, and at his urgent request I announced our last night in Manchester, after an exhibition of ten days. On the last night, as on each of the preceding ones, the room was quite full, and even so many were necessarily forbidden entrance, that they began a most ruinous warfare on the door from the outside, and to such a degree, that I was obliged to put the entrance to my premises in charge of the police, for protection. We were now prepared to move off to the metropolis, and I showed to Mr. Rankin, by his share of the profits of ten days, that he had already received more than he would have got in two months by the plan he had proposed, to hire the party to me for 100*l.* per month.

This seemed to please him very much, and we moved off pleasantly on our way to London, leaving the ungratified curiosity that remained in Manchester until a future occasion, when we might return again.

For our passage to London we had chartered a second-class carriage to ourselves, and in it had a great deal of amusement and merriment on the way. The novelty of the mode of travelling and the rapidity at which we were going raised the spirits of the Indians to a high degree, and they sang their favourite songs, and even gave their dances, as they passed along. Their curiosity had been excited to know how the train was propelled or drawn, and at the first station I stepped out with them, and forward to the locomotive, where I explained the power which pulled us along. They at once instituted for the engine, the appellation of the "Iron-horse;" and, at our next stopping-place, which was one where the engine was taking in water, they all leaped out "*to see the Iron-horse drink.*"

Their songs and yells set at least a thousand dogs barking and howling on the way, and as we came under the station at Birmingham, called up a fat old gentleman, who opened our door and very knowingly exclaimed, "What the devil have you got here? some more of them damned grisly bears, have you?" He was soon merged in the crowd that gathered around us, and, with doors closed, the Indians sat out patiently the interval, until we were under weigh again. Arrived at the Euston station, in London, an omnibus conveyed them suddenly to apartments in George-street, which had been prepared for them. They were highly excited when they entered their rooms, talking about the Queen, whom they believed had just passed in her carriage, from seeing two footmen with gold-laced hats and red breeches and white stockings, standing up and riding on a carriage behind, with large gold-headed canes in their hands : it proved, however, to have been the carriage of Lady S——n, familiarly known in that neighbourhood; and the poor fellows seemed wofully disappointed at this information.

The good landlady, who took a glance of them as they came in, was becoming alarmed at the bargain she had made for the rooms, and came to Mr. Rankin, expressing her fears that the arrangement would never answer for her, as "she did not expect such wild, black-looking savages from the Indies." Mr. Rankin assured her that they were quite harmless, and much more of gentlemen than many white men she might get in her house, and he would be responsible for all damage that they would ever do to her property, even if she left the whole of it unsecured by lock and key. So she said she would venture to try them for a week, and see how they behaved.   They were now in the midst of the great city of London, which they had been so anxious to see ; and, upon putting their heads out of the windows to take a first peep, the smoke was so dense that they could see but a few rods, when they declared that the " prairies must be on fire again."

Daniel was, at this time, remaining in Manchester to take down and bring on my collection, which it was agreed should be re-opened in London.   I was busy effecting a new arrangement for the Egyptian Hall, which I took for six months, and in a few days my collection was being replaced upon its walls.

The first visitor who came to see the party, and to wish them success in London, was my excellent friend the Hon. C. A. Murray, who was much pleased with them, and learning their desire to gain an audience of Her Majesty, he proposed, as the surest way to bring it about, that his Royal Highness the Duke of Cambridge should have an interview with them first, and then it would be easy to get Her Majesty to see them.   This plan was agreed to, and the next day Mr. Murray addressed me a note, saying that the Duke would meet them the next morning in the Queen's drawing-room, Hanover-square Concert-rooms.   I immediately made the arrangement with the proprietor of the rooms, and at the appointed hour the next morning was there with them, and met His Royal Highness the Duke of Cambridge, with the Hon. Mr. Murray and Baron Knesebeck, in attendance.   The Duke met them in the most familiar and cordial manner, offering them his hand, and smoking the Indian pipe with them.   He conversed a great deal with them through their interpreter, Cadotte ; and, after closely examining their costumes, weapons, &c., took a seat to see them dance.   They amused him with the war-dance and the *Wa-be-no* dance, giving several songs and the war-whoop ; after which they seated themselves on the

floor, and after a few minutes' rest, having passed the pipe
around, the old chief arose and said—

"Father, we are glad to see you and to take your hand ; we know that you
are uncle to our *great mother* the Queen, and we are happy to see you.
(' *How, how, how !*') We thank the Great Spirit for this ; he has kept us in
good health and safe over the great salt lake, and His eye is on us now, we
know, or we should not see our great father this day. We are poor,
ignorant children, and yet we hope the Queen, your niece, will be willing
to see us, when our hearts will be happy. (' *How, how, how !*')

"Father, my years, you see, are nearly spent. I have carried my
weapons and hunted for your enemies many years, and my warriors here
have many wounds they received in fighting for the Sag-a-noshes. (' *How,
how, how !*')

"I have no more words to say at present. (' *How, how, how !*') "

His Royal Highness graciously received the old Chief's
speech, and then examined the wounds pointed out on the
body of the War Chief; after which he replied to the
old man—

"My friends, I meet you here to-day with great pleasure, and *I* thank
the Great Spirit also, that He has guarded you and kept you safe over the
ocean. I hope your visit to England may be pleasant and profitable to you,
and that you may all get back safe to your children. (' *How, how, how !*')

"My friends, I will make known your wishes to the Queen, and I think
you will see her. (' *How, how, how !*') "

The Duke most kindly took leave of them, presenting
to the old chief ten sovereigns, which he divided equally
among the number, and sent them on the following day
ten pounds of the choicest smoking tobacco. On leaving
the Rooms he also thanked me for the treat I had afforded
him, and said, "Oh, the good fellows ! yes, the Queen will
see them."

The announcement of the arrival of the Ojibbeways
which had been made in the public papers, and the notice
also of their interview with the Duke of Cambridge, were
now gaining them a notoriety with the public ; and amongst
my personal friends, was announcing that I had returned to
London, which altogether brought me a flood of applicants
for private interviews with them. We had resolved not to

make any exhibition of their modes to the public, until after they had seen the Queen, and the month that we remained idle, and waiting for her Majesty's command, was rendered tedious and troublesome from the above causes. We were daily and hourly importuned for permissions to see them, which were in part granted, until it became quite necessary that I should absent myself from them, leaving instructions at the door that no communication could be had with them at present. Mr. Rankin during this time stayed constantly with them, and I occasionally spent an evening of gossip and smoked a pipe with them. We made use of most of the time in endeavouring to show them as much of the great city as possible, driving them out in a bus during the day, and several times taking them into the country to spend a day running over the fields for the benefit of their health.

After one of their first drives about the City, when they had been passed through Regent Street, the Strand, Cheapside, Oxford Street and Holborn, I spent the evening in a talk with them in their rooms, and was exceedingly amused with the shrewdness of their remarks upon what they had seen. They had considered the " prairies still on fire," from the quantity of smoke they met ; one of the women had undertaken to count the number of carriages they passed, but was obliged to give it up; " saw a great many fine houses, but nobody in the windows ; saw many men with a large board on the back, and another on the breast, walking in the street—supposed it was some kind of punishment ; saw men carrying bags of coal, their hats on wrong side before ; saw fine ladies and gentlemen riding in the middle of the streets in carriages, but a great many poor and ragged people on the sides of the roads ; saw a great many men and women drinking in shops where they saw great barrels and hogsheads ; saw several drunk in the streets. They had passed two *Indians* in the street with brooms, sweeping away the mud ; they saw them hold out their hands to people going by, as if they were begging for money : they saw many other poor people begging, some with brooms in their hands and others with little babies in their arms, who looked as if they were hungry for food to eat." They had much to say about the two Indians they had passed. " It could not be that white people would dress and paint themselves like Indians in order to beg money, and they could not see how Indians would consent to stand in the streets and sweep the mud away in order to beg for money." They appealed to me to know whether they were really Indians, and I said " Yes ; they are natives from the East Indies, called Lascars. They are naturally, most probably like yourselves, too proud to work or to beg ; but they have been left by some cruel fate, to earn their living in the streets of London, or to starve to death. and, poor fellows, they have preferred begging to starvation." The Indians seemed much affected by the degradation that these poor fellows were driven to, and resolved that they would carry some money with them when they went out, to throw to them.

I had about this time several communications from the Reverend Mr. S——, who was desirous, if possible, to have an interview with the Indians for the purpose of learning from them what notions they had of religion, if any ; and to endeavour to open their minds to a knowledge of the Christian religion, which it was the wish of himself and many others of his friends to teach to them for their eternal welfare. I at once wrote to those reverend gentlemen and assured them that their kind endeavours would be aided in every possible way by Mr. Rankin and myself; and I appointed an hour at once, when they could converse with the Indians on the subject. Their visit was made at the hour appointed, and the conversation was held in my presence. The reverend gentlemen most kindly and humanely greeted the Indians on their safe arrival in this country, where they were glad to meet them as brothers. They called upon them not in any way to interfere with their amusements or objects for which they had come to England, but to wish them all success, and at the same time to learn from them whether as poor children of the forests they had been kept in the dark, and out of the light of the true Christian religion, which it was their desire to make known to their minds. The old chief had lit his pipe in the meantime, and having taken a few moments to smoke it out, after the reverend gentleman had stopped, said (without rising up to speak) that he was much pleased to see them, and shake hands with them, for he knew their views were good and friendly. He said that they had heard something about the white man's religion in the wilderness where he lived, but they had thought it too difficult for them to understand. He said he was much obliged to them for offering to explain it at this time, but that they would take a little time to think of it first; and as they had not yet seen the Queen, they thought it best to do no more about it at present.

Poor fellows, they were daily asking for reports from the Palace, becoming impatient for the permission to see her Majesty. They had waited so long that they were beginning to think that their application had failed, and they were becoming dispirited and desponding.

I said to them one morning, " Now, my good fellows, don't despair—you have not tried what you can do yourselves yet; in your own country, if you wish it to rain, you have *Rain-makers* who can make it rain; if you wish it to stop raining, you have *Rain-stoppers*, who cook up a grand medicine feast and cause it to stop raining. If buffalos are scarce, your medicine-men can make them come: why not 'put on the Big Kettle,' and see what you can do in the present dilemma?—You have your *Medicine-man* with you, and your *Medicine-drum* and your *Shi-she-quoi* (mystery rattle); you are all prepared; go to work—you will certainly do no harm, and I fully believe you will bring it about.''

As I was leaving the room their interpreter overtook me, and said that the medicine man wanted the money to buy five fat ducks—that they had resolved on having a *medicine feast* that afternoon, and that they would expect me to be of the party to partake of it.

K 2

I came in at the hour appointed, and found them all with their faces painted black on one side and red on the other (their mode of ornamenting when they supplicate the Great or other Spirit for any gift or favour), and prepared to take their seats at the feast, which was then smoking, on the floor in the adjoining room.   Buffalo robes were spread upon the floor, on which we were seated, when the following dialogue took place between their kind (and now no longer terrified) landlady and the interpreter Cadotte :—" Why, " said she (as she was completing the last arrangement for our feast upon the floor), " you have left no room for the women, poor things." "Women!" said Cadotte, " why, do you suppose that women can eat at a *medicine feast?*" " Why not?" said the landlady, " are they not as good as the men? They are a nice set of women, and that little girl is a dear little creature.   I cooked the ducks as much for them as I did for you, and I think it would be cruel not to invite them to eat with you ; you are no better now than you were this morning ; they ate with you then.   If I had known this, I would have kept one of the ducks for them."   " Devil a bit !" said Cadotte, " do you know what *medicine* is ?" " No, I don't suppose I do ; but there are the three women all crying now in the other room, poor creatures."   " And there they are *obliged* to cry while we are in a *medicine feast,* or we have no luck."   " Oh, dear me, what a strange set of beings!" said the old lady, as she returned to the kitchen, " I won't interfere with them ; they must take their own way."

With closed doors we went through all the peculiar solemnities of this feast ; and, having devoured all the ducks, leaving "none for the poor women," the medicine man took about a quarter of an hour to recite a sort of prayer or thanks to the Great Spirit, which, from the extreme rapidity with which he repeated it, I supposed to be some established form peculiar to such occasions.   After this, and while the last pipe was passing around, my man

Daniel (in pursuance of my previous instructions) entered the room, and delivered to me a large letter, which he said he thought was from Mr. Murray, as it had the household stamp upon it. The most impatient excitement prevailed until I broke the seal and read as follows:—

"Buckingham Palace, Thursday morning.

"Dear Sir,—I have great pleasure in informing you that Her Majesty has expressed a desire to see the party of Ojibbeway Indians, and has appointed Thursday next, at two o'clock, as the hour when she will receive you with the party, in the Waterloo Gallery, Windsor Castle. I pray that you will be punctual at the hour, and I will meet you at the threshold, rendering all the facilities that may be in my power.

"Yours, sincerely,

"*To Geo. Catlin, Esq.*"   "C. A. MURRAY,

"*Master of H. M. Household.*"

The reader can readily imagine what was the *pleasure* of these poor people when they heard this letter read; but it would be difficult to know what were their feelings of *surprise*, that the efficacy of their *medicine* should have brought it in at that opportune moment. The reader will also suppose, what their superstition prevented them from ever imagining, that this letter was in my pocket several hours before the ducks were bought, and therefore cost me about twenty shillings.

A pipe was here lit by the old chief, and passed around, and smoked to the kind *Spirit* they had successfully invoked, and with it all the anxieties of this day passed away.

CHAPTER XIII.

Preparations for visiting the Queen—Amusing interview with Sykes, the porter—Mistaken by the old Chief for Prince Albert—Meet the Hon. Mr. Murray—The waiting-room—The Author conducts the party before Her Majesty and the Prince in the Waterloo Gallery—Their reception —Introductions and conversations — Indians give the war-dance—A smoke—The old Chief's speech to the Queen—Pipe-dance—Her Majesty and the Prince retire—Indians at a feast in the waiting-room—Drinking the Queen's health in Champagne—Indians call it " *Chickabobboo*"—Story of *Chickabobboo*, and great amusement—Indians return to London—Evening-gossip about the Queen and her *Chickabobboo*—First evening of the Indians in Egyptian Hall—Great excitement—Alarm—Tremendous applause—Old Chief's speech—Hon. Mr. Murray's letter to the old Chief, enclosing £20 from the Queen and other presents—Speech of the War-chief—Pipe-dance—Shaking hands—Curious questions by the audience—Ale allowed to the Indians at dinner and after supper—Their rejoicing—They call it *Chickabobboo*.

A NEW chapter commenced here with the Indians, as it commences with my book. All " omnibus drives" were postponed for the present; all communications with the world entirely interdicted; and all was bustle and preparation for the grand event which was to " cap the climax" of their highest ambition—the point to which they had looked ever since they had started, and beyond which, it is not probable, their contemplations had as yet visibly painted anything.

Colours, and ribbons, and beads, of the richest hues, were called for, and procured from various parts of the city ; and both night and day, all, men and women, were constantly engaged in adding brilliancy and richness of colour to their costumes.

The old chief was painting the stem of his pipe of peace (or calumet) sky-blue, emblematical of the feelings they carried in their breasts; and decorating it also with blue and red ribbons, as a suitable gift to royalty. The little girl, *Nib-nab-e-qua*, was crying, as she embroidered with red and white porcupine-quills, fearing that her new mocassins would not look so brilliant as she had sometimes made them. Her mother was arranging black mourning plumes in the cradle in which her infant had died, and which, by the custom of the country, she was obliged yet to carry on her back. The War-chief was repainting his shield, and arranging his scalps on a little hoop, to give proper effect to the scalp-dance. The *Medicine-man* was preparing his *wa-be-no* drum. *Gish-ee-gosh-ee-gee* was stringing beads with his wife; and *Sah-mah* was brightening his tomahawk and his scalping-knife for a glittering effect in the war-dance. Cadotte, during this time, was parading before the mirror, examining, arranging, and re-arranging the ostrich-plumes in his cap, and the fit of a laced frock he had just had made; and (I had almost forgotten myself) I was anxiously awaiting the arrival of a new coat I had ordered at my tailor's for the occasion.

On the morning appointed, all were satisfactorily pre-pared, and, being seated in an omnibus posted with four horses, we were on our way, and soon after that arrived at the gates of Windsor Castle. Descending from the carriage, the poor old chief, whose eyes were getting a little dim with age, was completely nonplused at beholding the magnificent figure (in scarlet and gold lace and powdered wig) of (his apparent Majesty) Sykes, the well-known porter of the palace, who had him by the elbow, and was conducting him and his heavy paraphernalia towards the door. The good old chief turned round and gave him his hand, not knowing as yet what to say, as they had none of them contemplated anything so brilliant aud dazzling, short of Majesty itself. He was at this moment, however, saved from committing himself or bestowing his pipe of peace by the sudden approach of several others of the household in liveries equally splendid, who conducted us into the hall, at which moment we met our friend the

Honourable Mr. Murray, whom we followed to the waiting-room adjoining to the Waterloo Gallery, in which our reception was to take place. Here we were seated, and awaited the anxious moment when it was to be announced that her Majesty was ready to see us.

The Indians were here parading before the large and splendid mirrors and adjusting their feathers and ornaments, and suggesting many surmises about the long table which was dressed out in the room where we were, and which they supposed was the place where the Queen and all her officers about her took their dinners. This, as the sequel will show, was a very great error, as it was preparing for another and entirely different purpose.

After waiting half an hour or so, an officer in full dress came into the room and informed us that the Queen was in the adjoining room, and ready to receive us, and showed us the way. There was a moment of jingling and rattling of trinkets as the Indians were throwing on their robes and gathering up their weapons; and when they responded to my question "if they were all ready?"—by their *"how! how! how!"* I led the way, and they followed into the Waterloo Gallery. They were now all at full length before her Majesty and the Prince, who most graciously received them. (*Plate No.* 5.) The Queen arose from a sofa in the middle of the room, having her Majesty the Queen Dowager and H. R. H. the Duchess of Kent by her side; and advancing towards the Indians, was joined by H. R. H. Prince Albert and the Hon. Mr. Murray. Her Majesty desired that the interpreter and myself should advance nearer to her, and at her request I introduced each individually by their appropriate names, explaining their costumes, weapons, &c. Her Majesty beckoned the little girl up to her, and held her some time by both hands, evidently much pleased with her appearance, and also the woman with the cradle on her back, in whom she seemed to take much interest. She asked many questions, as well as the Prince, relative to their costumes, modes, &c., and they then

took their seats on the sofa to witness the dances which the Indians had come prepared to give.

The Indians were at this time seated in a circle on the floor, when the *Medicine-man* gradually commenced tapping on his drum and singing in a low tone. In a few moments the house jarred with the leap of the War-chief, who was upon his feet, and after him all the party, in the din of the war-dance. (*Plate No.* 6.)

This dance finished, they were again seated on the floor, when the old chief, seventy-five years of age, having lighted his pipe and passed it around, arose and made the following address to her Majesty :—*

"Great Mother—I have been very sorrowful since I left my home, but the Great Spirit has brought us all safe over the great waters, and my heart will now be glad that we can see your face. We are now happy.

"These are all the words I have to say. My words are few, for I am not very well to-day. The other chief will tell you what I intended to say."

The War-chief then rose, and in a very energetic manner made the following speech, which was also literally interpreted to her Majesty :—

"Great Mother—The Great Spirit has been kind to us, your children, in protecting us on our long journey here. And we are now happy that we are allowed to see your face. It makes our hearts glad to see the faces of so many Saganoshes (English) in this country, and all wearing such pleasant looks. We think the people here must be very happy.

"Mother—We have been often told that there was a great fire in this country—that its light shone across the great water; and we see now where

---

* The poor old chief met with a sudden embarrassment at this moment that he had not thought of, and was not prepared consequently to know how to proceed. He had, according to the custom of his country, prepared and brought with him a beautiful calumet or pipe of peace to present, and on rising to make his speech (the moment when it is customary to present it) it for the first time occurred to him that he was about to present it to a woman, the impropriety of which was evident to him. He thought of the Prince, but as the pipe of peace can only be given to the highest in power, he had another misgiving; and, unlike to orators in the Indian countries, continued to hold it in his hand while he was speaking, and brought it away with him.

this great light arises.   We believe that it shines from this great wigwam to all the world.

" Mother—We have seen many strange things since we came to this country.   We see that your wigwams are large, and the light that is in them is bright.   Our wigwams are small, and our light is not strong.   We are not rich, but yet we have plenty of food to eat.

" Mother—Myself and my friends here are your friends—your children· We have used our weapons against your enemies.   And for many years we have received liberal presents from this country, which have made us quite happy and comfortable in our wigwams.

" Mother—The chief who has just spoken, and myself, have fought and bled by the side of the greatest warrior who ever lived—Tecumseh.

" Mother—Our hearts are glad at what we have this day seen—that we have been allowed to see your face.   And when we get home our words will be listened to in the councils of our nation.

" This is all I have to say."

After his speech the War-chief resumed his seat upon the floor ; and as her Majesty could not be supposed to reply to his speech, she called upon the Prince, who thanked them for the amusement they had afforded her Majesty, who felt a deep interest in their welfare, and thankful to the old chief for the noble and religious sentiments expressed in his remarks.

After this the Indians rose and gave their favourite, the PIPE DANCE, which seemed to afford much amusement to the Royal party.   The Queen and the Prince then graciously bowed and took leave, thanking them, through the inter-preter, for the amusement they had afforded them.   The Indians at the same moment shouldered their robes and retired, sounding their war-whoop to the amusement of the servants of the household, who had assembled to the amount of some hundreds in the galleries of the hall.

They were now in the waiting-room again, where, to their surprise (and no little satisfaction), they found that the table they had seen so splendidly arranged was intended for their own entertainment, and was now ready for the " set-to."   Mr. Murray announced it as ready, and we all went to work.   Mr. Rankin, who had been seated in the gallery during the presentation, having joined the party,

had now taken his seat with them at the table. With his usual kindness, Mr. Murray insisted on carving the roast-beef and helping them around, and next in drinking the Queen's health, which is customary at all public dinners. For this the first bottle of champagne was opened; and when the cork flew and the wine was pouring into glasses, the Indians pronounced the word " *Chick-a-bob-boo !*" and had a great laugh. A foaming glass of it was set be-fore each Indian; and when it was proposed to drink to Her Majesty's health, they all refused. I explained to Mr. Murray the promise they were under to drink no spirituous liquor while in the kingdom. Mr. Murray applauded their noble resolution, but said at the same time that this was not *spirituous liquor*—it was a light wine, and could not hurt them; and it would be the only time they could ever drink to Her Majesty so properly, and Her Majesty's health could not be refused by Her Majesty's subjects. When again urged they still refused, saying " We no drink—can't drink." They seemed however to be referring it to me, as all eyes were alternately upon me and upon their glasses, when I said to them—" Yes, my good fellows, drink; it will not hurt you. The promise you have made to Mr. Rankin and myself will not be broken—it did not con-template a case like this, where it is necessary to drink the Queen's health. And again, this is *champagne*, and not *spirituous liquor,* which you have solemnly promised to avoid."—" *How ! how ! how !*" they all responded, and with great delight all joined in "health to the Queen !" And as each glass was emptied to the bottom, they smacked their lips, again pronouncing the word " *Chick-a-bob-boo ! Chick-a-bob-boo !*" with a roar of laughter among themselves.

Mr. Murray and I becoming anxious to know the mean-ing of *chick-a-bob-boo*, it was agreed that the War-chief (who had a dry but amusing way of relating an anecdote) should give us the etymology of the word *chick-a-bob-boo*, which they said was manufactured but a few years since in their coun-try. The old Boy-chief, who was not a stranger to *chick a-*

bob-boo, nor to good jokes, said that the "War-chief couldn't tell a story well unless his lips were kept moist;" and he proposed that we should drink Mr. Murray's health before he commenced. So the champagne was poured again, and, the Hon. Mr. Murray's health being drank, the War-chief proceeded by saying—that " Only a few years since, when the white men were bringing so much rum and whiskey into the little village where he lives, that it was making them all sick, and killing a great many, the chiefs decided in council that they would tomahawk every keg of whiskey the white men should bring in ; and it had the effect of keeping them away, and their people, who had been drunk and sick, were getting well.

" Not long after that," continued he, " a little old man with red hair, who used to bring us bags of apples, got in the way of bringing in one end of his bag a great many bottles filled with something that looked much like whiskey, but which, when we smelled it, and tasted it, we found was not *fire-water,* and it was much liked by the chiefs and all ; for they found, as he said, it was good, and would not make Indians drunk. He sold much of this to the Indians, and came very often ; and when he had carried it a great way on his horse, and in the sun, it sometimes became very impatient to get out of the bottles ; and it was very amusing to see the little old man turn a crooked wire into the bottle to pull out the stopper, when one was holding a cup ready to catch it. As he would twist the wire in, it would go *chee—e—* ; and when he poured it out, it would say, *pop-poo, pop-poo.** This amused the women and children very much, and they called it at first *chee-pop-poo,* and since, *chick-a-bob-boo.* And this the old man with red hair told us at last was nothing but the juice of apples, though we found it very good ; and yet it has made some very drunk."

---

* This word must be *whispered,* as the War-chief gave it, and not *spoken,* to be appreciated—after the mode of Indians in their imitations, or exclamations of surprise.

This story of the War-chief amused Mr. Murray very much, and he ordered one of the waiters to "twist the crooked wire" into the neck of another bottle or two of the *chick-a-bob-boo* and "pull out the little stoppers," for he was going to propose that we all drink to the health of Prince Albert, who could never be neglected when her Majesty's health was drunk. This was done with enthusiasm; and the old chief soon proposed to drink Mr. Rankin's health, and my health, which were attended to; and he at length thought of the fat porter in scarlet and gold lace, whom he had passed at the door, and who at this moment, with several others in gold lace and powdered hair, were gathering around the table to take a glass or two of *chick-a-bob-boo* with them. This happened at a good time, and Mr. Rankin commenced the anecdote of the old chief having mistaken the porter Sykes for Prince Albert just as Mr. Murray and I withdrew from the room to proceed to town.

I visited the Indians in their rooms that evening, and found them in good spirits, having been well pleased by her Majesty's kind reception, and also delighted with the *chick-a-bob-boo*, and the liberal construction that had been put upon their sacred engagement "not to drink spirituous liquors." Mr. Rankin gave me an amusing account of the old chief's second interview with the porter Sykes, and their manner of taking leave when they were parting to meet no more. "Their pipes," he said, "were lit when they took their omnibus to return, and their joyful songs and choruses made it a *travelling music-box* the whole way to town."

I had come upon them at the moment when they were taking their coffee—a habit they had got into as one of the last things before going to bed. When they finished their coffee they lit the pipe, and there were many comments from different parts of the room upon what they had seen during the day. The Queen was of course the engrossing theme for their thoughts and their remarks; and though so well pleased with her kindness to them, they were evidently disappointed in her personal appearance and dress. Her

Majesty was attired in a simple and unadorned dress of black, and wore apparently no ornaments whatever at the time of their presentation, affording the poor fellows nothing either in her stature or costume to answer to the fancied figure of majesty which they had naturally formed in their minds, and were convinced they were going to see. They had, on first entering the room, taken the Duchess of Kent for the Queen, and said they were not apprised of their error until they heard me address the Queen as "Her Majesty."

They were advancing many curious ideas (over the pipe) as to the government of the greatest and richest country in the world being in the hands of a woman, and she no larger than many of the Indian girls at the age of twelve or thirteen years. I explained to them the manner in which she was entitled to the crown, and also how little a king or queen has actually to do in the government of such a country; that it is chiefly done by her ministers, who are always about her, and men of the greatest talents, and able to advise her. And the old chief, who had been listening attentively to me, as he was puffing away at his pipe, said, he was inclined to think it was the best thing for the country. "I am not sure," said he, "but it is the safest way; for if this country had a king instead of a queen, he might be ambitious as a great warrior, and lead the country into war with other nations : now, under her government there is peace, and the country is happy."

Many jokes were passed upon the old chief for having mistaken the porter Sykes for Prince Albert, and for having brought his pipe of peace back, having been afraid to present it. They had many remarks to make also upon the little girl whom her Majesty took by the hand; they told her she turned pale, and they were afraid she would grow up a white woman. They now, for the first time, thought of the Queen's little children, and wondered they had not seen them : they thought they ought, at least, to have seen the Prince of Wales. Daniel, they said, had long since told them how old he was, and that he was to be the next king of England.   He had also read to them his long names, which had pleased them very much, which they never could recollect, but would have written down.

The conversation again, and for some time, ran upon the deliciousness of her Majesty's chickabobboo, and also upon the presents which they had imagined would have been made to them, and which I assured them they might feel quite easy about, as they would come in due time according to the custom.   So were they whiling away the evening of this memorable day, and I left them.

The grand point having been made, their visit to the Queen, the Indians seemed in good spirits to meet the greetings of the public, amongst whom the daily paragraphs in the papers, and their occasional drives through the streets, had excited the most intense curiosity.   The place for their operations was prepared for them in the Egyptian Hall; and in the midst of my Indian collection, as in Manchester, a platform was erected on which their dances and other amusements were to be given.

Having been without any exciting occupation for more than a month, in daily anticipation of their visit to the Queen, the Indians had become, as well as the public, impatient for the opening of their exhibition, which seemed requisite for their amusement as well as necessary for their accustomed bodily exercise.

Their first evening's amusements being announced, the large room of the Egyptian Hall was filled at an early hour, and the Indians received with a roar of applause as they entered and advanced upon the platform.   I came on by their side, and after they had seated themselves upon the platform, entered upon my duty, that of explaining to the audience who these people were, whence they came, and what were their objects in visiting this country.   I also introduced each one personally by his name, to the audience, and briefly described their costumes, weapons, &c., and they were then left to commence as they chose, with their dances and other amusements. Indian looks and Indian costumes, &c., were supposed to have been pretty well understood before this, by most of the audience, who had studied them at their leisure in my rooms on former occasions; but Indian dances and Indian yells, and the war-whoop, had been from necessity postponed and unappreciated until the present moment, when the sudden yell and scream of the whole party (as they sprang upon their feet) announced the war-dance as having commenced. The drum was beating, rattles were shaking, war-clubs and tomahawks and spears were brandishing over their heads, and all their voices were shouting (in time with the beat of the drum and the stamps of their feet) the frightful war-song!

With the exception of some two or three women (whose nerves were not quite firm enough for these excitements, and who screamed quite as loud as the Indians did, as they were making a rush for the door) the audience stood amazed and delighted with the wildness and newness of the scene that was passing before them; and, at the close of the dance, united in a round of applause, which seemed to please the Indians as much as seeing the Queen.

Like all actors, they were vain of their appearance, and proud of applause, and (rather luckily for them, and unlike the painful excitements that fall to the lot of most actors' lives) they were sure of the applause which sympathy brings, and exempt from that censure which often falls heavily upon those whose acting the audience is able to criticise.

According to their custom, after the war-dance was finished, the Indians seated themselves upon the platform and lit their long pipe, which they were almost constantly smoking. This pipe was filled with their own native tobacco (k'nick-k'neck), and passed around from one to the other for a few whiffs, according to the usage of all the American tribes. I took this opportunity of explaining to the audience the meaning of the war-dance, the war-whoop, &c., and whilst I was up, was so overwhelmed with questions (all of which

I felt disposed to answer) that I found it exceedingly-difficult to sit down again. These questions were put for the purpose of gaining information which it was my wish to give; and having patiently answered a number of them, I stated to the audience that I believed the explanations I should throw out in the course of the evening in my own way, would answer nearly every question that they would be disposed to put, and I begged they would allow me as much time and opportunity to give them as possible. This was responded to by acclamation all around the room, and the exhibition proceeded by the Indians wishing me to announce that they were to give the *wa-be-no* (or mystery) dance. This eccentric and droll dance caused much merriment among the audience, and gained them hearty applause again; after which, they being seated as usual, with the pipe passing around, I proceeded with my explanation, which done, I was requested by the interpreter to announce that the old chief had something which he wished to say to the audience, and was going to make a speech. There was a great expression of satisfaction at this, evinced among the crowd, which seemed to give fire to the eye, and youth to the visage of the old man as he rose and said,—

" My friends—It makes our hearts glad when we hear your feet stamp upon the floor, for we know then that you are pleased, and not angry." (Great applause.)

The old man then straightened himself up in the attitude of an orator, and, throwing his buffalo robe over his shoulder, and extending his right arm over the heads of his audience, he proceeded :—

" My friends and brothers—These young men and women and myself have come a great way to see you, and to see our GREAT MOTHER THE QUEEN. The Great Spirit has been kind to us, for we are all well, and we have seen her face. (' *How, how, how!*')

" My friends—We know that the Saganoshes in our country all come from this place; they are our friends there, and we think they will not be our enemies here. (' *How, how, how!*' and immense applause, with ' Hear, hear, hear,' from the audience.)

" My friends—You see I am old, and my words are few; some of my younger men may talk longer than I can. I hope our noise is not too great. (' No, no,' from every part of the room : ' The more noise the better, my good fellows.')

" Brothers—My young men will finish their dances in a little while, when we will be glad to give you our hands." (" *How, how, how !* " great applause, and " Hear, hear.")

The venerable old man then resumed his seat; and at that moment, as the pipe was preparing, Daniel was making his way through the crowd, with one hand raised above the heads of the audience, conveying a large square letter, which he was endeavouring to hand to me. On opening the letter and reading, I found it was from the Honourable Mr. Murray, and, with permission of the audience, I read thus :—

" Dear Sir,—I have great pleasure to inform you that I am instructed by Her Majesty to transmit to you the enclosed 20*l.* note to be given to the Ojibbeway chiefs ; and also to say that Her Majesty has instructed me to order to be made, as soon as possible, an entire piece of plaid, of Her Majesty's colours, which is also to be presented to them in her name, as an evidence of Her Majesty's friendship for them, and solicitude for their welfare. I have transmitted the order for the plaid, and as soon as it can be prepared I shall send it to them.

" I have the honour to be, dear Sir, yours, &c. &c.

" CHAS. AUG. MURRAY,
" *Master of Her Majesty's Household, Buckingham Palace.*
" *To Geo. Catlin, Esq.*"

The reading of this letter called forth a round of applause, which the Indians did not seem to understand until its contents were interpreted to them by Cadotte, when they received the bank-note with a yell or two, and then gathered around it to examine it, and to make out, if they could, how it could be a present of 20*l.*, or (in American currency, which they were a little more familiar with) 100 dollars. That they might better appreciate it, however, I sent Daniel to the door with it, who in a few moments brought back twenty sovereigns, which were placed in the chief's hand, and, being better understood, were soon divided equally, and put into the pouches which were attached to their belts.

The War-chief (who was not much of an orator, and always seemed embarrassed when he spoke) then rose, and advanced to the front of the platform to offer his acknowledgments. He held his long pipe to his lips, and, drawing several deep breaths of smoke to his lungs, and pouring it out through his nostrils, at length began :—

" My friends—I can't speak—I never speak. (Great applause, and he smoked again.)

" My friends—My heart and my tongue were never made to live together. (Roar of applause, and ' *How, how, how!* ') Our chief is old, and his words few : he has told you that the Great Spirit has been kind to us, and that we have seen the face of our Great Mother the Queen. We have all thanked the Great Spirit for this, and we all wish to thank our Great Mother now for the presents she has sent us. She is not here, and we can't thank her ; but we see these presents pass through your hands, and we wish to thank you. (' *How, how, how!* ' and ' Hear.')

" Brothers—I have no more to say, but I shall be glad in a little time to offer you my hand." (" *How, how, how!* " and applause.)

The audience were now prepared, and the Indians also, for the *pipe-dance*, one of the most spirited and picturesque of their dances, and which they gave with great effect. It was then announced that the Indians would seat themselves on the front of the platform, where all the visitors who desired it might have an opportunity to advance and shake hands with them. This afforded the visitors a gratifying opportunity of getting nearer to them, and disposed many to be liberal to them, who gave them money and trinkets to a considerable amount.

Thus passed their first night of exhibition in London. The audience gradually drew off, and the Indians, at length seeing a space through which they could pass, gathered up their weapons, &c., and retired to their private rooms, leaving Daniel to answer to, and explain, all the curious surmises and questions that had been raised in the minds of the audience during the evening, and not explained ; amongst whom (he told me the next day) there were at least a dozen who wished to know "in what way the Indians were *taken*—whether with a lasso or in a sort of pit," as they had heard of their taking wild oxen, &c. Half a dozen inquired what part of the Indies they were from ; twenty or more " whether Cooper's descriptions of the Red Indians were true ;" several " whether they eat the scalps ;" and one desired to be informed " if it was actually necessary to cross the ocean to get to America, or whether it was not attached to the mainland." Several ladies were waiting to inquire " whether the Indians actually had no beards ;" and a great number of women after these, some of whom lingered patiently until all other questions had been answered, begged to know "whether the interpreter and the handsome little fellow *Sah-mah* were married."

Mr. Rankin and myself, as usual, went into the Indians' apartments to smoke a pipe with them after the fatigues of the evening were over, and we found the poor fellows in an unusually pleasant humour, counting over and showing the money and trinkets which they had received from the visitors, and also the money sent by the Queen, which, to be divided more exactly *per capita* (their mode of dividing presents), they had got changed into silver.

Their high excitement and exhilaration convinced us that it was the very sort of life they required to lead to secure their health ; and their remarks upon the incidents that had transpired in the room, as well as things they discovered in the crowd, were exceedingly amusing and caused them a great deal of merriment whilst they were repeating them over. In the midst of all this they often uttered the exciting word *Chickabobboo;* and it occurred to Mr. Rankin and myself as a suitable occasion to explain to them that we had no objection to their having each a glass of ale at their dinner, and also after the exceeding fatigues of their dances at night. We told them " that, in binding them in the promise they had made, and so far kept, it never entered our heads that they were not to be allowed an occasional glass of wine or ale—luxuries of which nearly all the good people of England, ladies as well as gentlemen, and even divines, partook in a moderate way. We believed that they would use as much discretion in taking those things as English fashionable people did, and felt quite sure they would keep their promise with us. I told them that this ale which I had just mentioned was a very fine drink, and we thought that, though it was not quite as good as the Queen's *chickabobboo,* yet they would like it, and that a glass of it at dinner, and also after their night's fatigues, would give them strength and be of service to them. I told them also that we had just sent for a jug of it (at that moment coming in), that they might try it, and see whether they liked it." "*How, how, how!*" resounded through the whole house; and each, as he emptied his glass, shouted " *Chickabobboo! chickabobboo! ne-she-sheen! ne-she-sheen!*" (good, good). So we agreed that, if on the next morning they should pronounce its effects to be pleasing, they should be allowed a similar quantity every day at dinner, and also at night, instead of the strong coffee they were accustomed to drink before going to bed.

We then left them ; and thus finished our first day's labours and excitements at the Egyptian Hall.

CHAPTER XIV.

THE morning after their first interview with the public at the Egyptian Hall having been deemed a proper time for a visit to them, the Rev. Mr. S—— and a friend called on me with a view to a further conversation with them on the subject of religion, which had been postponed at their request until after they had seen the Queen, which honour they had now had. I spoke to the chiefs about it, and they said, " It is very difficult now, for we have not time. Mr. Rankin has gone for the carriage, and we are just going out to ride, but you can bring them in."

The old chief received them very kindly, and gave them seats, when the Rev. Mr. S—— addressed them through the interpreter in the most kind and winning manner. " My friends, I have been delighted to see by the papers that your Great Mother the Queen has graciously received you and made you some valuable presents ; and I hope the time is come now when your minds are at ease, and we can have some conversation on that great and important subject that I proposed the other day."

The old man was at that moment painting his face with vermilion and bear's grease, as he sat on the floor with a small looking-glass between his knees, and the palms of both hands covered with his red paint, which he was plastering over his face, and impressing on his naked arms and shoulders. He was not in a condition or mood to make a speech, or to hold a long talk; but he replied in a few words: "You see, my friends, that it is impossible to talk long now, for my young men, like myself, are all dressing and painting to take our ride, which we take every morning at ten. We are going now to the show of wild beasts, and we can't wait long; if we do, we may not see them." The reverend gentleman very pleasantly and patiently said to him, that he did not wish to take up any of their time when they had amusements or exercise to attend to; but he hoped they would keep the subject in mind, and give them some leisure hour when they could listen to him; and proposed the next day at twelve o'clock. The old man said, "No; at twelve they were to give their exhibition, which was, after that day, to be given in the day and evening also."—"Well, at two?"—"At two we dine."—"Well, what do you do after dinner?"—"Sleep."—"Not all the afternoon?"—"Pretty much."—"Well, in the morning, at eight?"—"*In bed* at eight."—"What time do you breakfast?"—"About nine."—"Well, then, say ten?"—"Well, ten."—"To-morrow?"—"No, next day." The reverend gentleman then said, "Well, my good friends, we will come and see you the day after to-morrow, at ten; and we hope you will think of this important subject in the mean time." The chief said, "He would be glad to see them, as he had promised; but they had so much to see and to think of, that it was not probable they could have much time to think about it; and as the Queen did n't say anything to them about it, they had n't given it any thought since they last met."

The Indians took their customary omnibus drive —

not on this morning, as the old chief anticipated, to the menagerie, but to the Thames Tunnel and London Bridge. To these they were accompanied by Mr. Rankin, and looked upon them both as the wondrous works of white men's hands, which they could not comprehend. When they entered the Tunnel, and were told that they were under the middle of the Thames, and that the great ships were riding over their heads, they stood in utter astonishment, with their hands over their mouths (denoting silence), and said nothing until they came out. They called it the *" Great Medicine Cave,"* and gave the medicine (or *wa-be-no*) dance at the entrance of it. Mr. Rankin made a speech here to the thousands assembled, which I believe was never recorded. They were met with much kindness at that place, where they received some fine presents, and were treated, they said, to some very good *chickabobboo.*

The scene at the Egyptian Hall on this evening was again very exciting, the Hall being as full as it could pack, and the Indians in great glee, which insured much amusement. I accompanied the Indians on to the platform as before, and, as usual, introduced them to the audience, and explained the objects for which they had come to this country, &c. : they then proceeded with their amusements by giving a dance, accompanied by their customary yells and the war-whoop, which was followed by thundering applause. They then seated themselves and smoked their pipes, while I explained the nature and object of the dance they had just given. While I was thus engaged, some decided opposition to the nature of the exhibition manifested itself, which might well exist in the minds of persons unacquainted with the relative position in which these Indians and my- self stood ; and which objections I felt quite willing to meet at that moment.

The first interruption that I met with was from a man who had taken his position in front of me, and whom I had seen several times endeavouring to obtain a hearing. He at length took an opportunity when he could be distinctly heard, and addressed me thus:—" Do you think it right, Sir, to bring those poor ignorant people here to dance for money?" There was a cry of " Put him out! put him out!" but as soon as I could restore silence I said, " No, my friends, don't put him out; I wish to answer such questions." At that moment another rose in an opposite part of the room, and said—

" I think it is degrading to those poor people to be brought here, Sir, to be shown like wild beasts, for the purpose of making money; and I think, more than that,—that it is degrading to *you*, Sir, to bring them here for such a purpose; and the sooner it is stopped the better."

The audience, at my request, had held silence until this speech was finished, when there was a general cry of " Turn him out! turn him out! Shame! shame!" &c.

I waited as patiently as I could until silence was restored, when I was enabled to get every ear in the house to listen to me; and I then said—

" My friends, I beg that there may be no more disposition to turn any one out, for, if I can be heard a few moments, I will save all further trouble, and, I venture to say, make those two gentlemen as good friends to the Indians, and to myself, as any in the room. The questions which they have naturally put are perfectly fair questions, and such as I am anxious everywhere to answer to. The position in which I stand at present is not, I grant, ostensibly, the one in which my former professions would place me. I have been several years known to the British public, from my labours and my professions, as an advocate for the character and the rights of American Indians. This position I have taken, and still claim, from a residence of eight years amongst the various tribes where I have travelled, at great expense, and hazard to my life, acquainting myself with their true native dispositions, whilst I was collecting the memorials of these abused and dying people, which you see at this time hanging around us. In the eight years of my life which I have devoted to this subject, I have preserved more historical evidences of these people, and done more justice to their character, than any man living; and on these grounds I demand at least the presumption that I am acting a friendly part towards them, who have in their own country treated me with genuine hospitality. (Hear, hear! and immense applause.)

" My friends, we come now to the facts, which it is my duty to mention, and which I presume those two gentlemen are not acquainted with. In the first place, I did not bring these people to this country, but have always been opposed to such parties going to a foreign country for such an object.* These Indians are men, with reasoning faculties and shrewdness like to our own, and they have deliberately entered into a written agreement with the person who has the charge of them, and who is now in the room, to come to this couutry, stimulated by the ambition of seeing Her Majesty the Queen, whose lawful subjects they are, and make, if possible, by their humble and honest exertions, a little money to carry home to their children. (Immense applause.)

" These people are the avowed friends of the English in their own country, and several of them are here to show the frightful wounds they received in fighting Her Majesty's battles in the war of 1812 . (Applause, and Hear !)

" When they arrived, their first object was to see my collection, which is known (at least by report) to almost every Indian to the Pacific coast ; and when they were in it, they decided that there was the appropriate place for their dances, &c., and insisted upon my conducting their exhibitions. By this it is seen that I met these persons in this country ; and in the belief that my countenance and aid would render them subjects of greater interest, and therefore promote their views, I have undertaken to stand by them as their friend and advocate—not as wild beasts, but as men (though perhaps ' degraded,' as civilized actors degrade themselves on foreign boards) labouring in an honest vocation, amid a world of strangers, wiser and shrewder

---

* On a subject of so much importance to me, I deem proof admissible and necessary, and therefore offer to the reader the following letter from the former Secretary at War, Mr. Poinsett, to whom I had written on the subject of an expedition, fitting out in the United States, for such a purpose, several years since :—

My dear Sir, Washington City, October 19th, 1839.
    I received your letter of the 11th instant, and am much obliged to you for the information of the contemplated speculations with Indians in foreign countries. I have taken precautions to defeat all such enterprises, and will prosecute the speculators, and saddle them with heavy costs, instead of gains, if I can detect them. I consider such proceedings are calculated to degrade the Red Man, and certainly not to exalt the whites engaged in them.

               With great regard,
                  Yours very truly,
To Geo. Catlin, Esq.   J. R. POINSETT, Sec. at War.

A few days after I received the above letter an order was issued from the department of war to all the surveyors of Atlantic ports, prohibiting Indians from being shipped to England, or other foreign countries, for the purposes of exhibitions, without the consent of the Government of the country.

than themselves, for the means of feeding their wives and little children. (Hear, hear, hear.)

"These people are here at an enormous expense, and the gentleman to whom they have intrusted themselves has a tremendous responsibility on his hands, for he must return them safe home, at his own expense, after sharing the receipts of the expedition with them. They are free men, and not slaves; and in a free country like this, who will have the cruelty to say to them, 'Stop your vocation, and go to the streets, like the poor Lascars, with brooms in your hands;' or the kindness to say, 'Quit your dancing, and we will pay your expenses to the shores of Lake Huron, and give you money to buy blankets and food for your wives and little children'? (Hear, hear! and applause.)

"As for 'degradation,' I only hope, my friends, that I may always live as free from it as I consider myself whilst by my exertions I am promoting the honest views of these simple and unoffending people; and for the name and honour of civilization I only wish that the thousands of the enlightened world who are led into the Indian countries by the passion to make money, would make it in as honest a way, and as free from degradation, as the one in which these poor fellows are labouring here to make a little." (Cheers and immense applause, and cries of "No reply, no reply!")

My two opponents by this time had lowered their heads and were lost sight of amidst the crowd, and no other objections were heard from them; and the poor Indians, who had enjoyed a good pipe in the mean time, without knowing the nature of our debate, were rested and prepared for their next dance. The audience at this time were all standing, and wedged together, as it were, in every part of the room; and amongst such a crowd, so closely packed, there were many occurrences in the course of the evening which afforded much amusement to the Indians, who were overlooking the whole of it from their platform. The screams of one woman, who announced that "she should faint unless she could get out," stopped all proceedings for a few moments. It was decided on all hands to be impossible for her to reach the door; and, being near the platform, she was at length lifted on to it by the joint aid of the Indians and those below, and she then took a conspicuous seat, as she supposed, for the rest of the evening. Another now hallooed for help and fresh air, and, not being so near the platform, was told that it was entirely impossible to get out, unless she was lifted over the heads f the crowd. "Never mind," said she, "I must go!" So she was raised by many hands, amidst a roar of laughter and fun, every one over whose head she was passed, being quite willing and ready to lend a hand, with a "Lay hold here! pass her along," &c. The "jolly fat dame" (as she was afterwards called), who had escaped from the surges and squeezes of the mass below, now comfortably seated on the edge of the platform, and briskly plying her pocket-handkerchief by way of fan, began to imagine her condition in no way improved, inasmuch as her back was towards her friends the Indians, and her jolly red face, of necessity, under the intense glare of the chandelier, and exposed to the gaze of the audience, who she imagined were passing their criticisms on her "good looks." (*Plate* No. 7.) More and more annoyed every moment at the idea that her ruddy face was growing redder and redder as it was just in the focus of all eyes in the room, and at the instant thought also that (considering she was only coming into a crowd) her stays had been left off, and her new poplin dress, with lace frill in front, not prudent to wear, she had silently and unadvisedly resolved upon resuming her old position, and with that view unceremoniously launched herself, feet foremost, amongst the crowd of gentlemen below. Owing to several circumstances— the density of the crowd, her rotund and unwedge like form, &c.,—there was an insurmountable difficulty (which she probably had not anticipated) in bringing down with her feet to the floor, or anywhere in that direction, the voluminous paraphernalia with which she was circumvested. This state of semi-suspension (her toes merely occasionally feeling the floor) became instantly alarming to her, as well as conspicuous and amusing to the Indians and the audience; and whilst she was imploring one party in the name of Heaven to lift, and the other to pull, the strong and muscular arms of the interpreter, Cadotte, gracefully raised her out of the abyss below, and, leading her across to the back

part of the platform, gave her a comfortable seat, squatted behind, and in the shadow of the Indian group, amongst shields and war-clubs, and other implements used by the Indians in their various amusements.

All was mirth and amusement during the remainder of the evening; and the last position of the "jolly fat dame" (who it would seem had strolled in on the occasion alone) proved exceedingly gratifying to her, as it afforded her an opportunity of a few words of conversation now and then with Cadotte, and of bestowing upon him a very splendid bracelet which she took from her own arm, saying, as she gave it, "Look here; you will always know me in a crowd, for on my left arm I have the fellow to it, and I will always wear it for your sake, that you may not lose sight of me." This gush of kindness had suffused the uninvaded soul of this simple and fresh-grown young man, and, when the exhibition had closed, gained her the kindness of his strong grip again in easing her down upon the floor. His backwoods gallantry could not allow her to wander about alone and uninstructed, and he glided down from the platform on his soft mocassined feet, and, with his eagle and ostrich plumes waving six feet and a half from the floor, was strolling around by her side as the audience were withdrawing from the room, and enlightening her by his descriptions of the paintings and Indian curiosities covering the walls of the Hall.

The Indians in the mean time had shaken hands with the audience, and received many fine presents, and having gathered their robes and their weapons, and Mr. Rankin having announced to Cadotte that "the carriage was ready," the poor fellow turned upon his heel and said, "I am obliged to go." "I am so sorry," she exclaimed; " but look ye, can you read?" " Yes, ma'am." " But can you read writing?" " Yes, a little." " Oh, well, never mind, I'm going to be here every night—oh! it is so charming to me! Good night, good night!"

The Indians were now off to their lodgings, and the

greater part of the audience also, leaving poor Daniel, as usual, in the midst of some dozen or two of the most inquisitive and knowledge seeking and devouring, to answer the accustomed routine of inquiries reserved for this (to them) most profitable part of the exhibition.

He was assuring the crowd around him that " these people were *not* taken with a lasso, nor were they taken in a pit (as some had conjectured), but that they had *come in* of their own accord," &c.   He was also showing the *real lasso*, and explaining that it was only a cord with a noose at the end of it, which the Indians throw over the wild horses' necks to catch them, and not " a *net* or a *hammock*," to both of which he pointed, and which it seems many had mistook for lassoes.

He had also commented upon several *real scalps* which he had taken down and was holding in his hand, saying, " Gentlemen, what nonsense to talk about Indians eating the scalps!   You see the scalp is nothing but a small piece of the skin from the top of the head, with the hair on it, and dried as hard as a bit of sole-leather : there couldn't be any pleasure in eating a thing of that sort."

About this time the "jolly fat dame," having edged up in his vicinity, touched Daniel on the shoulder, and at her nod and wink he followed her to the other side of the room, when she said, " Well, you know *me*, don't you, Daniel?"   " Yes, madam, I recollect you very well ; you used to come here, some months ago, very often, to see the collection and the tableaux."   " Well, now," said she, " look here : those shoats there will worry you to death ; I'd let them alone ; they'll go in a minute.   Ah, what a delightful scene this has been to-night!   The *real Indians* after all!   what I never expected to see.   I never was so happy and so much delighted before—oh, dear me! they are *such fine* fellows!   I shall be here every night.   I can't keep away.   How happy they seem!   they are clever —ah, that they are!   I venture to say they are very clever men.   That Interpreter!—what's his name?   for I have forgotten." "His name is Cadotte, madam." "Ah, yes; stop a moment till I write it down, lest I should forget. I don't like to forget things — I can't say that I like to forget. How do you say? Cado—with two t's, or one?" "I believe it is spelt with two t's, madam." "Yes, I dare say—*Cadotte!*—now I have it! Well, it is wonderful! What a fine-looking fellow that Cadotte is — ha! — what a tremendous powerful man! Oh, law me! he made nothing of taking me up there. I suppose you saw him?" "No, madam, I was 'tending door; but I heard of it." "Why, bless me! I was no more than a pocket-handkerchief to him as he lifted me on to the platform; and you see I'm not a thing for the wind to blow away—oh dear!—and what a tremendous hand he has! I never saw the like. When he took hold of my arm it seemed as if he could have crushed it in a moment. I am sure he is six feet and a half high." "No, not quite that, madam, but pretty near it." "Well, really he is a giant, almost; and yet I am sure he is young—not over 20 I am quite sure!" "No, madam, he is but just turned 18 I believe." "Oh, charming! and how wonderful! But you are jesting, Daniel?" "No, madam, I may be mistaken, but I believe I am right." "He can't be married yet?" "Oh, no, you may be sure of that—I don't suppose he ever thought of a woman yet." "Bless me!—ah, well!—did you see the present I made him, Daniel?" "No, madam, I have not." "Look there! I gave him the fellow to that. He'll recollect me, won't he? I took it off, and tried to buckle it on his wrist myself; but, law me, what a tremendous arm he has got! it wouldn't go much more than half way around! I thought *I* had a pretty lusty arm, Daniel?—feel it—clasp it round—take hold higher up—up there—I never wear sleeves!—that's lusty, is'nt it?" "Yes, by jolly!" said Daniel, as he was making a careful estimate of it; "that's a stout arm, madam." "Well, mine is a baby's arm to that ' boy's,' as you call him. Ah, well, Daniel, I am taking up your time, and I must go. I shall be here every night, I assure you ; and you will always let me in early ?   You see I am not half dressed to-night.   I want to get as near that corner of the platform as possible when I come."   "I understand." " Good night !"   " Good night ! madam."

At this moment, or a moment after, Daniel closed the door upon the last remaining visitors, and I stepped out from behind a green curtain at one end of the platform, forming a little retreat into which I was in the habit of withdrawing myself to avoid the crowd at the close of the exhibition.   Owing to this little accident, therefore, the reader is in possession of the above ejaculatory conversation between the "jolly fat lady" and Daniel; for as, in taking him to the "other side of the room," she had most fortunately placed her back within a few inches of the screen that was before me, bringing poor Daniel's eye to mine directly over her shoulder, I was enabled to record, *verbatim et literatim* (which it might have puzzled poor Daniel to have done from recollection, after the excitement of her jolly fat arm), precisely all that was said and done on the occasion, as above related.

" Why," said I, " Daniel, that lady seems to be quite ' taken' with Cadotte."   " Taken ! she's more than that— she's dead *in love* with him.   I'll be shot if ever I saw the like in my life—the woman is perfectly mad after him—and she's the same lady that used to come to the *tableaux* so often when you gave them in the Egyptian Hall, and was repeatedly asking (as you'll recollect I told you) whether you were actually married ; and when I told her you were, she wouldn't believe it.   She's the same identical woman.   I knew her in a moment, for I have talked hours with her in the exhibition rooms; and didn't you hear her call me Daniel when she spoke to me to-night ?   She appears to be quite a lady.   She used to come in quite a respectable carriage ; and I'll venture to say it has been standing at the door all the evening, and I'll be shot but it will be there every night for a fortnight to come."

" Well, it is quite a curious case ; but let us treat her respectfully, and with politeness, on all occasions." " Oh, yes, certainly ; she is very civil and polite, and you may be sure, Mr. Catlin, that she will receive no other treatment from me."

Under an agreement with Mr. Rankin and the Indians to meet them at their lodgings after the exhibition, I repaired to their rooms, and found them just finishing their beefsteaks and their jug of *chickabobboo*. They were all in a merry humour, talking over the curious scenes they had witnessed in the crowd. They said they thought the Englishwomen loved to be squeezed in a crowd, for there were a great many there, and they seemed to be very happy and goodnatured. They were sure that they saw several persons quite drunk in the room, and also believed that many of the ladies there must have been drinking *chickabobboo*. They had several hearty laughs about the poor woman who was passed over the people's heads ; and also about the "jolly fat dame," who was lifted on to the platform by Cadotte ; and they teazed him a long time with their jokes about her, and the beautiful present he had received from her, and which they had seen her a long time trying to fasten on to his arm.

Their jokes, which they were thus innocently enjoying, and their *chickabobbo*, seemed to make them cheerful and happy ; and I returned home, myself pleased, and went to bed.

My desk was now becoming loaded with communications relative to the Ojibbeway Indians, with more inquiries about their domestic habits and warfare than I could possibly find time to answer, and more invitations to dinners and parties than they could attend to ; and on the next day, amongst numerous applications for private interviews, were two notes from reverend gentlemen, wishing opportunities to converse with them. To them I answered that I should feel much satisfaction in affording them every opportunity and every facility in my power, and I recommended that they should come the next day at ten o'clock, when the Indians were, by appointment, to meet several clergymen to converse upon the subject of religion. One of those reverend gentlemen replied to my note, saying, that "he should prefer a different audience from that which I had named, and should feel as if I had acted entirely up to the professions of my first note if I would use my endeavours to obtain it;" to which I answered that "my only reason for recommending that occasion was, that, as they had already had several short interviews with clergymen, and had fixed upon that morning for a final interview, I thought it probable it would be the only opportunity he could have of hearing them state their religious belief." I never received any further communication from this reverend gentleman, nor did he attend the meeting named; and if I gave him any offence, it was done while I was giving him what I thought to be the most friendly advice.

The next night of their exhibition at the Egyptian Hall passed off much like the preceding one; the Hall was crowded, and in the midst of the crowd, at the end of the platform (as she had desired it), appeared the *"jolly fat dame"* in *full* dress, and fully equipped and prepared for any emergency. She was in her *"stays"* and her *poplin* and *lace*, and loaded with trinkets; and although it was now the middle of winter, that she might not suffer quite so much as she had done the night before, she had brought a large fan, which the heat of the room and its excitements made it necessary to keep constantly in motion. Daniel had placed her where she could get some support by leaning on the platform, and once in a while whisper a word to Cadotte, whose beautifully embroidered mocassins were near to her nose when he leant forward to listen to her, with the eagle plumes and ostrich feathers of his cap falling gracefully down over her shoulders. She looked altogether more lovely and "killing" that night than on the first; and, while she kept more cool and considerate, was not lessening the progress which her fascinations were making upon the heart of poor Cadotte, nor curtailing the draughts of admiration which she was taking in at every breath she inhaled, and at every glance that she had of his manly and herculean figure as it moved before her.

What transpired in the bosom and the brain of this fair dame during the evening, none but herself can exactly know; but, from the lustre of her eyes, and the pleasure beaming from every part of her jolly face, it was evident that peace and happiness, for the time, reigned within.

The dances and other amusements of the evening pleased all of the audience well, and the "jolly fat dame" *supremely*. The Indians returned to their apartments, and delighted themselves by counting over their money and trinkets, with which they were well pleased, and drinking their *chickabobboo*.

The next morning at ten o'clock, the hour appointed, the Rev. Mr. S—— and friend called, and were conducted by me to the Indians' apartments. They were met with cordiality by the Indians and by Mr. Rankin; and when the kind and reverend gentleman reminded them of the promise made him for that morning, they all responded "*How, how, how!*"

They then, at the order of the chief, all spread their robes upon the floor, upon which they took their seats, and at once were in *council*.

The reverend gentleman then, in a tone and a manner the most winning, and calculated to impress upon them the sincerity of his views, told them "he was aware that they were religious, that they all worshipped the Great Spirit, but that he did not exactly know in what way; that he did not come here to tell them anything to give them offence, but with the hope of learning something more of their belief and modes of worship, of which he confessed he was ignorant, and also of explaining to them what he and the other divines in the civilized world believed to be the best, if not the only true religion." (Here the old chief lighted his pipe, which he commenced smoking.)

The reverend gentleman then explained, in the briefest manner possible, and in the mode the best calculated for their understanding (and which was literally interpreted

M 2

them), the system of the Christian religion and the mode of redemption.

When the reverend gentleman had finished his remarks, the old chief filled his pipe again, and, sitting with his eyes cast down until he had smoked it partly out, he handed it to the War-chief, and (instead of rising, as an Indian does to speak on any other subject) the old man rested his elbows on his knees and answered as follows :—*

" My friends—We feel thankful for the information and advice which you come to give us, for we know that you are good men and sincere, and that we are like children, and stand in need of advice.

" We have listened to your words, and have no fault to find with them. We have heard the same words in our own country, where there have been many white people to speak them, and our ears have never been shut against them.

" We have tried to understand white man's religion, but we cannot—it is *medicine* to us, and we think we have no need of it. *Our* religion is simple, and the Great Spirit who gave it to us has taught us all how to understand it. We believe that the Great Spirit made our religion for us, and white man's religion for white men. Their sins we believe are much greater than ours, and perhaps the Great Spirit has thought it best therefore to give them a different religion.

" Some white men have come to our country, and told us that if we did not take up white man's religion, and give up our own, we should all be lost. Now we don't believe that ; and we think those are bad or blind men.

" My friends—We know that the Great Spirit made the red men to dwell in the forests, and white men to live in green fields and in fine houses ; and we believe that we shall live separate in the world to come. The best that we expect or want in a future state is a clear sky and beautiful hunting-grounds, where we expect to meet the friends whom we loved ; and we believe that if we speak the truth we shall go there. This we think might not suit white people, and therefore we believe that their religion is best for them.

---

* The numerous conversations held on the subjects of religion and education with the three different parties of Indians, in various parts of England, as well as on the continent, I consider form one of the most interesting features of this work ; and as I have been present at them all, I have taken down all the Indians' remarks on those occasions, and I have inserted them in all cases in this book as I wrote them from their lips, and not in any case from recollection.—AUTHOR.

" If we follow the religion of our fathers we shall meet them again : if we follow a different religion we are not sure of it.

" My friends—We are here but a few, and we are a great way from our homes, and we shall have but little time to waste in talking on this subject. When a few white men come into our country to make money, we don't ask them to take up our religion. We are here away from our wives and children to try to get some money for them, and there are many things we can take home to them of much more use than white man's religion. Give us guns and ammunition, that we can kill food for them, and protect them from our enemies, and keep whisky and rum sellers out of our country.

" My friends—We love you, and give you our hands ; but we wish to follow the religion of our fathers, and would rather not talk any more on the subject." (' *How, how, how !*')

When the old man had thus closed his remarks, *Gish-ee-gosh-ee-gee* took the pipe and puffed away a few minutes as hard as he could, when he spoke as follows :—

" My friends—The words of our chief, which you have just heard, are good—they are the words of nearly all of our nation. Some of the Ojibbeways say that the words of the white people are the best ; but we believe that they have two tongues.

" My friends—A few years ago a *black-coat* came amongst us in the town where I live, and told us the same words as you have spoken this morning. He said that the religion of the white men was the only good religion ; and some began to believe him, and after a while a great many believed him ; and then he wanted us to help build him a house ; and we did so. We lifted very hard at the logs to put up his house, and when it was done many sent their children to him to learn to read, and some girls got so as to read the ' good book,' and their fathers were very proud of it ; and at last one of these girls had a baby, and not long after it another had a baby, and the *black-coat* then ran away, and we have never seen him since. My friends, we don't think this right. I believe there is another *black-coat* now in the same house. Some of the Indians send their boys there to learn to read, but they dare not let their girls go.

" My friends, this is all I have to say." (' *How, how, how !*')

The reverend gentlemen kindly thanked the Indians for their patience, and, telling me that it would be cruel and useless, under their present circumstances, to question them longer, thanked Mr. Rankin and myself for the kind assistance we had rendered them, and retired, leaving with them as a present several very handsome Bibles. As I was leaving the room I heard the old chief complaining that talking made his lips very dry, and Mr. Rankin ordered for them a jug of *chickabobboo.**

---

* The minds of the Indians had been so much engrossed for several days with the subject of religion, that the inventive powers of the little *Sah-mah* (Tobacco) had been at work ; and when I called on them the next morning one of them handed me his ideas, as he had put them on paper with a lead pencil, and I give them to the reader (Plate No. 8) as near as my own hand could copy them from his original sketch now in my port-folio. If the reader can understand the lines, he will learn from it something of the state of the arts in the Indian country, as well as their native propensity to burlesque.

CHAPTER XV.

Exhibition rooms—Great crowd—The " jolly fat dame"—Her interview
with Cadotte—She gives presents to all the Indians—Excitement in the
crowd—Women kissing the Indians—Red paint on their faces and dresses
—Old Chief's dream and feast of thanksgiving—An annual ceremony—
Curious forms observed—Indians invited to the St. George's archery-
ground—They shoot for a gold medal—They dine with the members of
the club—The " jolly fat dame " and Cadotte—She takes him to his
lodgings in her carriage—Cadotte (or the " Strong-wind ") gets sick—
Is in love with another !—Daniel unfolds the secret to her—Her distress
—She goes to the country—The " jolly fat dame" returns—Cadotte's
engagement to marry—Rankin promotes the marriage—The Author dis-
approves of it.

THE reader will easily imagine the position of the Indians
at this time to have been a very pleasant and satisfactory
one to themselves—all in good health; having seen and
pleased the Queen ; having met the public several times in
the great city of London, where their Hall was crowded
every night, and was likely to continue so ; where everybody applauded, and many bestowed on them presents in
trinkets and money ; with plenty of roast beef, and withal
indulged in their *chickabobboo*. The old chief had finished his
talks on religion, and Cadotte was in the delightful state of
incubation under the genial warmth of the wing of the jolly
fat dame.

The Hall on this evening was as overflowing as on the
previous nights. The "jolly fat dame " had been the first
one at the door, and, by the power of her smiles upon
Daniel's gallantry, she had passed in before the hour for ad-
mitting the public. This had most luckily (and *bewitchingly*,
as she did not expect it) allowed her a delightful *tête-à-tête*
of a few minutes with Cadotte, who happened to be saunter-

ing about in the half-lighted hall of the exhibition, while
the Indians were in an ante-chamber, putting on their streaks
of paint, and arranging their locks of hair and ornaments for
the evening. Lucky, lucky hour! What passed there in
these few minutes nobody knows. *One thing*, however, we
may presume, *did pass* in that short time. Upon Daniel's
authority she had a letter in her hand when she entered, and
which was never identified on her person afterwards, though
a similar one poor Cadotte was seen poring over for several
subsequent days, at odd spells, like a child at its task in its
spelling-book. As she was first in, she took her old position,
which had afforded her so much pleasure the evening before. As her heart was more smitten, her hand became more
liberal : she had come this night loaded with presents, and
dealt them out without stint to the whole party. As each
one received his brooch, or his pin, or his guard-chain, he
held it up and gave a yell, which made the good lady's kindnesses subjects of notoriety ; and we believed, and *feared* also,
that her vanity was such, that, to make the most of the
occasion, she drew upon some of the most costly of the ornaments that adorned her own ample person. During the
excitement thus produced by the distribution of her trinkets, some female in the midst of the crowd held up and
displayed a beautiful bracelet "for the first one who should
get to it." Three or four of the young fellows, with their
naked shoulders and arms, leaped with the rapidity almost
of lightning into the screaming mass. The little *Sah-mah*,
who was the *beau-ideal* of Indian beauty among them,
bore off the prize. As there was not the same inducement
for retracing their steps, and they were in the midst of
strong inducements to stay in the crowd, it became exceedingly difficult to get them back, and to resume the amusements of the evening. Many ladies were offering them their
hands and trinkets : some were kissing them, and every kiss
called forth the war-whoop (as they called it, " a *scalp* ").
The women commenced it as *Sah-mah* had dashed into
the crowd ; and as he was wending his way back, finding it

had pleased so well, he took every lady's hand that was laid upon his naked arm or his shoulder as a challenge, and he said that he kissed every woman that he passed. This may or may not be true; but one thing is certain, that many there were in the room that evening who went home to their husbands and mothers with streaks of red and black paint upon their cheeks, which nothing short of soap and water could remove. And, curious to relate, when the amusements were finished, and the audience nearly withdrawn, and the "jolly fat dame" was strolling about the room, she met her two maids, to whom she had given their shillings, and told them to "go and see the Indians." These two buxom young girls had been in the midst of the crowd, and, both of them having met with the accident I have mentioned above, the good-natured fat lady glowed into a roar of laughter as she vociferated, "Why, girls, you husseys, you have been kissing those Indians! Bless me, what a pretty figure you cut! why, your faces are all covered with red paint!" "And *your* face, mistress! Look here! all one side of your face, and on your neck! Oh, look at your beautiful new lace!" And *it was even so;* but *how* it happened, or where, or in what part of the excitement, or by whom, is yet to be learned.

Leaving these excitements for a while, which were now become of nightly occurrence, we come to one of a different character and of curious interest. It is impossible for me to recollect the day, but it was about this time, the old chief related to Mr. Rankin a dream which he had had the night before, which made it incumbent upon them to make a feast, and of course necessary for Mr. Rankin and myself to furnish all the requisite materials for it.

In his dream (or "vision," as he seemed disposed to call it) he said the Great Spirit appeared to him, and told him that he had kept his eye upon them, and guarded and protected them across the great ocean, according to their prayers, which he had heard; that he had watched them so far in this country; that they had been successful in seeing their Great Mother the Queen, and that they were now all happy and doing well. But in order to insure a continuance of these blessings, and to make their voyage back across the ocean pleasant and safe, it now became necessary that they should show their thankfulness to the Great Spirit in giving their great annual Feast of Thanksgiving, which is customary in their country at the season when their maize is gathered and their dried meat is laid in and secured for their winter's food.

This injunction, he said, was laid upon him thus, and he could not from any cause whatever neglect to attend to it; if he did, he should feel assured of meeting the displeasure of the Great Spirit, and they should all feel at once distressed about the uncertainty of their lives on their way back. This Feast of Thanksgiving must be given the next day, and they should wish us to procure for them a whole goat, or a sheep, and said that it must be a *male,* and that they would require a place large enough to cook it without breaking a bone in its body, according to the custom of their country.

The request of this good old man was of course granted with great pleasure; and Mr. Rankin, in a short time, returned from the market with the sheep, which, on close inspection, seemed to please them; and a large chamber in the Egyptian Hall, which Mr. Clark, the curator of the building, had placed at their service, was decided on as the place where the feast should be prepared and partaken of. Mr. Clark and his wife, who are kind and Christian people, afforded them all the facilities for cooking, and rendered them every aid they could in preparing their feast; and the next day, at the hour appointed, it was announced to Mr. Rankin and myself that the " feast was ready, and that we were expected to partake of it with them."

When we entered the room we found the feast arranged on the floor, in the centre of the large hall, and smoking, and the men all seated around it on buffalo robes; and the only two guests besides ourselves, my man Daniel and Mr.

Clark, who were also seated. Two robes were placed for Mr. Rankin and myself, and we took our seats upon them. The three women of the party came in after we were all arranged, and, spreading their robes, seated themselves in another group at a little distance from us. A short time before the feast was ready, they sent Cadotte to me to request that I would buy for them a small cup of whisky, which was to be partaken of, "not as *drink* for the *belly*, but as drink for the *spirit*," which by the custom of their country was absolutely necessary to the holding of their Feast of Thanksgiving. In this they were also, of course, indulged; and when we were seated, we found the whisky standing in front of the medicine-man in a small pewter mug.

Everything now being in readiness, the pipe was lit by the war-chief, who rose up with it, and, presenting its stem towards the *north* and the *south*, the *east* and the *west*, and then upwards to the Great Spirit, and then to the earth, smoked through it himself a few breaths, and then, walking around, held it to the lips of each one of the party (the women excepted), who smoked a whiff or two through it; after which he made a short and apparently vehement appeal to the Great Spirit to *bless* the food we were then to partake of. When he had taken his seat, the medicine-man took his *wa-be-no* (*medicine-drum*) and commenced beating on it as he accompanied its taps with a *medicine* song to the Great Spirit. When the song was finished he arose, and, shaking a rattle (*she-shee-quoin*) in his left hand, and singing at the same time, he handed the cup of whisky around to the lips of each guest, all of whom tasted of it; it was then passed to the women, who also tasted it, and returned it to its former position but partially emptied.

The War-chief then rose upon his feet, and, drawing his large knife from his belt, plunged the thumb and fore finger of his left hand into the sockets of the sheep's eyes, by which he raised the head as he severed it from the body with his knife, and held it as high as he could reach. At this moment he returned his knife to its scabbard, and, seizing the *she-shee-quoin* (or rattle) in his right hand, he commenced to sing a most eccentric song as he shook his rattle in one hand and brandished the sheep's head in the other, and danced quite round the circle between the feast and the guests, going so slow as to require some eight or ten minutes to get round. Having got round to his seat, he gave a frightful yell, and, raising the sheep's head to his mouth, bit off a piece of it, and again danced until he had swallowed it. He then laid the head and the rattle at the feet of another, who sprang upon his feet, and, taking the sheep's head and the rattle, performed the same manœuvre, and so did a second and a third, and so on until each male of the party had performed his part. After this, the flesh was carved from the bones by the War-chief, and placed before us, of which we all partook. Parts of it were also carried to the women, and after a little time the greater part of the flesh of the carcase had disappeared.

It is worthy of remark, also, that at this strange feast there was nothing offered but the flesh of the sheep; but which was cooked in a manner that would have pleased the taste of an epicure.

When the eating was done, the war-chief took the rattle in his hand, and, lightly shaking it as a sort of accompaniment, took at least a quarter of an hour to repeat a long prayer, or return of thanks, to the Great Spirit, which was spoken (or rather *sung* than *spoken*) in a very remarkable and rapid manner. After this the pipe was lit, and, having been some three or four times passed around, the feast was finished, and we took leave.

I leave this strange affair (having described it as nearly as I possibly could) for the comments of the curious, who may have more time than I can justly devote to it at this moment, barely observing that the old chief, after this, seemed quite contented and happy that he had acted in conformity to the sacred injunction of the Great Spirit, and strictly adhered, though in a foreign country, to one of the established and indispensable customs of his race; for which, and for another cogent reason (that "his lips were getting very dry after eating so much"), he thought we would be willing (as of course we were) to let Daniel go for a jug of *chickabobboo.*

The whole party now seemed to be completely happy, and in the midst of enjoyment. They were excited and amused every night in their exhibitions, which afforded them wholesome exercise; and during the days they took their drives through the city and into the country, and beheld the sights of the great metropolis, or reclined around their rooms on their buffalo robes, enjoying their pipes and counting their money, of which they had received some thirty or forty pounds, presented to them in the room at various times, independent of that received from her Majesty, and their wages, and trinkets, and other presents.

Of their drives, one of the most exciting and interesting that they had or could have in London was about this time, when her Majesty rode in state to the opening of Parliament. They were driven through the immense concourse of people assembled on the line and along Parliament-street, and conducted to a position reserved for them on the roof of St. Mary's chapel, near Westminster Abbey. From this elevated position they had a splendid bird's-eye view of the crowd below, and the progress of the Queen's state carriage, as it rolled along on its massive wheels of gold, and drawn by eight cream-coloured horses. So grand a pageant filled their rude, uncultivated minds with the strangest conjectures, which were subjects for several evenings' curious gossip. And what seemed to please them most of all the incidents of the day was, as they said, "that her Majesty and the Prince both most certainly looked up from their golden carriage to see them on the top of the church."

They were also most kindly invited by the members of the St. George's Archery Club to witness their bow-and-arrow shooting on one of their prize-days. This was calculated to engage their closest attention; and at night they returned home in great glee. They had been treated with the greatest kindness by the gentlemen of that club. They had put up a gold medal for the Indians to shoot for, which was won by *Sah-mah* (Tobacco), and other prizes were taken by others of the party.* The first shot made by the young man who bore off the golden prize was said to have been one of the most extraordinary ever made on their grounds; but in their subsequent shooting they fell a great way short of it, and also of that of the young gentlemen belonging to the club. After the shooting of the Indians, and also of the members of the club, contending for their valuable prizes, the Indians were invited to their table, where a sumptuous dinner was partaken of. Many toasts were drunk, and many speeches made; and, to their agreeable surprise, as they said, they had plenty of the *Queen's chickabobboo!*

They continued their amusements nightly, much in the same way as I have above described, with full houses and similar excitements, all of which and their effects we will imagine, as I pass over a week or two of them without other notice than merely to say that the "jolly fat dame" still continued to visit them, as she had promised, and nightly to strengthen the spell she seemed

---

* It was stated in some of the papers of the day that the Indian won the golden prize from the members of the club, which was not the case. It was put up, most liberally, by the young men of the society for the Indians to shoot for among themselves, and won in this way, not from the members of the club.

There are no Indians in North America who can equal the shooting of these young gentlemen, who practise much this beautiful and manly exercise. I have often, at their kind invitations, visited their grounds, and I have had the opportunity of seeing the shooting amongst most of the American tribes. The Indian tribes who use the bow and arrow at the present time are mostly the Prairie tribes, who are mounted, and, from their horses' backs, at full speed, throw their arrows but a very few paces, and use a short bow of two feet or two feet and a half in length, and therefore never practise at the target at the distance of one or two hundred yards. Their skill and power, however, in that mode of using the bow is almost inconceivable, and might puzzle the best archers in England or in the world to equal.

to be working upon the heart of poor Cadotte. She was elegant, but rather fat. She rode in a good carriage. She bestowed her presents liberally, and on all; and insisted the whole time that " it was the most interesting exhibition she ever saw," and that "Cadotte was almost a giant ! " " She could not keep away, nor could she keep the Indians out of her mind." All were inquiring who she could be, and nobody could tell. She had delivered three or four letters into Cadotte's hand in the time ; and, though " her carriage could put him down at his door quite easy," she had driven him home but one night, and then he was landed quite quick and quite safe. The Indians talked and joked much about her, but Cadotte said little. He was young, and his youth had had a giant growth in the timid shade of the woods. He was strong; but he knew not the strength that was in him, for he had not tried it. He was like a mountain torrent—dammed up but to burst its barriers and overflow. The glow of this fair dame upon him was a sunshine that he had never felt, and, like the snow under a summer's sun, he was about to have melted away. In the simplicity of his native ambition, he had never aspired to anything brighter than his own colour ; and few were dreaming till just now that the warrior Cupid was throwing his fatal arrows across the line. Nor did those who suspected them (or even *saw* them), from the source that has been named, know more than half of the shafts that were launched at the " *Strong-wind* " at this time, nor appreciate more than half the perplexities that were wearing away his body and his mind. *He* knew them, poor fellow, and had *felt* them for some time ; but the world saw no symptom of them until his treatment of this fair dame on one night set them inquiring, when they found that she, with her little *archer*, was not alone in the field.

Reader, we are now entering upon a drama that requires an abler pen than mine, which has been used only to record the dry realities of Indian life, stripped of the delicious admixture which is sometimes presented when Cupid and civilization open their way into it.

I regret exceedingly that I cannot do justice to the subject that is now before us ; but, knowing the facts, I will simply give them, and not aspire to the *picture*, which the reader's imagination will better paint than my black lead can possibly draw.

On the unlucky evening above alluded to the "jolly fat dame" had made her appearance at the rooms half an hour before the doors were to open ; and, with Daniel's usual indulgence, she passed into the room, in the hope, as she said, to have a few words with the Indians, and shake hands with them all, and bid the good fellows good by, as she was going into the country for a few days. She loitered around the room until it began to fill with its visitors for the evening, without the good luck to meet the "*Strong-wind,*" as she had been in the habit of doing, before the chandelier was in full blaze, and while the Indians were in their adjoining room, putting on their paint and ornaments. This disappointment, for reasons that she probably understood better than we can, seemed to embarrass her very much, and most likely, even at that early stage, carried forebodings of troubles that were "brewing." In the embarrassment of these painful moments, not being able to spend the evening in the exhibition, as usual, but under the necessity of returning to pack her things and complete her preparations for her journey, she was retreating towards the door as fast as the audience filled in in front, determined to hold a position in the passage where she could shake hands with the Indians as they passed in, and drop a little billet into the hands of the "*Strong-wind,*" which, if received, was intended only to stop a sort of palpitation there would be in the side of her breast, in case she should have gone off to the country without informing the "*Strong-wind*" of it, and that she was to return again in a very few days.

Unlucky device ! The Indians all passed by, excepting

the "*Strong Wind,*" and, as each one shook her hand, he saluted her with a yelp and a smile. All this was gratifying to her, but added to the evident fever that was now coming on her. She paced the hall forward and back for some time, living yet (and thriving) upon the hope at that moment raised in her mind, that he ("noble fellow!") was hanging back in order to have a moment of bliss alone with her in the hall, after the gazing visitors had all passed by. This hope sustained her a while, and she many times more walked the length of the passage, but in vain. At this moment the sound of the drum and the echoing of the war-whoop through the hall announced their exhibition as commenced; and the liberal dame, advancing to the door, and standing on tiptoe, that she might take a peep once more at the good fellows over the heads of the audience, beheld, to her great astonishment, the noble figure of the "*Strong-wind,*" swinging his tomahawk, as he was leading the dance! Unhappy dame! the room was closely stowed, and not the possibility left of her getting half way to her old stand by the end of the platform, if she tried.

This dilemma was most awful. The thought of actually "going off to the country, as she had promised, for several days, without the chance to say even good bye, or to shake hands, was too bad,—it was cruel!" She went to the door to see Daniel, and said, "Well, this is very curious; I wanted to have seen Cadotte for a moment before I went away, and I can't stay to-night. I shook hands with all the rest as they went in, but I did not see Cadotte. I don't understand it." "Why," said Daniel, "the poor fellow is not here to-night; he's getting sick: he was here when you first came in, but he *shot out* a few moments afterwards, and told me to tell you, if you came, that he was too unwell to be here to-night. He is looking very pale and losing flesh very fast, and his appetite is going. He has only danced once or twice in the last week." "Poor fellow! I am sorry. What a pity if he should get sick! I don't see what they would do without him; he is worth more than the whole party besides. He's a fine young man. What an immense fellow he is! Did you examine his hand? What a grip he has got—ha! I *may* not go to-morrow, but if I *do*, it will only be for a few days. I have *promised* to go, and you know it is wrong to break promises, Daniel. If anything should prevent me from going to-morrow I shall certainly be here again to-morrow night. Poor fellow! I *hope* he won't get sick: I think a little ride in the country would do him good. Mr. Catlin ought to send him into the country for a while. That's what he should do, shouldn't he? I won't stand here too long, Daniel; it's rather a cold place: so good night."

It *was* a *fact* that the "*Strong Wind*" was getting sick; and a fact also that Daniel thought he had gone home, as he told the good lady; and two other facts followed the next day—the one was, that the journey to the country was not made that morning; and the other, that the "jolly fat dame" was at the Hall at an early hour of the evening as usual. Her visit was carefully timed, so as to allow her a little time for gossip with Daniel at the door, and to subject her to the delightful possibility of accidentally meeting the "*Strong Wind*," as she had sometimes done, in the half-lighted hall.

"You see, Daniel, that I didn't get off this morning; and when I am in London I cannot keep away from those curious fellows, the Indians. They are here, I suppose, before this?" "Yes, madam, they have just come in in their bus." "Well, how is Cadotte? he is *my* favourite, you know." "Well," said Daniel, "I don't think he's any better: I believe there is but one thing that will cure him." "Bless me, you don't say so! What do you think is the matter with him?" "Why, I think he is in love, madam; and I don't believe there is anything under heaven else that ails him." "Oh! now, but you *don't think* so, do you, really?" "I do, indeed, madam; and I don't wonder at it, for there are charms that are lavished upon him that are enough to——" "Oh! come, come, now, Daniel, don't give us any of your dry compliments. He's a fine man, certainly—that

I *know*, and I should be sorry if he should get sick. He will be in the exhibition, I suppose, to-night?" " No, madam, I saw him a few minutes since, and he had lain down on his buffalo robe on the floor, and I heard him tell Mr. Rankin that he should not go into the room to-night; that he did not feel well enough." " So, you cruel man, you think the poor fellow is in love, do you?" " I am *sure* of it, madam : in the next house to where the Indians lodge there is one of the most beautiful black-eyed little girls that I have seen since I have been in London, and, by putting her head out of the back window to look at the Indians, and by playing in the back yard, she long since showed to everybody who saw her that she was fascinated with Cadotte. She used to kiss her hand to him, and throw him bouquets of flowers, and, at last, letters." " Pshaw!" " It's true! And, finally, she and her sisters got in the habit of coming in to see the Indians, and, at last, the father, and mother, and brother; and they all became attached to Cadotte, and invited him to their house to take tea with them and spend the evenings; and he has at last become so perfectly smitten with the girl that he is getting sick: that is the reason why he is not at the Hall more than three evenings in the week; he spends his evenings with her, and often don't get home before twelve and one o'clock." " Oh, but you shock me, you *shock* me, Daniel—but I don't *believe* it—I *can't believe* it—he *couldn't* be *led away* in that silly manner—*I don't believe a word of it*. You say he is in the dressing-room?" " Yes, madam, I know he is there." " You don't think he'll come into the exhibition-room to-night?" " No, I know he will not." " You don't think he would come out a minute? I can't stay to-night, and I shall certainly go in the morning. I *must* go—you *don't think* he would come out?" " I don't know, madam; I will ask him if you wish." " Well, *do*, Daniel; come, that's a good fellow—or, stop!—look here—just hand him this note; it is merely to say good bye : give it to him, and only tell him I am here, will you, and going out of town to-morrow morning?"

Daniel took in the note to the "*Strong Wind*," who was lying on his robe, and in a minute returned with the note and this awful message:—"Tell her she *may* go out of town—I don't wish to see her." This was as much of his ungallant message as Daniel could venture to bear to the good lady, though the "*Strong Wind*" continued to say, "Take the note back to her: she is making too free with me, and all the people see it. She wants a husband too bad, and I hope she will soon get one." Daniel returned the note, and apologized for being the bearer of such a message to her; but he said, as he had carried her message to Cadotte, he felt bound to bring his message back. "Certainly, certainly," said she; "I can't blame you, Daniel; but this is strange—all this is strange to me; it's quite incomprehensible, I assure you. The crowd is coming in, I see, Daniel; and I can't possibly be here through the evening. I'll be here as soon as I come back. Good night."

One can easily imagine how the peace of the bosom of this good-natured unoffending lady was broken up by the abrupt way of the "*Strong Wind*," and how unhappy might have been the few days she was to spend in the country, and which she could not then fail to do, as she had made a promise to friends, that she could not break. By her absence from the exhibition-room for a week or more, it was evident that she was accomplishing her visit to the country; and, though her little *archer* was unemployed in her absence, it would seem as if the very show of so many bows and arrows in the great city of London had suddenly called into existence, or into service, a reinforcement of those little marksmen, who were concentrating their forces about this time, and seemed to be all aiming their shafts at the breast of the "*Strong Wind*." There were several fair damsels who nightly paid their shillings, and took their positions near the platform, in a less conspicuous way, though not less known to the "*Strong Wind*," than our friend who had "gone for a while to the country." From the fair hands of these he had received, unobserved, many precious and sly gifts, and amongst them several little billets of the most sentimental nature, containing enclosures of beautiful little stanzas, and cards of address, &c.

Among this jealous group of inveterate gazers and admirers was always, though most coy and least noticed, the sweet little "black-eyed maiden" of whom I have said Daniel gave some account to the good lady who has gone to the country, as having "kissed her hand and thrown bouquets of flowers" to the "*Strong Wind*" from the back windows of her father's house in George-street. The whole soul of the "*Strong Wind*," which, until now, had been unchained and as free as the mountain breeze, was completely enveloped in the soft and silken web which the languishing black eyes, the cherry and pulpy lips, and rosy cheeks of this devouring little maid had spun and entwined about it. He trembled when he straightened his tall and elegant figure above the platform, not that he was before the gazing world, but because *her* soft black eyes were upon him. His voice faltered and his throat was not clear when he brandished his glistening tomahawk and sounded the shrill war-whoop. This was not that the ears of hundreds, but that the ears of ONE, were open to catch the sound.

His heart was now free, for a few days at least, from the dangers of the first siege, the guns of which for the time were all silent. The glances of his eyes and his occasional smiles were less scrupulously watched ; and now and then they could be welcomed by sweet returns. He had now but one *real* enemy in the field, and *his* shafts, though they went to his inmost soul, were every one of them welcome messengers of peace and love.

Thus besieged, thus pierced and transfixed, the "*Strong Wind*" did as much as he could to continue his natural existence, to eat his accustomed meals, and to act his customary parts in the dance ; but efforts all seemed in vain.

The sweet and balmy sleep that had been the pleasure of his untaught youth had fled ; roast beef and plum-puddings, his favourite bits, had ceased to please him ; sighs and long breaths had taken all the place of peaceful and equal respiration ; the paleness of his face showed there was trouble within ; his noble frame and giant strength were giving way ; and, save the devouring pleasure that was consuming him, nothing was acceptable to him but seclusion and his occasional mugs of *chickabobboo*.

All things at the Egyptian Hall went on as usual for several days, the Indians giving their nightly entertainments, but without the aid of the " *Strong Wind*," and consequently without the presence of the "languishing little black eyes" that used to be seen peeping over the corner of the platform. The reader (who has heard already that the " *Strong Wind*" loved to ride home with this sweet little creature—that he took his dishes of tea in her father's house, which was next door—and that he often stayed there until twelve and one o'clock at night) can easily understand how the time now passed with the " *Strong Wind*," and how hopeless were to be the chances of the good dame who had " gone to the country but for a few days, where she had promised to go, but from which she was soon to return." The reader who is old enough will easily understand also why the " *Strong Wind*" grew pale ; how it was that everything ceased to taste good— beautiful things to look pretty ; and why I had to translate, as well as I could, the speeches of the Indians, who now had no better interpreter.

The exhibition-room continued to be filled night after night without the presence of the " *Strong Wind;*" and at length, on one of these occasions, the "jolly fat dame," who had gone to the country for a few days, presented herself at the door as usual before the audience had assembled. She was admitted by Daniel's kindness ; and as she got into the passage, the party of Indians came in from their omnibus, and, passing her, gave her their hands, and as they passed on each one gave a hideous yell. She seemed delighted at this, and, turning to Daniel, said, "Oh, did you hear the poor fellows rejoicing? they are delighted to see me back again." "Why, madam," said Daniel, "that was the *war-whoop;* and when that is given, the tomahawk always follows." She seemed a little startled at this; "But," said she, "the good fellows, I have lots of fine presents here for them to-night; I can make it all right with them I think. But I don't see Cadotte—I hope he's not sick—he's a splendid fellow—I have not seen a man like him in all my travels in the country, and I have been a great way. I have a nice present for him, d'ye see?—is'nt that a fine brooch? I know he'll like it." "But I fear you are too late, madam—I believe it is all over with him." "What! you don't mean to say that he is dead?" "No, he's not dead, but he's nearly as bad—he don't come here at all—he don't eat or drink—he's pining away for that pretty little girl I told you of. It's been all her doing : the foolish girl fell in love with him, and is determined to have him, and I believe he will marry her." "Oh, pshaw! fie on it! I don't believe a word of it;—they will get over it all in a day or two." The kind lady after this took her position in the Hall as usual, and during the exhibition smiled on all the group, and dealt out her presents to them, and went home as usual well pleased.

Most curiously, all this affair of Cadotte's and the sweet-mouthed, black-eyed little girl, had passed unnoticed by me, and I had of course entirely mistaken his malady, having sent my physician to attend him. His symptoms and the nature of his disease were consequently fully understood by examinations of the patient and others who had watched closely all the appearances from the commencement of his attack. Getting thus a full report of the case, I held a conversation with Mr. Rankin, who at once told me that it had been well understood by him for some time, and that Cadotte had asked for his consent to marry the young lady, and that he had frankly given it to him. I told him I thought such a step should be taken with great caution, for the young lady was an exceedingly pretty and interesting girl, and, I had learned, of a respectable family, and certainly no step whatever should be taken in the affair by him or me without the strictest respect to their feelings and wishes. He replied that the mother and sisters were in favour of the marriage, and had been the promoters of it from the beginning ; that the father was opposed to it, but he thought that all together would bring him over. I told him that I did not know either the father or the mother, but that, as long as there was an objection to it on the part of the father, I thought it would be cruel to do anything to promote it ; and that, much as I thought of Cadotte, I did not feel authorized to countenance an union of that kind, which would result in his spending his life in London, where his caste and colour would always be against him, and defeat the happiness of his life; or she must follow him to the wilderness of America, to be totally lost to the society of her family, and to lead a life of semi-barbarism, which would in all probability be filled with excitements enough for a while, but must result in her distress and misery at last. To these remarks his replies were very short, evidently having made up his mind to let them raise an excitement in London if they wished, and (as I afterwards learned) if he could possibly bring it about.

CHAPTER XVI.

At the commencement of this chapter we find the Indians still proceeding with their amusements at the Egyptian Hall, riding out during the day for fresh air and to see the city, and enjoying their roast beef and *chickabobboo ;* the interpreter laid up, as described, and Mr. Rankin labouring to promote, and preparing for, an event that was to give greater notoriety to himself and his party, and ensure more splendid success through the kingdom, as the sequel will show.

My opposition to his views in promoting the marriage of this love-sick pair afforded him the suitable occasion of calling on me one morning and advising me of a course which "he had been, he said, recommended by many of his friends to pursue, which was, that (as he had now heard me lecture on the modes of the Indians until the subject had become sufficiently familiar to him to enable him to give the lectures well enough himself) he could promote his

own interest much better by taking the Indians to the
provincial towns, meeting all the expenses, and taking all
the receipts, instead of sharing with a second person, which
his friends thought was a great pity he should any longer
do." He represented that by such a course he could
afford to do better by the Indians, and he thought it would
be decidedly for the interest of both, and he had resolved
to do it. I said to him that it was, to be sure, a resolve
which he could easily make, as we were under no other than
a verbal agreement, and entirely confidential, so that, if his
interest urged it sufficiently strong, there was no doubt
that he could do as he pleased, and that, under any circumstances, I should have but one anxiety, and that would be
for the welfare of the Indians under his charge. I had so
far done all I could to introduce them and him properly. I
had added my collection to their exhibition, to give it additional interest. I had devoted my best efforts in lecturing
on them and their customs, and had succeeded (after lying
still with them for a month in London) in getting for
them an audience of the Queen. By these means I had
rendered him and them a service, for which I wanted no
other return than the assurance that, wherever he went with
them, he should take good care of and protect them.

He said he had made up his mind to take them on his
own hands in that manner after an exhibition for ten days
longer in the Egyptian Hall, when he was to leave London
on a tour to the provincial towns ; and he wished me to
advertise these exhibitions positively to close on a certain day.
I then informed him that I should do so, and should freely
yield to his proposition to sever in the manner he had proposed, on account of the accomplishment of the marriage,
which he had assured me was just at hand, and in the responsibility of which I was determined to take no part. This I
told him was an argument sufficiently strong, without further
comment, to incline me to meet his proposition without the
slightest objection.

I therefore advertised, as he had suggested, that the

Indians could only be seen in London that number of days ; and from night to night announced the same thing from the platform when giving my lecture ; and to the last day, at his request, stated that the Indians were positively to leave London at that time. The next morning after we had made this final close, and I had announced it as such to the audience, advertisements appeared in the papers that "he had rented the adjoining room to Mr. Catlin's, and on the same floor, for two months—a much finer room, where ladies and others would be much better accommodated; where the lectures in future would be given by Mr. Rankin, *himself,* who had *lived all his life among the Indians.*" And in his advertisements, a few days after, he had the imprudence to state that "*hereafter the beautiful and interesting bride of the 'Strong Wind,' the interpreter, will make her appearance on the platform with the Indians, and preside at the piano.*"

This extraordinary advertisement, which of course was after the consummation of the marriage, was inserted in all the London daily journals, and was at once a key to all the absurd and disgusting efforts that had been used to create an excitement on the occasion of the wedding. It had been carefully announced that the wedding was to take place at a certain hour in the day in St. Martin's church, that ten thousand people might be waiting there for a chance to see the novel spectacle of a beautiful London girl married to an Indian from the wilds of America, and then to trumpet it through the city and through the land where they were going, that the shillings might the more abundantly pour in for a sight of the extraordinary pair that were united in St. Martin's church in London, and the "beautiful and interesting bride who was to preside at the piano" while the Indians danced.

To make this affair more exciting, and its disgusting humbug more complete, several omnibuses and coaches, drawn by four-in-hand, were employed to convey the "beautiful and interesting bride" and bridegroom, and Mr. Rankin and his attendants, through the streets to and from the church where the ceremony took place. Each of these splendid affairs was decorated with evergreens, ribands, &c.; and on their tops, bands of music playing through the streets, and other attendants, covered with belts and ribands, waving flags of various and brilliant colours. These carriages were directed to be driven through the principal thoroughfares of London, that the excitement and hubbub might be the more complete, and that the greater number of shillings might be turned into the exhibition-room.

The scheme, as a business one, was not without some ingenuity, but, most unluckily for its projector, it did not exactly succeed. There was too much sagacity in the London people and the London press not to detect the object of the scheme, and too much good taste to countenance and patronise it. The result was, and deservedly so, that it was condemned by the press, and the project and its projectors held up to public view in the light that they deserved.

The next day after his advertisement that "the beautiful and interesting bride was to appear and preside at the piano," he put forth another advertisement, stating that the bride *would not* appear, as announced the day before, owing to objections raised by some of her friends, &c. These friends were nearly all the press in London, as well as her father and her husband, who had never been consulted on the subject, who were indignant at the step he had taken, and ordered him to countermand his advertisement.

He then commenced his exhibition of the Indians in his new quarters, and under the new auspices, necessarily without the additional attraction of the new and beautiful bride, and also without the aid of his interpreter Cadotte, whom he had turned out of his employment, and to whom he had refused admission to the house to see his fellow Indians or to hold any communication with them. Cadotte was thus driven to his father-in-law's house, where he took up his residence, and Mr. Rankin proceeded with his exhibitions, himself lecturing on their customs and *interpreting* their speeches to the audience, and all the various communications of the audiences and the public to them, wherever they went, without knowing five words of their language.

The extraordinary announcement which he had put in the papers of the appearance of the " beautiful and interesting bride upon the platform" had drawn a great crowd together at his first exhibition under the new arrangement, and, from the odd mixture of people it had brought together, begat some very amusing incidents worth recording. On ascending the platform for his first lecture, amidst a room densely packed, chiefly with working men and working women, whose application to their tasks during the day had prevented them from getting a glimpse of the beautiful bride of the " *Strong Wind*," and had now handed in their hard-earned shillings, he soon found himself in the midst of difficulties which it would seem that he had not anticipated.

In such a city as London there are always enough who do not read the *contradictions* of announcements (with those who won't believe them if they do read them) to fill a room; and of such was his room chiefly filled on this occasion—all impatient to see the beautiful bride of the Indian, and full of expectation, though his second advertisement had announced that " she would not appear." One can easily imagine the difficulties with which he was surrounded, and the perplexing materials with which he was about to contend in presenting himself as the expounder of Indian modes, and that in the absence of the " beautiful bride."

Curiosity to hear him give his first lecture on the customs of the Indians, " who had spent all his life amongst them," led me into the crowd, where I caught the following amusing incidents, which are given as nearly as I could hear them amidst the confusion that soon took place. Mr. Rankin had proceeded but a few sentences in his elucidations when a voice from a distant part of the room called out, " Rankin! Mr. Rankin!" " Well," inquired the lecturer, " what's wanted of Mr. Rankin?" " Why, Sir, Mr. Rankin is advertised to lecture, and we expect to hear him." " My name is

Rankin—I am Mr. Rankin. Sir." "No, you are not Mr.
Rankin neither: why do you tell us that nonsense? Come
now, *Arthur;* you know me, old fellow : don't set yourself up
for Mr. Rankin here ; you'll get yourself into trouble if you
do." (Uproar, and cries of " Turn him out, turn him out.")
The voice continues, " Mr. Rankin ! Mr. Rankin ! what has
lived all his life with the Indians !" (Uproar.) " I am Mr.
Rankin, Sir : what do you want?" " You are *not* Mr. Rankin;
are Mr. Arthur Jones, or was so when I knew you in New
York." (Cries of " Turn him out—shame, shame ! the bride,
the bride !" and hisses.) The lecturer here advanced to the
front of the platform and endeavoured to frown the crowd
into silence, but got nothing in return but " The bride, the
bride !" and hisses from various quarters. One of the men
in his employment unluckily at that moment seized hold
of a little square-shouldered working-man, standing just
before me, who was hissing, and was hauling him towards
the door. The little man gathered himself up, and brought
his antagonist to a halt before he was half way to the door.
While grasping each other by the collar, the little man, who
was nearly lost sight of in the crowd, demanded the cause of
this violence on his person. " Why, Sir, you was hissing
the lecturer, and I was ordered to put you out of the room
—that was all."

" So I did iss im, Sir, hand I'll iss again, hif I choose——
ands hoff ! hif you please!" " You must go out, Sir." " Hout,
Sir ! [in a tremendous voice.] I'll hax this haudience hif I
am to go hout, or whether they would prefer to ear the hob-
servations I hintend to make." There was a general uproar
here for a few moments, and the friends of the little man
seemed to predominate as they were gathering around him,
and the cry of " Hands off !" freed him from the difficulties
with which he had been beset, and encouraged him to demand
an audience for a moment, which was carried by acclamation all around the room. By stepping on to the end
of a bench near by, he become conspicuous above the heads
of the audience, and continued :—·

" Ladies hand Gentlemen, I opes I ave your haprobation ?" (Shouts of approbation from all parts of the room ; the Indians seated on the platform, and Mr. Rankin allowing the little working gentleman to proceed.)

" My friends, I am a poor and to speak, and I did not hanticipate an event hov this sort. I came ere, like the rest of you, an ard-working man, to spend my shilling, hand for wot? To be umbugged, gentlemen ? (Great applause.) To be oaxed, gentlemen ? I calls it an impudent oax ! I olds in my and the adwertisement of that gentleman, haxing us to pay our shillings to see the bride of the Hindian wot was married yesterday ; and we are now told that she is not to be ere, and that this is ol notbink. —I say it is *somethink*, gentlemen. (Great applause.) Wen it was said that this couldn't be elped, I issed im, and ee *hought* to be issed, for I saw we was oaxed : I was then dragged by the andkerchief in a wiolent manner, but I hescaped unurt, and I am thankful that my woice can now be eard.

" Hif this gentleman is really Mr. Rankin, or hif ee is not, its hol the same—wot's the hods ? he as inwited us ere, to inale the ot hatmosphere of the Hegyptian All, to see the ' beautiful bride,' oom ee as been hinstrumental in leading up to the halter of Ymen, after making a great ubbub about it; and I esitate not to pronounce it an underanded business, that umbles a man in my hestimation, and I think it would ave been better for im to ave ushed up the wole think holtogether. (Applause.)

" Gentlemen, I am appy to see that I ave your haprobation. Wen I look around me, I see that you are all working men like myself, and able to hunderstand me. You all know it's werry ard to be oaxed out of our shillings — wen prowisions is igh—wen work is scarce—wen we ave little to heat, and hobliged to lie hidle." (Applause, and Hear, hear.) A voice. " Mr. Rankin ! Mr. Rankin !" A hundred voices ! " The bride ! the bride !—Turn him out !—Bagh !—The Indians ! the Indians !—The workee ! hear him out !—Mr. Rankin !—The Indians ! the Indians ! Police ! the police !—Turn him out !—The bride ! the bride ! the bride ! the bride !" &c. &c.

In the midst of all the din and confusion which it seemed now impossible to suppress, the sudden expedient of Mr. Rankin succeeded, and was probably the only one that could have done it. He thought of his Indians, who were quietly seated on the platform, and prepared for the war-dance ; and the signal given, and " Sound trumpets, sound !" they all sprang upon their feet and soon drowned the din and confusion in the screams and yells of the war-dance.

By the time the brandishing of tomahawks and spears and war-clubs and scalping-knives of this noisy affair was done, the attention of the visitors had become so much engrossed with the spirit and novelty of the scene, that they seemed generally disposed to dispense peaceably with the expected treat of seeing the beautiful bride, and were quiet. The little pugnacious working-man, however, arose again, as soon as silence was restored, to resume his speech ; and, asking " if he should go hon," the response from every part of the house was, " No ! no ! " to which he pertinaciously replied, " Well, then, I'll go ome, and see if I can hearn hanother shilling in the place hov the one I ave given to see those ill-looking wild hanimals, the Hindians."

The reader can easily understand why Mr. Rankin's stay with the Indians in London after this was very short. Of his career and theirs in the provincial towns, other historians will probably give some account, and I refer the reader to them, being unable to give more than a very imperfect account of it myself.

This sudden break-up of our establishment at the Egyptian Hall, just at the commencement of the fashionable season, when considerable outlay had been made, and the receipts daily increasing, was disastrous to all parties, and particularly so to me, who had the Hall, at a heavy rent, for three months longer, left on my hands. The excitement of the exhibition being thus removed, my Indian collection, which had already been three years in the same building, scarcely drew visitors enough to meet its expenses, and I left its management entirely to my faithful man Daniel, while I devoted my time, in an adjoining room, to getting out my second book, shortly after published at the Egyptian Hall—a large illustrated work, entitled ' *Catlin's Hunting Scenes and Amusements of the North American Indians.*' Several months being necessary for the completion of this work, I resolved to hold my collection in the Hall, as it was, until the expiration of my lease, and then pack it up and return to the United States.

I was then, for a while, free again from the yells and stamps of the Indians, and the excitements and anxieties attending their exhibitions; and my exhibition room became a quiet and pleasant salon in which to meet my friends, who frequently called, and I found were glad to see me, even though I had no Indians with me. My work was advancing fast, and I devoted my whole time to it, excepting when old friends or persons of distinction called, when I endeavoured to be with them, leaving the management of the room and entertainment of visitors mostly to Daniel, who by this time was a perfect key to everything in the room, provided he was turned the right way. He had all sorts of visitors however—those who came for useful information, and others merely to hear the war-whoop, and see the war-dance, supposing the Indians to be still there. These, feeling provoked at their disappointment, often took revenge on poor Daniel, by torturing him with questions about the Yankees, repeal, &c., which would lead at last to most exciting discussions on slavery, poor-laws and poorhouses, United States Bank, national debt, annexation, wars in Afghanistan, the Oregon question, the income-tax, and repudiation. As I have before said, Daniel, with a strong mind, and well fortified with the facts and dates relative to these subjects, was quite able to surprise his assailants with his information on all these points, and of course to provoke them in return. The consequence was that these debates often ran too high, and, as soon as they arrived at a pitch of indiscretion, I generally heard something of them in the adjoining room, and, leaving my work, showed myself in the exhibition, which brought them to an amicable issue.

There were others, again, who came to talk and learn more about the Indians, whom they knew had gone away. Among such was one day the " jolly fat dame," who stepped in merely to have a little chat with Daniel; and, as will be seen, she was lucky in finding him alone, and just in the humour to talk with her. There happened to be no cart or carriage passing at the moment, to prevent me from hearing her melodious voice, as she entered, and rolled along, with her parasol swinging in her hand.—"Well, Daniel" (who happened to be at the farther end of the room), " I am so lucky to find you all alone for once, for you always have such a possee around you! Daniel, you know you and I have always agreed very well." "Yes, madam, I don't know why you and I should have a falling-out." "Ah, well, we'll drop that, Daniel—I believe I'll take a chair, I am so fatigued with those plaguy stairs. Well, oh, but what a wonderful collection this is—Ha? what a curiosity that man is—Mr. Catlin, I mean—what a life he *has* led, to be sure! Don't you think he has been married to some of those little squaws? I'll be bound he has." "No, madam, I should doubt whether he has. I think Mr. Catlin went into the Indian country, determined to make this collection and to immortalize himself; and I have many a time heard him say that he resolved never to get into any difficulty with them about their women; and I think it was one reason why he succeeded, and was everywhere treated with friendship." "Ah, well! may be so. But, look ye, Daniel; that's been a sad affair with poor Cadotte, has it not? what a foolish man, ha!"

"Why, I don't see that it was so foolish on his part as on that of the girl."

"Oh, tush! but she's a silly little thing. She's pretty enough; but what's that to such a man as Cadotte? She's no substance. He's a giant, almost—what a grip!—I never felt the like in my life! Ah, well, I am sorry—I felt quite an interest in Cadotte."

"I feel more sorry for the foolish girl," said Daniel, "for falling in love with him—it was all her doing—she would have him, and wouldn't take 'No' for an answer. I never saw the like in my life. She seemed crazy for him; and they both cried like children about it for weeks, and he was good for nothing else. She has got him now; and, as I said before, I pity her, for she don't know what country she is going to, nor what society she will have instead of that of

her parents, and sisters, and friends in London. The girl
don't know what she will come to, and therefore I pity
her."

"Well, *I* don't pity her a bit. Ah, yes, I am sorry she
has been so silly; but I pity *him* the most. I care nothing
about her; or—that is—she ought to know better; but she's,
as I told you, a silly little thing. Ah, well, I have only
been one night to see them since they left Mr. Catlin. What
a foolish thing that was! It will be the ruin of them all.
I am afraid they will come to want, poor things! I have
only been there one night! Cadotte was not there."

"No, madam, he won't join them any more. Rankin has
turned him out of the house, and out of his employ, because he wouldn't let his wife appear in the exhibition and
play the piano, as he had advertised."

"Noble fellow! I like him for that. Isn't that a fine
spirit? I knew he had it. But that little silly thing, she
can't play. What do the public care about a foolish girl's
playing upon the piano?—Ridiculous! Well, they have
all gone, I suppose?"

"All but Cadotte and his wife, madam; they have not
gone."

"What! you don't say so? Cadotte has not gone?"

"No; they are living together with the girl's father.
Rankin has left him, without anything but his wife, to get
home to his own country in the best way he can."

"Well, there's a brute for you; is'nt he—that Rankin?
I always hated his looks, d'ye see. Not gone, ha? What
is he to do here? Will he stay in London? Can't Mr.
Catlin do something for him? He'd be just a good hand
now, to help you here, Daniel—to explain: you can't
always be here—there should be two of you. He comes
here occasionally?"

"Oh, yes, he's here every day,"

"Well, look ye, Daniel, I'll call again and see Mr. Catlin
about it. Something should be done. Mr. Catlin is a
good fellow I know. I want a long talk with him; he shall

know my whole mind on this affair. I can't stay now—I must go; but what a pity—ha, Daniel! Good day."

"Good day."

She was very near discovering me as she turned round and passed my door; but Daniel smiled after she had gone out, and said he was quite sure she had not seen me, as he had kept her conversation directed to him, so that she should not turn her face round suddenly on me.

I was sorry that I had overheard this dialogue; but, as it had fallen thus into my possession, I resolved to make the most prudent use of it, believing it to contain the sum total of all she wished to say in her "long talk" with me; and I directed Daniel, when she should call to see me, to announce me "out of town," and himself to engross all that she had to say, saving me from entering again upon an unpleasant subject, which I considered now at an end.

Thus continued my labours and Daniel's, each one in his department, for three months or more after the Indians had left, by which time my large work was ready for publication (like the first one, " to be published by the Author, at the Egyptian Hall, price five guineas in printed tints, and eight guineas coloured), with a subscription-list headed by the illustrious names of—

HER GRACIOUS MAJESTY THE QUEEN,
LOUIS PHILIPPE, KING OF THE FRENCH,
THE EMPEROR OF RUSSSIA,
THE KING OF THE BELGIANS,
H.R.H. THE DUKE OF CAMBRIDGE,
AND MANY OF THE NOBILITY OF ENGLAND.

The Emperor of Russia was at this time paying his visit to the Queen of England; and my dear wife and myself took the occasion of the grand pageant when the Emperor, with Prince Albert and the Duke of Wellington, reviewed 10,000 troops at Windsor, to obtain a view of his Imperial Majesty, which we did during the review, and, still more to our satisfaction, after it was over, from behind the post of the gate opening into the great park, where we had stationed ourselves, and where his Imperial Majesty passed within reach of us. When the Emperor and suite had passed by, I suddenly perceived in the passing throng J. W. Webb, Esq., editor of the 'New York Inquirer,' and endeavoured, but unsuccessfully, to overtake him.

A few days after this, the Honourable Mr. Murray was kind enough to deliver to the Emperor the copy of my work subscribed for by his Majesty; and, in a few weeks after that, sent me the following very flattering communication :—

" Dear Sir,   " Buckingham Palace, June 14th, 1844.
        " The Emperor of Russia, having inspected your PORTFOLIO OF INDIAN HUNTING AND OTHER SCENES, was so much pleased with their spirit and execution, that he desired Count Orloff to send me a gold snuff-box, to be presented to you as a mark of his Majesty's gratification derived from the efforts of your pencil.

" I acquit myself of this agreeable commission by sending you herewith a Russian box of gold and blue enamel, set in pearls, which will, I trust, prove to you a gratifying reminiscence of the Emperor's visit to England.

                        " I am, my dear Sir,
                                " Very faithfully yours,
" *To Geo. Catlin, Esq.*"   " C. A. MURRAY.

This most gratifying testimony of the Emperor's satisfaction with my work was unexpected by me; and future pages will show that I received evidences equally flattering from their Majesties the King of the French and the King of the Belgians.

My large work being now published in London, and, like my former one, kindly noticed and highly approved by the press, I felt as if my labours in England were coming near to a close : and, having a little leisure, I was drawing my little children (of whom I now had four) nearer to me than ever, and with my dear Clara was endeavouring to see the remainder of the sights of London before our departure for our native land. This desired event was yet to be delayed a little, however, by a circumstance that I must here narrate, not to leave the reader in the dark as to the curious incidents and impulses of this transatlantic part of my chequered life.

About this period occurred an unparalleled destruction of life at sea : the " Solway " and other noble vessels striking on sunken rocks, and going down in smooth water in sight of land, and hundreds of human beings sinking with them to eternity. Human invention, roused by human sympathy, was everywhere labouring to devise means for the preservation of life in such cases ; and my brain, like the brains of hundreds of others, was busy in the same cause, when a plan suddenly suggested itself, which appeared more practicable the more I contemplated it. I deliberated on it much, and threw in my own way all the arguments I could possibly raise against it ; and amongst them, as the strongest, the blind and deaf enthusiasm, which leads too many inventors to ruin. No objections that I then raised or can yet raise, however, have created in my mind a doubt of the feasibility of my plan, or of its immense and never-ending importance to the human race. And, as the sequel will show, I give the following information concerning it to the world, not on my own account, but for those who may possibly be benefited by it, or whom it may in any way concern.

On mature deliberation I decided, like other inventors, to avail myself of a patent for my discovery ; and, with that view, called upon a patent-agent, who had been recommended to me by the highest authority. On stating to him the object of my visit, I was invited to a private room, where he stated that it was necessary that he should hear a distinct description of my invention before he could tell whether it was new, and whether it was a fitting subject of a patent. I replied as follows :—" I believe, Sir, that there is but one effectual way of saving the lives of the greater number of persons on board steamers and other vessels sinking or burning at sea, and that an invention applicable, for such a purpose, to all vessels (as there is never to be an end to the increase of vessels and exposure of life on the ocean) would be of the greatest importance to mankind, and would most richly repay the inventor. A plan has suggested itself to me which I think will have this effect; and if, after hearing it explained, you should decide that it is new and of sufficient consideration, I beg you to procure me a patent for it as soon as it can be obtained."

I then proceeded—"The patent I should ask for would be for ' *disengaging and floating quarter-decks of steamers and other vessels for the purpose of saving human lives at sea.*' These I would propose to build of solid timber or other material, resting upon and answering all the purposes of quarter-decks; and, in case of the sinking of a vessel, to be disengaged by means which I would set forth in the specification, and capable of floating, as rafts, with all the passengers and crew upon them. These rafts might easily be made of sufficient strength to resist the force of the most violent sea; and their shape being such as to prevent them from capsizing, there would be little difficulty in preserving life for many days upon them. They might be made to contain within them waterproof cases of sheet iron or tin, to carry provisions and liquors, and also rockets for signals, valuable papers, money, &c.; and, when driven on shore, would float safely over a reef, where vessels and life-boats go to pieces and the greatest loss of life generally takes place. In case of a vessel on fire at sea, when it should be found that all exertions to extinguish the flames were unavailing, all hands might retreat to the quarter-deck, and the vessel be scuttled and sunk by slinging a gun and firing a shot through her bottom, or by other means; and as she goes down the flames of course are extinguished, and her passengers and crew, and valuables, might be saved on the raft, as I have described."

When I had thus explained the nature of my invention, I asked the agent whether he considered it new, and fit to be patented, to which he at once replied, " You may rely on it, Sir, it is entirely new: nothing of the kind has been patented; and it is a subject for which I think I can get you what we call a 'clean patent.'" Upon this I at once authorized him to proceed and procure the patent in the quickest manner possible, saying that the money required for it should be ready as fast as he should call for it. After this, and in further conversation about it, he said, " I think remarkably well of the invention, and, though I am not in the habit of giving encouragement to my employers, I say to you, frankly, that I believe that when we have obtained the patent, the Admiralty will buy it out of your hands and give it for the benefit of the world at large."

Being thus authorized, he proceeded, and the patent was obtained in the space of two months, and for which I paid him the sum of 130*l.* After I had received my patent, I met a friend, Mr. R——, to whom I explained the nature of my invention; and, when I had got through, he asked me who had been my agent in the business, and I told him; to which he replied that it was very strange, as he believed that a friend of his, a Captain Oldmixon, had procured a patent, in London, for a similar thing, some five or six years before. He said he was quite confident that it was the same thing, for he had heard him say a great deal about it, and recollected his having advertised and performed an experiment on a vessel in the river below the city; and advised me to call on my agent and put the question to him. I did so, and he referred to the published lists of patents for ten or twelve years back, and assured me that no such name was on the list of patentees, and that I might rest satisfied that no such patent had ever been taken out.

I then returned to my friend Mr. R——, and informed him of this, telling him that he *must* be mistaken. To which he replied, "No; since you have been absent I have recollected more. I have found the address of Captain Oldmixon's attorney who procured the patent for him, which I give you; and I wish you would call on him, and he will correct me if I am wrong."

I took the address and called on the attorney, whom

I found in his office. I asked him if he had taken out a patent for Captain Oldmixon five or six years ago, and he replied that he had. I asked him if he would be kind enough to tell me the nature of it, and he instantly replied that it was for "disengaging and floating quarter-decks for saving life." I then asked him if he had completed his patent by putting in his specification, and he replied that he had, and that if I would ask for it in a registry of patents in Chancery-lane I could see it. I then inquired if it had been published in the manner that the law requires, and he assured me it had. He further stated that he had been for several years, and still was, engaged with it for Captain Oldmixon before the Committee on Shipwrecks, with a prospect of getting the Admiralty to take it up. With this information I returned immediately to my agent, and, having explained it to him, he accompanied me to the registry in Chancery-lane, where, on being asked if they had the specification of a patent in the name of Captain Oldmixon, one of the clerks instantly replied " Yes," and unrolled it upon the counter.

I read it over, and, finding it almost word for word like my own, and the invention exactly the same, I said to my agent, " I have nothing more to say or to do, but to go home and attend to my business." Nor have I ever taken further pains about it. My agent, at a subsequent period, wrote me a letter, expressing his regret that such a thing should have happened, and enclosing a 10*l.* note, the amount, he said, of his fees; stating that the rest had all been paid into different offices, for which there was no remedy.

I have mentioned the above circumstance, as forming one of the many instances of ill luck that have been curiously mixed with the incidents of my life ; and also to show the world how much circumspection and caution are necessary in guarding one's interest, even amidst the well-regulated rules and formalities of this great and glorious country.

Captain Oldmixon has my hearty wishes for the success of his invention; and I hope that my allusion to it in the above manner will do him no injury, but may be the cause of turning the attention of the world towards it as a means of benefiting the human race.

I have informed the reader already that, just before completing the above adventure, the Ojibbeways having left London, and my large work being published to the world, I was turning my eyes to my native country again, where, with my little ones and my collection, I was preparing to go; but even this *was not to be* as we had designed it, for it was announced, just then, that another party of fourteen Indians had arrived in Liverpool, and were on their way to the metropolis! Life has its chapters, like the chapters of a book; and our days are like the leaves we turn in reading it. We peruse one page ignorant of what is contained in the next; and, as the chapters of life are often suddenly cut short, so this chapter of my book must end here; and the reader will start with me afresh, in a second volume, which commences with a new enterprise.

APPENDIX.

APPENDIX.—(A.)

OPINIONS OF THE PRESS

ON

CATLIN'S NORTH AMERICAN INDIAN MUSEUM.

THE following are a few of the very numerous eulogiums which the Press has passed upon the merits of this Collection, in England, France, and the United States, where it has been exhibited.

LONDON PRESS.

THE QUARTERLY REVIEW.

MR. CATLIN'S object in visiting England with his Indian Gallery, it would seem, is to sell his collection to our Government, and we most sincerely hope that his reliance on the magnanimity of the British people will not be disappointed. As a man of science, of enterprise, and of true philanthropy, he is justly entitled to be considered as a citizen of the world ; and, although he reflects especial honour upon the intelligent nation to which he is so proud to declare that he owes his birth, yet, for that very reason, we are confident, a generous feeling will universally exist to receive him with liberality here.

But, leaving the worthy artist's own interests completely out of the question, and in the cause of science casting aside all party feeling, we submit to Lord Melbourne, to Sir Robert Peel, to Lord Lansdowne, to Sir R. Inglis, and to all who are deservedly distinguished among us as the liberal patrons of the fine arts, that Mr. Catlin's Indian collection is worthy to be retained in this country as the record of a race of our fellow-creatures whom we shall very shortly have swept from the face of the globe. Before that catastrophe shall have arrived, it is true, a few of our countrymen may occasionally travel among them ; but it cannot be expected that any artist of note should again voluntarily reside among them for seven years, as competent as Mr. Catlin, whose slight, active, sinewy frame has peculiarly fitted him for the physical difficulties attendant upon such an exertion.

Considering the melancholy fate which has befallen the Indian race, and which overhangs the remnant of these victims to our power, it would surely be discreditable that the civilized world should, with heartless apathy, decline to preserve and to transmit to posterity Mr. Catlin's graphic delineation of them ; and if any nation on earth should evince a desire to preserve such a lasting monument, there can be no doubt that there exists none better entitled to do so than the British people ; for with feelings of melancholy satisfaction, we do not hesitate to assert that throughout our possessions on the continent of America, we have, from the first moment of our acquaintance with them to the present hour, invariably maintained their rights, and at a very great expense have honestly continued to pay them their annual presents, for which we have received from them, in times of war as well as of peace, the most unequivocal marks of their indelible gratitude. Their respect for our flag is unsullied by a reproach—their attachment to our sovereign is second only in their breasts to the veneration with which they regard their " Great Spirit "—while the names of Lord Dalhousie, of Sir Peregrine Maitland, and of Sir John Colborne, who for many years respectively acted towards them as their father and as their friend, will be affectionately repeated by them in our colonies until the Indian heart has ceased to beat there, and until the Red Man's language has ceased to vibrate in the British " wilderness of this world." Although European diseases, and the introduction of ardent spirits, have produced the lamentable effects we have described, and although as a nation we are not faultless, yet we may fairly assert and proudly feel that the English government has at least made every possible exertion to do its duty towards the Indians ; and that there has existed no colonial secretary of state who has not evinced that anxiety to befriend them which, it is our duty to say, particularly characterized the administration of the amiable and humane Lord Glenelg.

THE LITERARY GAZETTE.

Catlin's Indian Gallery, Egyptian Hall.—We have now to announce the opening of this exhibition, from visits to which every class of the community, old as well as young, will reap much instruction and gratification. Having recently described, from an American journal, Mr. Catlin's seven or eight years' sojourn among the red races of North America, we need now only say that his representation of them, their country, their costumes, their sports, their religious ceremonies, and in short their manners and customs, so as to enable us to form a complete idea of them, is deserving of the utmost praise. There are above 500 subjects in these spacious rooms, from a wigwam to a child's rattle ; and everything belonging to the various Indian tribes are before the spectator in their actual condition and integrity. There are, besides, a multitude of portraits of the leading warriors, &c. &c., and other pictures of dances, ball-play, ambuscading, fighting ; and the whole supplying by far the most ample and accurate history of them that has ever been published to the world. No book of travels can approach these realities; and after all we had read of the red men, we confess we are astonished at the many new and important points connected with them which this Gallery impressed upon us. We saw more distinctly the links of resemblance between them and other early and distant people; and we had comparisons suggested of a multitude of matters affecting the progress of mankind all over the earth, and alike illustrated by similitudes and dissimilitudes. Indeed the philosophical inquirer will be delighted with this exhibition, whilst the curious child of seven years of age will enjoy it with present amusement and lasting instruction.

THE ATHENÆUM.

The Indian Gallery.—This is the collection mentioned heretofore by our American correspondent (No. 609), and a most interesting one it is. It contains more than 300 portraits of distinguished Indians, men and women of different tribes, all painted from life; and in many instances the identical dress, weapons, &c. are exhibited which they wore when their portraits were taken; and 200 other paintings, representing Indian customs, games, hunting-scenes, religious ceremonies, dances, villages, and said to contain above 3000 figures: in brief, it is a pictorial history of this interesting and fast-perishing race. It includes, too, a series of views of the Indian country; and we have seen nothing more curious than some of the scenes on the Upper Missouri and Mississippi, the general accuracy of which is beyond question. Mr. Catlin has spent seven years in wandering among the various tribes, for the sole purpose of perfecting this collection. As he observes, " it has been gathered, and every painting has been made from nature, by my own hand; and that, too, when I have been paddling my canoe or leading my packhorse over and through trackless wilds, at the hazard of life. The world will surely be kind and indulgent enough to receive and estimate them as they have been intended, as true and fac-simile traces of individual and historical facts, and forgive me for their present unfinished and unstudied condition as works of art."

The value of this collection is increased by the fact that the red men are fast perishing, and will probably, before many years have passed, be an extinct race. If proof of this were wanting, we have it in the facts recorded in the catalogue, of the devastation which the smallpox has lately spread among them. Of one tribe, the hospitable and friendly Mandans, as Mr. Catlin calls them, 2000 in number when he visited them and painted their pictures, living in two permanent villages on the Missouri, 1800 miles above its junction with the Mississippi, not one now exists! In 1837 the smallpox broke out among them, and only thirty-five were left alive; these were subsequently destroyed by a hostile tribe, which took possession of their villages: and thus, within a few months, the race became extinct—not a human being is believed to have escaped.

THE ART-UNION.

Mr. Catlin's Indian Gallery.—Circumstances have hitherto prevented our noticing this most admirable exhibition ; but we have examined it in all its parts with very minute attention, and have been highly gratified, as well as much informed, by doing so. Mr. Catlin's collection is by no means to be classed among the ephemeral amusements of the day ; it is a work of deep and permanent interest. Perceiving that the rapid destruction of the aboriginal tribes by war, disease, and the baneful influence of spirituous liquors, would soon cause all traces of the red men to be lost, Mr. Catlin determined on proceeding through their still untrodden wildernesses, for the purpose of gaining an intimate acquaintance with their manners and customs, and of procuring an exact delineation of their persons, features, ceremonies, &c., all which he has faithfully and perfectly accomplished at no small hazard of life and limb. It was not a common mind that could have conceived so bold a project, nor is he a common man who has so thoroughly accomplished it.

The arms, dresses, domestic implements, &c. &c. collected by the industry of this most energetic of explorers are precisely as they have been manufactured and used by their Indian owners, and form a collection which every succeeding year will render more and more valuable. The portraits of distinguished warriors, &c., the representations of religious ceremonies, war-dances, buffalo-hunts, &c. &c., are depicted by Mr. Catlin himself, and that with a force and evident truth that bring the whole detail of Indian life in eloquent reality before the eyes of the spectator. We have no hesitation in saying that this gallery supplies the most effective and valuable means for acquiring an exact acquaintance with the great American continent that has ever been offered to the hunger and thirst after knowledge, so prevailing a characteristic of the age. Mr. Catlin is about to publish the details of his eight years' sojourn among the interesting people with whom his portraitures have made us so familiar ; and we have no doubt that this work will render the stores of information he has opened to us in his gallery entire and complete. As works of art their merit depends chiefly on their accuracy, of which no doubt can be entertained.

LA BELLE ASSEMBLÉE.

Mr. Catlin's Gallery of North American Indians.—Of all the exhibitions that have been brought forward for the amusement of the public, we must give this of Mr. Catlin the preference in every point of view ; it possesses not only present but future interest, for perhaps not many generations may flourish and fade before nearly the whole of the aboriginal tribes will be wholly extirpated. Wherever the imprint of the white man's foot has flattened the grass of the prairie, it may be looked upon as an ominous token to the unsuspecting native. The broad lands of the owners of the soil are daily passing into the hands of the stranger, and desolation comes where lowly comfort dwelt.

As historical records, these pictures, from the faithful pencil of Mr. Catlin, are invaluable, inasmuch as they may be considered, in all probability, the last and almost the only authentic remains of ancient tribes, that are slowly but surely leaving nothing but a name behind.

THE TIMES.

Mr. Catlin's North American Indian Gallery.—A very curious exhibition is opened in the Egyptian Hall, Piccadilly. It consists of above 500 portraits, landscapes, views of combats, religious ceremonies, costumes, and many other things illustrative of the manners and customs, and modes of living and of battle, &c. of the different tribes of North American Indians. Some of these pictures are exceedingly interesting, and form a vast field for the researches of the antiquary, the naturalist, and the philosopher. The numerous portraits are full of character; they exhibit an almost endless variety of feature, though all bearing a generical resemblance to each other. The views of combats are very full of spirit, and exhibit modes of warfare and destruction horribly illustrative of savage life. The method of attacking buffaloes and other monsters of the plains and forests are all interesting; the puny process of a fox-chace sinks into insignificance when compared with the tremendous excitement occasioned by the grappling of a bear or the butting of a bison. These scenes are all accurately depicted, not in the finished style of modern art, but with a vigour and fidelity of outline, which arises from the painter having actually beheld what he transmits to canvas. The most curious portion of this exhibition is, however, the representations of the horrible religious ceremonies of several of the Indian tribes, and the probationary trials of those who aspire to be the leaders amongst them. These representations disclose the most abhorrent and execrable cruelties. They show to what atrocities human nature can arrive where the presence of religious knowledge is not interposed to prevent its career. The exhibition also contains tents, weapons, dresses, &c. of the various tribes visited by Mr. Catlin. These are curious, but of secondary importance. The catalogue, which is to be had at the exhibition-room, is a very interesting *brochure*, and will afford a great deal of novel but important information.

MORNING CHRONICLE.

The Aboriginal Tribes of North America.—A pictorial exhibition of a singularly interesting description has just been opened in the Egyptian Hall, Piccadilly. It consists of portraits, landscapes, costumes, and other representations of the persons, manners, and customs of the North American

Indians, painted by Mr. Catlin, an American artist, during eight years' travel amongst their various tribes.

On Monday a numerous assemblage, comprising many distinguished members of the fashionable as well as the literary world, visited this extraordinary collection, and listened with the utmost curiosity and interest to the details and explanations given by Mr. Catlin in illustration of some of its most remarkable objects.

Mr. Catlin modestly apologizes for the unfinished character of his pictures, considered as works of art. They are sketches rapidly and roughly executed, as might be expected from the circumstances under which they were made ; but they are freely drawn with a strong tone of colour ; and being drawn and coloured immediately from nature, there is a graphic truthfulness about them which places, as it were, the very objects themselves before the eye of the spectator, and fills the imagination with images of these ancient lords of the western continent, now reduced to scattered remnants and fast disappearing from the earth, a thousand times more distinct and vivid than could be produced by volumes of description.

THE MORNING POST.

Catlin's Indian Gallery.—This is a very extraordinary collection, consisting of an immense number of portraits, landscapes, costumes, and representations of the manners and customs of the North American Indians, among whom the artist-collector travelled for eight years, extending his researches through forty-eight tribes, the majority of whom speak different languages. The long room on the groundfloor of the Egyptian Hall is covered from the roof to the floor, and nearly the floor itself, by some thousands of specimens, real as well as pictorial, of these interesting races, many of whom are now, alas! nearly extinguished, under the civilizing influences of fire-water, smallpox, and the exterminating policy of the government of the United States, in which treachery has recently played a counterpart to the most gratuitous despotism. " I have seen them in their own villages," says Mr. Catlin, " have carried my canvas and colours the whole way, and painted my portraits, &c. from the life, as they now stand and are seen in the gallery."

The collection contains 310 portraits of distinguished men and women of the different tribes in the British, United States, and Mexican territories ; and 200 other paintings descriptive of river, mountain, forest, and prairie scenes ; the village games, festivals, and peculiar customs and superstitions of the natives, exhibiting in all above 3000 figures; all, Mr. Catlin assures us, were taken from nature, and all by his own hand! a truly Herculean undertaking, and evidently sustained by an enthusiastic spirit, as well as a share of unconquerable perseverance, such as falls to the lot of few artists in any country to boast of.

THE MORNING POST.

Catlin's Indian Gallery.—This valuable collection of portraits, landscapes, scenes from savage life, weapons, costumes, and an endless variety of illustrations of Indian life, real as well as pictorial, continues to attract crowds of spectators. We are happy to find our prediction fully borne out by fact, that the exhibition only required to be fully made known to the public to be properly appreciated. The most pleasing attention is paid by Mr. Catlin and his assistants to gratify the curiosity of visitors, to point out to notice the peculiarities of the various subjects through which they wander, and to explain everything which strikes the eye and attracts the observer to inquire into its use or meaning. During our visit on Saturday the company were startled by a yell, and shortly afterwards by the appearance of a stately chief of the Crow Indians stalking silently through the room, armed to the teeth and painted to the temples, wrapped up in a buffalo robe, on which all his battles were depicted, and wearing a tasteful coronet of war-eagle's quills. This personation was volunteered by the nephew of Mr. Catlin, who has seen the red man in his native wilds, and presents the most proud and picturesque similitude that can be conceived of the savage warrior. His war-whoop, his warlike appearance and dignified movements seem to impress the assemblage more strikingly with a feeling of the character of the North American Indian than all the other evidences which crowded the walls. Subsequently he appeared in another splendid costume, worn by the braves of the Mandan tribe, also remarkable for its costly and magnificent head-dress, in which we see " the horns of power" assume a conspicuous place. The crowds that gathered around him on each occasion were so dense that Mr. Catlin could scarcely find space to explain the particulars of the costumes; but we are glad to find he is preparing a central stage where all may enjoy a full and fair sight of " the Red Man " as he issues from his wigwam, clad in the peculiar robe and ornaments of his tribe, to fight, hunt, smoke, or join in the dances, festivals, and amusements peculiar to each nation.

THE GLOBE AND TRAVELLER.

Indian Knowledge of English Affairs.—Mr. Catlin, in one of his lectures on the manners and customs of the North American Indians, during the last week, related a very curious occurrence, which excited a great deal of surprise and some considerable mirth amongst his highly respectable and numerous audience. Whilst speaking of the great and warlike tribe of Sioux or Dahcotas, of 40,000 or 50,000, he stated that many of this tribe, as well as of several others, although living entirely in the territory of the United States, and several hundred miles south of her Majesty's possessions, were found cherishing a lasting friendship for the English, whom they denominate Saganosh. And in very many instances they are to be seen wearing about their necks large silver medals, with the portrait of George III. in bold relief upon them. These medals were given to them as badges of merit during the last war with the United States, when these warriors were employed in the British service.

The lecturer said that whenever the word Saganosh was used, it seemed to rouse them at once ; that on several occasions when Englishmen had been in his company as fellow-travellers, they had marked attentions paid them by these Indians as Saganoshes. And on one occasion, in one of his last rambles in that country, where he had painted several portraits in a small village of Dahcotas, the chief of the band positively refused to sit, alleging as his objection that the Pale-faces, who were not to be trusted, might do some injury to his portrait, and his health or his life might be affected by it. The painter, as he was about to saddle his horse for his departure, told the Indian that he was a Saganosh, and was going across the Big Salt Lake, and was very sorry that he could not carry the picture of so distinguished a man. At this intelligence the Indian advanced, and after a hearty grip of the hand, very carefully and deliberately withdrew from his bosom, and next to his naked breast, a large silver medal, and turning his face to the painter, pronounced with great vehemence and emphasis the word Sag-a-nosh ! The artist, supposing that he had thus gained his point with the Indian Sagamore, was making preparation to proceed with his work, when the Indian still firmly denied him the privilege—holding up the face of his Majesty (which had got a superlative brightness by having been worn for years against his naked breast), he made this singular and significant speech :—" When you cross the Big Salt Lake, tell my Great Father that you saw his face, and it was bright !" To this the painter replied, " I can never see your Great Father, he is dead !" The poor Indian recoiled in silence, and returning his medal to his bosom, entered his wigwam, at a few paces distant, where he seated himself amidst his family around his fire, and deliberately lighting his pipe, passed it around in silence.

When it was smoked out he told them the news he had heard, and in a few moments returned to the traveller again, who was preparing with his party to mount their horses, and inquired whether the Saganoshes had no chief. The artist replied in the affirmative, saying that the present chief of the Saganoshes is a young and very beautiful woman. The Sagamore expressed great surprise and some incredulity at this unaccountable information ; and being fully assured by the companions of the artist that his assertion was true, the Indian returned again quite hastily to his wigwam, called his own and the neighbouring families into his presence, lit and smoked another pipe, and then communicated the intelligence to them, to their great surprise and amusement; after which he walked out to the party about to start off, and advancing to the painter (or Great Medicine, as they called him) with a sarcastic smile on his face, in due form, and with much grace and effect, he carefully withdrew again from his bosom the polished silver medal, and turning the face of it to the painter, said, " Tell my Great Mother that you saw our Great Father, and that we keep his face bright!"

THE GLOBE AND TRAVELLER.

North American Indians.—An exhibition has been opened consisting of portraits, landscapes, costumes, implements of war, articles of commerce, and a variety of curiosities, illustrating the manners, habits, and customs of forty-eight different tribes of the North American Indians The collection, which must prove highly interesting to all who take an interest in the various modes of life existing among our fellow-creatures in the different states and stages of savage life, or comparative civilization, consists of 310 portraits of distinguished men and women of the different Indian tribes, and 200 other paintings descriptive of Indian countries, villages, sports, and pastimes; the whole of which were painted by Mr. Catlin during a residence of eight years among the different tribes. An additional interest is given to the paintings by the various implements used by the natives, such as bows, arrows, tomahawks, and scalping knives. There are even human scalps, which illustrate one of the paintings representing the scalp dance, in which the victors of one tribe exhibit, in one of their war dances, the scalps of another whom they have vanquished. Among the most spirited of the paintings, as works of art, may be enumerated those of the voluntarily inflicted torments to which some of the tribes subject themselves as proofs of their courage; those of the buffalo hunts, buffalo fights, and of the prairies, which are all highly characteristic productions. In speaking of the different items of interest in this exhibition, Mr. Catlin and the cicerone should not be forgotten, as they amuse the visitors with many of those interesting personal anecdotes which travellers always abound in.

THE SPECTATOR.

Catlin's Indian Gallery, at the Egyptian Hall, Piccadilly, is a museum of the various tribes of North American Indians.

Mr. Catlin is an enterprising American artist, who has devoted eight years to the delineation of scenes and persons, and the collection of objects to form a permanent record of the characteristic features and customs of the different tribes of Indians in North America, now fast becoming extinct by the combined operation of smallpox, spirit-drinking, and war. The walls of a room 106 feet in length are entirely covered with portraits of Indian men, women, and children, in their respective costumes, some small whole-lengths, others busts the life-size, to the number of 310; and 200 views of landscape scenery, native villages, games, customs, and hunting-scenes, all painted on the spot. Besides the pictures, the dresses worn by several tribes, and a numerous collection of weapons, pipes, ornaments, &c., are arranged round the room; and in the centre is set up a wigwam of the " Crow " tribe, a conical tent twenty-five feet high, made of buffalo-skins, dressed and painted, supported by thirty poles meeting at the top, and capable of sheltering eighty persons.

To attempt anything like a detailed description of the contents of such a museum would require a volume; to characterize it generally in our limited space is difficult. It would require hours of attentive study to become fully acquainted with the multifarious articles. The several tribes are distinguished in the catalogue: the dresses are all so fantastic, and the physiognomies so varied, that it would be difficult to class them.

The dances and other amusements appear anything but gamesome; and the religious ceremonies of the Mandans, of which there are four scenes, are horrible in the extreme. It is their annual custom to assemble the young men in the "Medicine" or "Mystery" Lodge—the medicine-men are a sort of mixture of the doctor, priest, and sorcerer—and after being starved for four days and nights, they are tortured in the most cruel manner to test their powers of endurance. The animal character, sharpened and sometimes ennobled by the influence of moral qualities, is strongly expressed in all the heads.

The scenery on the Missouri and Mississippi is remarkable for the mixture of beauty and desolation, and an appearance of cultivation in the wildest parts. Mr. Catlin's views bear the impress of fidelity that belongs to pictures painted on the spot; and their freshness and characteristic spirit more than atone for any defects of execution. The scenes of buffalo-hunting are full of movement and energy; and the groups of Indians are sketched with so much life and action, that the scene appears to pass before you. Numerous certificates attest the accuracy of the portraits and views. The robes and the tent covering exhibit come curious specimens of the pictorial skill of the Iudians, which reminds one of the Egyptian and Mexican paintings; the outline being strongly defined, and with attention to the characteristic points. The dresses are very tastefully decorated with beads, feathers, and skins; and the pipes, war-clubs, lances, bows, quivers, and shields are profusely ornamented: the cradles are really beautiful.

Mr. Catlin is about to publish an account of his expedition, in which the various objects in his museum will be more fully explained than in the catalogue; previously to which he intends giving a sort of lecture in the room descriptive of the people. In the mean time, a visit to this "Indian gallery" will give a more lively and distinct idea of the aborigines of North America, than a whole course of reading.

THE CONSERVATIVE JOURNAL.

Catlin's Indian Gallery.—This is, we believe, the first time that the British public have had a fair opportunity, upon an extensive scale, of making themselves acquainted with the personal appearance of the various tribes of North American Indians, once constituting the noblest race of savages that are mentioned in history, but of late years sinking into all the depravity which the wicked race of white traders has inflicted on them. These manly natives of the woods and prairies of America, "the red men," as they are properly denominated, are sinking fast in character, and gradually fading from human existence, through the sordid and base traffic of the "pale-faces," who drive an infamous trade by bartering the execrable "fire-waters" (rum and whisky) amongst these children of the wood, for the furs and other produce of their hunting expeditions. Once these vile poisons are swallowed by the aborigines, they lose all their manly and martial energies, become sottish, feeble, and enervated in mind and body, and appear as if conscious of their self-debasement.

With respect to the subjects of exhibition, they are chiefly portraits of the most noted chiefs of the various tribes that formerly roamed at large over the vast territory of which they were the natural proprietors. There are also some of the females of note and others in early life, who display attractions of feature and expression which would not discredit the most civilized people. Amongst the chiefs of greatest notoriety here is the celebrated chief "Black Hawk," on whose keen eye and determined brow "no compromise" is plainly written by the hand of nature. The eldest and second sons of this chief are here also, and are worthy of the sire from whom they sprung. There are also several other distinguished warriors of this tribe, which is denominated the Sacs (Sauskies). There also are distinguished chiefs and warriors of the following nations: the Konzas, Osages, Camanchees, Pawneepicts, Sioux, Missouries, Mandans, Black Feet, A'assin-ne-boins, Delawares, Choctaws, Cherokees, &c., amounting to some hundred portraits; besides views of fine scenery, buffalo-hunting, war and other dances; a variety of weapons, dresses, some scalps, a wigwam, &c. We hope soon to give a few interesting details.

ATLAS.

Catlin's Indian Gallery, Egyptian Hall.—A room 106 feet in length and of proportionate breadth and height, is occupied exclusively with this most interesting exhibition. Its pictorial portion consists of a vast series of portraits of the chiefs, the braves, the medicine-men, and squaws of the numerous tribes and nations of Indians—the aborigines of North America. Another lengthened series consists of landscape views of scenery, the rivers, mountains, and prairies—the homes and hunting-grounds of the Red Men. Illustrations of manners and customs, including some of the most curious and valuable portions of the gallery, form a third series of pictures, and these efforts of the pencil extend to upwards of 500. They are not offered as specimens of the art, although in that light they are by no means unworthy of attention, but as a pictorial history of nations about to be swept by the tide of civilization from the surface of the earth. As these bold sketches were executed in the wigwam, in the tent, in the steam-boat, in the forest, in the canoe, in storm and sunshine, amid strife and smoke, and every possible variety of interruption and annoyance, their existence is a miracle, and the artist may be proud of the fire and spirit, the truth and energy, yes, and the freedom and power with which he has, under such circumstances conveyed to canvas the vivid impress of the ancient nobles of the forest and the prairie.

In eight years Mr. Catlin visited 48 tribes, including 300,000 Indians; has painted 310 portraits from life, and all the scenic accounts we have noticed. For the sake of the pictures, of the exhibition itself, which is intensely interesting, and yet more for the important lesson it teaches, we earnestly recommend the Indian Gallery to the attention of the reader.

THE BRITANNIA.

Egyptian Hall, Piccadilly.—The suite of apartments composing this unique building has been opened for the exhibition of Catlin's Gallery of North American Indians, which comprises a museum of the various articles used in domestic life and in war by the aborigines who inhabit the Texas and adjoining country. Besides the articles of dress and ornament, the instruments of chace and warfare, the walls of the apartment are hung with a collection of 500 paintings, which represent the figures of living Indian chiefs, their battles, festivities, and domestic habits, as well as the scenery of the country in the "far west," and the animals which inhabit it, being a faithful representation of those distant regions.

At the farther end of the room is a wigwam of buffalo-hide, pitched in the manner in which the natives arrange it; namely, in the form of a tent, but somewhat more conical. The owner of this interesting exhibition, Mr. Catlin, spent several years among the Pawnee, Sioux, Crow, and other tribes, for the purpose of taking accurate delineations of the noble races of Indians who still wander through the extensive prairies in all their primary freedom and independence. The exhibition will amuse the mere lounger as much as it will interest the curious and reflecting.

EAST INDIA CHRONICLE.

North American Indians.—Of late years Cooper's American novels, and various works of travels; and, more recently, the Hon. Mr. Murray's and Captain Marryat's attractive volumes, have deeply interested us respecting the Red Indians of North America, their derivation, manners, customs, &c. Mr. Catlin, however, who has devoted eight years of his life to these miscalled savage people, who are now rapidly fading away from the face of the earth, sad victims of oppression, European vice and European disease, is enlightening us still further upon the subject. He has opened an exhibition at the Egyptian Hall, Piccadilly, in which are assembled (all of his own painting) about 500 portraits of Indian chiefs, warriors, squaws,

&c. ; landcapes and other scenes, illustrating their warlike and religious ceremonies, their customs, dances, buffalo hunts, &c. The portraits, many of them valuable even as works of art, excite a strong and vivid interest from the almost exhaustless variety and force of character which they display. Many of the heads are bold and highly intellectual, and remarkable for their phrenological developments. Several of the young squaws, too, have considerable pretensions to beauty, with abundance of archness, vivacity, and good humour. Then again there is an immense collection of their weapons, pipes, musical instruments, dresses, &c. ; amongst them a child's cradle, or whatever it may be termed, in which the women carry their children at their backs. It is impossible for persons of any age to find themselves otherwise than instructed and gratified by this exhibition. Besides what we have mentioned, Mr. Catlin lectures thrice a week in the evening, with the assistance of living figures for additional illustrations.

THE JOHN BULL.

Catlin's Indian Gallery.—Mr. Catlin is an American artist, who, after eight years' toilsome travel, during which he visited forty-eight tribes of the aborigines of his native land, and traversed many thousands of miles, appearing to have crossed in nearly every direction the vast plains which lie between the semi-civilized border and the Rocky Mountains, has succeeded in forming a collection which he truly terms " unique," and which ought to be so secured by the purchase of some Government or other, as to be rendered what he fondly calls it, " imperishable." He thus explains the motives which induced him to undertake this labour :—" Having some years since become fully convinced of the rapid decline and certain extinction of the numerous tribes of the North American Indians, and seeing also the vast importance and value which a full pictorial history of these interesting but dying people might be to future ages, I set out alone, unaided and unadvised, resolved (if my life should be spared), by the aid of my brush and my pen, to rescue from oblivion so much of their primitive looks and customs as the industry and ardent enthusiasm of one lifetime could accomplish, and set them up in a gallery, unique and imperishable, for the use and benefit of future ages."

A proof of the utility of his undertaking is the fact that one of the most singularly interesting tribes which he visited, the Mandans, who numbered 2000 souls in 1834, have been since wholly destroyed, not a remnant of their race left—name, and line, and language utterly extinct. Of the other tribes, too, many thousands have perished since the period of his visit by the smallpox, which deadly disease sweeps them off by wholesale ; by the ardent spirits, still deadlier, introduced among them by the traders, and by war. The red man seems doomed to inevitable destruction ; and despite the philanthropist, no long period of time, it is to be feared, will elapse before he will exist only by the aid of the " brush and pen."

Mr. Catlin has made 310 portraits of distinguished individuals of the various tribes, and 200 other paintings illustrative of their manners, games, religious and other customs, as well as portraying some of the most remarkable scenery of the prairies and wilderness. They are roughly executed, but are the more valuable as being evidently faithful transcripts from the life. They occupy the entire of the large room of the Egyptian Hall, covering the walls on either side, whilst in the centre a long table is covered with Indian habiliments and weapons, which likewise hang with bears' and other skins in profusion from the ceiling, whilst the whole is crowned by a wigwam, a veritable wigwam, brought from the foot of the Rocky Mountains. Will or can any one with a spark of curiosity, not to name enthusiasm, in his composition, begrudge a shilling for the sight?

———————

THE COURT JOURNAL.

Catlin's Indian Gallery.—We must confess that, after the many failures of exhibitions analogous to this, we did not go to it prepared either to be pleased or to glean from it any novelty of information; but we were most agreeably disappointed, and can assure our readers that a more attractive exercise for the mind could not well have been devised. We may, without hesitation, describe this immense collection of portraits, landscapes, costumes, and representations of manners and customs, as embracing a view of all the North American Indian tribes (resident in the British and Mexican territories, and those of the United States) now unexterminated! Out of the entire nations swept away by whiskey, smallpox, and the aggressions of the whites, about 300,000 souls remain; and of these the numbers become every year more and more reduced, so that ultimately we may calculate with certainty that they will

" Leave not a wreck behind."

Under this impression Mr. Catlin has done well and wisely to " devote more than eight years of his life to the accomplishment of so great a design " as that of creating their pictorial history.

Mr. Catlin states that every painting has been made from nature, and by his own hand, many of them in the intervals of paddling a canoe, or leading a packhorse through trackless wilds, at the hazard of his life; that he has visited these people in their own villages, and painted their portraits (certificated by the United States authorities) on the spot.

The room in which this exhibition takes place is on the ground-floor of the Egyptian Hall, and is 106 feet in length. In the centre is a very handsome " Crow lodge or wigwam," brought from the foot of the Rocky Mountains. It is made of buffalo-skins garnished and painted. The pine-poles are thirty in number, and the interior will hold eighty persons. On a table near this tent are lances, calumets, tomahawks, scalping-knives, and scalps; and above, men's and women's dresses, bows, spears, shields, moccasins, war-clubs, drums, &c. Around are hung the numerous paintings in oil, comprising portraits, landscapes, ceremonies, games, manual occupations, hunting excursions, councils, and feasts.

The portraits are very characteristic, the men being for the most part ugly, with one or two striking exceptions, and the young women remarkably handsome. The landscapes are clearly painted, and the ceremonies are very amusing in some instances and very horrible in others. Those which please us most are the hunting and travelling sketches, and one or two of " the fury of the fight !" For instance, No. 486, " Bogard, Batiste, and I, chasing a herd of buffalo in high grass, on a Missouri bottom," is one of the most spirited things that can be imagined ; and so also is No. 471, " A Camanchee warrior lancing an Osage at full speed."

The great merit of these oil sketches is their manifest correctness, not to a line or the mere making out of a horse's head or some portion of dress, but to the action and the scene. Not only the portraits, but the landscapes and groups, have a certificate of identity.

We recommend to all the " Descriptive Catalogue," which is very amusing, and is necessary to the elucidation of customs and localities. At the private view to which we were invited on Tuesday there was a very numerous assemblage of persons of distinction.

NEW COURT GAZETTE.

Catlin's Indian Gallery.—This interesting exhibition consists chiefly of portraits of the most distinguished warriors and chiefs of the various tribes, besides views of fine scenery, buffalo hunting, war and other dances ; a vast variety of weapons, dresses, some scalps, a wigwam, &c. The collection also contains some of the females of note, who display attractions of feature and expression which would not discredit the most civilized people. Amongst the chiefs of greatest notoriety here is the celebrated chief " Black Hawk." The eldest and second sons of this chief are here also, and are worthy of the sire from whom they sprung. There are several other distinguished warriors of this tribe and others, amounting to some hundred portraits. We can strongly recommend our readers to attend ; they will then, for the first time, become acquainted with the real manners and customs of these " before-misrepresented people," who are fast sinking from the face of the earth.

LONDON SATURDAY JOURNAL.

Mr. Catlin's Indian Gallery.—In visiting it, indeed, the town-bred admirer of the freedom and grandeur of " savage life" might find somewhat, at first sight, to feed his sentimental fancies. Round the room, on the walls, are portraits of Indians, remarkable specimens of the true animal man; arrayed in their holiday dresses, tricked out in all the variety of savage fancy, and many of them as evidently and consciously "sitting for their portraits," as the most pedantic and affected superficialist of civilization. With these we have many glimpses of the scenery and state of existence connected with " life in the wilds." The far-stretching prairie; the noble river and its " reaches," and " bluffs," and waterfloods; the shaggy bison, whose tremendous aspect makes him fearful, even in the stillness of a picture; the more terrible grisly bear; the Indian " at home," and the the Indian "abroad," with stirring hunting scenes, enough to rouse one's blood, and to make an unfledged adventurer long to dash away, and try one's skill and courage in an encounter with horned monsters, or even that " ugly creature " before whom the " strongest bull goes down."

KIDD'S LONDON JOURNAL.

Catlin's Indian Gallery, Egyptian Hall.—By a visit to this exhibition, every class of the community, old as well as young, will derive much instruction and gratification. Mr. Catlin's representation of the red races of North America, their country, their costumes, their sports, their religious ceremonies, and, in short, their manners and customs, so as to enable us to form a complete idea of them, is deserving of the utmost praise. There are above 500 subjects in these spacious rooms, from a wigwam to a child's rattle; and everything belonging to the various Indian tribes are before the spectator in their actual condition and integrity. There are, besides, a multitude of portraits of the leading warriors, &c., &c., and other pictures of dances, ball-play, ambuscading, fighting; the whole supplying by far the most ample and accurate history of them that has ever been published to the world. No book of travels can approach these realities; and after all we had read of the red men, we confess we are astonished at the many new and important points connected with them which this gallery impressed upon us. We saw more distinctly the links of resemblance between them and other early and distant people; and we had comparisons suggested of a multitude of matters affecting the progress of mankind all over the earth, alike illustrated by similitudes and dissimilitudes.

SCOTSMAN—EDINBURGH.

Mr. Catlin's Lectures on the North American Indians.—Numbers of fashionable persons still continue to attend the Rotunda to inspect the varied curiosities belonging to this interesting tribe. We have much pleasure in publishing the following testimonial from a gentleman well qualified to pronounce an opinion, on the remarkable fidelity and effect of Mr. Catlin's interesting and instructive exhibition :—

" Cottage, Haddington, 15th April, 1843.

" DEAR SIR,—I have enjoyed much pleasure in attending your lectures at the Waterloo Rooms in Edinburgh. Your delineations of the Indian character, the display of beautiful costumes, and the native Indian manners, true to the life, realised to my mind and view, scenes I had so often witnessed in the parts of the Indian countries where I had been ; and for twenty years' peregrinations in those parts, from Montreal to the Great Slave River north, and from the shores of the Atlantic, crossing the Rocky Mountains, to the mouth of the Columbia River, on the Pacific Ocean, west, I had opportunities 'of seeing much. Your lectures and exhibition have afforded me great pleasure and satisfaction, and I shall wish you all that success which you so eminently deserve, for the rich treat which you have afforded in our enlightened, literary, and scientific metropolis.

" I remain, dear Sir, yours very truly,
" To George Catlin, Esq."   " JOHN HALDANE."

The following is an extract of a letter received some days since by a gentleman in Edinburgh, from Mr. James Hargrave, of the Hudson's Bay Company, dated New York Factory, Hudson's Bay, 10th December, 1842 :—

" Should you happen to fall in with ' Catlin's Letters on the North American Indians,' I would strongly recommend a perusal of them for the purpose of acquiring a knowledge of the habits and customs of those tribes among whom he was placed. Catlin's sketches are true to life, and are powerfully descriptive of their appearance and character."

UNITED STATES PRESS.

THE UNITED STATES GAZETTE.

Catlin's Indian Gallery.—The conception and plan of this gallery are in a high degree ingenious and philosophical. While it seems to the careless visitor to be only a very animated representation of some of the most striking incidents in Indian life, it is in fact so contrived as to contain an intelligent and profound exposition of all that characterizes the savage in mind, in memory, and in manners ; a revelation of the form and qualities of his understanding, of the shape and temper of his passions, of his religious impressions and the traditions which have given them their hue, and of the mingled ferocity and fun, barbarity and *bonhomie*, which streak his character. These are the matters that are brought out by a study of these pictures ; and they show, on the part of the originator of this museum, a comprehension and reach of understanding which of themselves merit the name of genius. The execution is as happy as the purpose is judicious. No artist in this country possesses a readier or more graphic pencil ; perhaps no one, since Hogarth, has had in so high a degree the faculty of seizing at a moment the true impression of a scene before his eyes, and transferring it to the canvas. And as a refined and finished portrait-painter, his large picture of Osceola alone sets him on a level with the most accomplished professors in any part of the States, and shows what eminence and what emolument might have been achieved by him had he devoted himself to that narrower branch of his art. The great and unshared merit of these sketches lies in the circumstance that there is nothing either in the grouping or the detail in anywise imaginary, but that every scene which his collection contains was copied by him from life, while the original was before him. Of the tribes thus represented, some have already, in the interval since these drawings, been entirely swept away from the earth, and it is plain that others, who escape that fate, will, as they are more nearly approached by the whites, lose much that is distinctive in their character and habits, and in a few, probably a very few years, the only memorial of the bravery, the sufferings, the toils, sports, customs, dresses, and decorations of the Indians, will be Catlin's Gallery.

We feel great pride in stating that Mr. Catlin is a native of Pennsylvania. His birthplace, we are informed, is the valley of the Wyoming. There, probably, he acquired that fondness for the free wild life of the huntsman and forester that has led him so far from the tame continuance of cities, and has made the privations of that remote existence tolerable. There, too, he must have imbibed in early youth that love of the chace, and that sympathy with its noble excitements, which has made him out of sight the best ex_hibitor of the sports of the West that ever yet employed pen or pencil in illustration of the magnificent diversions that gave a dash of sublimity to the occupation of those dwellers by the sources of the Father of Waters. We, too, have seen something of that stirring Western life, and have had a taste of its delights and dangers, though we pretend not to a tithe of the lore here brought out. We know, perhaps, enough to judge of what is well done in this department, and we can testify strongly to the prodigious superiority of Mr. Catlin in the conception of the hunting-scenes, in the appreciation and selection of its strongest points and most interesting moments, and in the vigour and power with which the whole is presented, over Mr. Irving. Mr. Irving's style is, at all times, nicer and more fastidious than suits our taste ; certainly it is too dainty to be capable of expressing the roughness and energy of those exhibitions. It may be that we ought not to have Indian life at all, but if we are to have it, let us have something of the heartiness and strength which make it what it is, and let there be some harmony between the subject and the manner. In Irving's dialect there are no terms for the utterance of what is most peculiar on those occasions ; the harp-like gentleness of his tones and regularity of his pauses cannot present the hurry, helter-skelter dash and drive of those impetuous onsets and those breathless contests. His descriptions of the buffalo-hunt remind us of Finden's engraving of a ragged peasant, wherein the ravelled coat seems fringed with lace, and the cap seems tasselled with flakes of the ermine. Catlin brings forward the scene in all the rudeness and the raciness of reality.

Upon the whole, Mr. Catlin has accomplished a work which will for ever associate his name in the highest rank of honour, with a subject that will interest the civilized world every year more and more through all coming time. We have learned with great regret that he will certainly take his museum to England in the course of a few weeks. We know too well how it will be valued there, to imagine that it will ever be permitted to come back.

THE PHILADELPHIA GAZETTE.

Catlin's Indian Gallery.—We cannot notice this collection too often. It is one of those productions which illustrate, in an eminent degree, the observation of Playfair, that when the proper time has arrived for some great work to be performed, some individual is raised up by Providence whose position and character and capacity precisely fit him for accomplishing the design. For reasons that will be appreciated by the philosopher, the philanthropist, and the theologian, as well as considerations that address themselves to the curiosity of the man of general knowledge, it was particularly desirable that a full and authentic record should be given to the world of the national characteristics of a race whose history is so peculiar, whose condition is so curious, and whose speedy extinguishment is so certain, as those of the North American Indians. Accordingly, when it is plain that the moment has arrived beyond which the portraiture of their state cannot any longer be delayed, if it would be known that they are in that native predicament which has been in nowise modified by European intercourse, a man appears whose birth in a spot of which the traditions are so strongly interfused with the memory of the Indian (the Wyoming Valley), has caused his imagination to be deeply impressed, even from his earliest youth, by the character and actions of this people; who is endowed by nature with the hand and eye of a painter, and who passes through a professional education which advances his talent to the skill of an accomplished artist, and who has inherited a fortitude of spirit, an elevation of purpose, and a vigour of limb, which render him competent to encounter the dangers, the discouragements, and the difficulties which of necessity lie along the path to the object in question. The man is willing to devote the best years of his life to the task of working out a great picture of those tribes of savages which are separated by 2000 miles from the farthest settlement of his nation.

One of the most remarkable tribes which has yet been found on this continent was that of the Mandans. They were more advanced in the knowledge of domestic comforts, and were distinguished for more intelligence and a higher sense of honour than any of their brethren. They possessed certain very extraordinary and interesting annual religious celebrations, which were in part a commemoration of the Deluge, and contained, amongst other things, an allusion to the twig which the dove brought back from Noah to the earth. Mr. Catlin was the first white man who was ever admitted to inspect these ceremonies in the sacred hall in which they were performed for four days. He made several large and very copious paintings of the scenes which were presented to him; and he sketched almost all that was striking in the character of this tribe. The next year the whole of this nation was swept away by the smallpox; not an individual man, woman, or child survives; and the world possesses no other knowledge of this people or their traditions than is contained in these pictures in the gallery of Catlin. Fortunately they present us with as full and satisfactory a representation as could be desired.

We believe that all who have visited this collection have formed but one opinion as to its interest and excellence. We would remind our readers that this gallery will remain open for their inspection but a short time longer before its final removal to England.

Mr. Catlin's Gallery of Indian Paintings.—We congratulate our citizens on the opportunity they have now presented to them of witnessing the results of Mr. Catlin's labours and travels among the tribes of Aborigines inhabiting the Rocky Mountains and the prairies of "the far West." Mr. Catlin spent many years among these tribes, at the imminent risk of his life, and at an incalculable cost of comfort, solely with the view of taking likenesses and sketches from life and nature, and of representing these "children of the forest" in their own peculiar costumes, and as he found them in their own native wilds.

Of the accuracy of his likenesses we have the most undoubted testimony; and of the sketches of scenery, dances, hunting parties, &c., we may venture to say they are graphic, bold, and free. We know of nothing from which one who has never seen the Indian in his untamed character can derive so accurate a knowledge of these fast-disappearing natives of the soil as from this gallery.

We would throw in a word in favour of the young—let them by all means see this gallery.

THE PHILADELPHIA WEEKLY MESSENGER.

Catlin's Indian Gallery.—Mr. Catlin's gallery of Indian pictures and curiosities has recently been opened at the Arcade for the inspection of the citizens of Philadelphia. In common with other lovers of amusement, we have visited this collection, and have found that it fully justifies whatever has been said by those who visited it in Boston and New York, and described it as the most surprising, entertaining, and instructive exhibition which the efforts of American genius have ever brought before the country. . . . .

In this stage of human knowledge Catlin resolved to devote the labours of his life to exploring the condition, customs, character, and conduct of this people, and to bring home a record of their being, which should be to the world a possession for ever. He has fulfilled this purpose. He has lifted the veil on which was written "ignorance," and he has shown to his countrymen the peculiarities of a life which is competent to instruct philosophy with conclusions that it has never dreamt of, and entertain curiosity beyond the compass of the wildest fables.

THE PHILADELPHIA EVENING POST.

The subjects of Mr. Catlin's pencil, his histories and delineations, are of a noble race. The Camanchees, the Mandans, the Pawnees, the Blackfeet, Sioux, Crows, Assiniboins, Omahaws, &c. &c., who have not yet sunk beneath the withering associations of white people, who on their native prairies stalk with noble pride and independence, who manufacture their own dresses from the skins of the mountain sheep and buffalo, and use their spears, bows and arrows, in preference to fire-arms, and with courtly pride and hospitality welcomed the artist, and honoured him for his talents of delineation, as a nobleman of nature, infinitely superior to the mercenary race of traders and Indian agents, who plunder and cheat them when opportunity offers.

The Indian is truly fortunate in having so faithful and industrious a champion, historian, and painter as Mr. Catlin, who will no doubt rescue their name from the mass of trading libellers that have so long corrupted and then slandered them. With a remarkable assiduity and perseverance he has devoted many years of his life, and much pecuniary means, in preparing a magnificent collection of their dresses, instruments, ornaments, portraits, &c. For ourselves, we anticipate one of the most original and curious works that has been issued from the press for many years, for Mr. Catlin has struck out a new path to fame and fortune, and while he leaves a memorial of the true Indian uncorrupted native character, he makes a lasting name for himself.

THE NEW YORK EVENING STAR.

Catlin's Indian Gallery.— We would remind those who have not yet visited this extraordinary collection, that it will be closed after the lapse of a single week, and that it will never again be exhibited in America. There will never be presented to our citizens an opportunity of inspecting one of the most remarkable and entertaining works that the genius and labour of an individual has created in this age and country ; and those who neglect this occasion of examining this most curious monument of talent and enterprise will have missed for ever one of the noblest spectacles at which patriotism can refresh its pride, or reason can inform its curiosity. Mr. Catlin has received permission from the English Chancellor of the

Exchequer to import his museum into England free from duty, a saving to him of about two thousand dollars. He will sail for that country in the course of the summer, and the indifference of America will have surrendered to her rival what the labour of an American had created for herself.

In our opinion nothing could redound more to the patriotism, national pride, and honour of our country, than the purchase by Congress of this rare collection of aboriginal curiosities, to enrich a national museum at Washington. Such an object is by no means unworthy the attention of the nation; and as in the lapse of a few more years all traces of this interesting people will have passed away, or but a small remnant of them remain in their wilderness asylum almost beyond the ken of civilized man, such a depository of the relics peculiar to this wonderful people would possess an interest which would be immeasurably enhanced when their existence as a nation was for ever blotted out, as from present indications it inevitably must be. Located at the capital, members of Congress and public-spirited citizens of the far West could from time to time contribute to the common stock, until, in the course of a few years, a national museum of Indian curiosities would be formed to perpetuate their manners, customs, and costumes, that would be a monument to the taste and public spirit of the nation to the latest generation. The facilities possessed by the Government for the successful prosecution of so noble a design commends it forcibly to the consideration of Congress. And as it is not yet too late, we trust, to secure the co-operation of Mr. Catlin in furtherance of an object so congenial with his views, and which would at the same time ensure him a just reward for his enthusiastic devotion to this noble enterprise, without being compelled to seek it in a foreign land, we would fain hope that his stay among us would be prolonged until measures were taken to call the attention of Congress to the subject. Should this suggestion be favourably received, and it be found that the engagements of Mr. Catlin do not preclude its being carried out, we trust the project will enlist warmly the interest of our public-spirited and patriotic citizens at an early day.

We have already spoken once or twice at some length of the value and interest of this exhibition. It addresses itself to the feelings of the rudest observer, and engages the imagination of the idlest visitor, by revealing, with amazing copiousness, the whole interior life and customs of a people singular and striking beyond the speculations of romance, and so separated by position, by distrust, and enmity, that no one has ever before seen what this man has sketched. To the philosopher, the philanthropist, the moralist, and the man of science, it presents matter equally attractive and important, in those higher regards with which they are conversant, with that which amuses the fancy of the rude. By all it will be found a storehouse of wonders, which will surprise the mind in present observation, and gratify the thoughts in all future recollection.

THE UNITED STATES GAZETTE.

Catlin's Indian Gallery.—I am grieved to see that this noble product of American genius is in a few days to leave its native soil, without any effective efforts having been made to ensure its permanent return.

I did hope that individual disposition would be matured into common action, and that at any price a treasure so honourably, so peculiarly American, would be kept from passing into European hands.

Is it *yet* too late to avert such a result ? Cannot we yet prevent such a spot upon our city's bright escutcheon ?

With what feelings will our descendants enter some department of the British Museum, or some *Palais* or *Musée* in the city of Bourbons, to see a treasure thus surrendered by their fathers ? Can they boast of Catlin's *powers* as a national glory ? Others can point to the possession of the *fruits* of them as our national disgrace.

Whether in justice or in wrong, our treatment of the Indian nations has been a reproach to us through the world. Let it not be in a stranger's power to show how noble and how elevated a race we are thus accused of having injured.

Let it not be said that while America has extirpated them from existence, France or England has preserved the only memorial of what they were.

It is at all events yet in the power of each to *visit* the collection in his own country. Let no man who bears the honoured name of an American fail to do so. He has no idea of what the rude forefathers of his forests were. He has never had Indian existence in its varied forms presented to him in such life-like reality, never before so much relating to this people so systematically brought together. In the labours of Catlin's hand and in the achievements of his pencil, we and our descendants must now look for the history of our national ancestry.

THE AMERICAN SENTINEL.

Catlin's Gallery.—Mr. Catlin's extraordinary exhibition of Indian curiosities and paintings will be closed, as we learn from his advertisement, in the course of a few days. This is the last exhibition that will be made of this wonderful collection in the United States, as it will be taken to England at once and there be disposed of. We trust that every one who has a spark of rational curiosity or national pride will visit a work which, above every other that we are acquainted with, is fitted to gratify both.

We do not think that, all the circumstances being taken together, there has been produced in this age any work more wonderful or more valuable. The hardy enterprise of the forest-born adventurer must unite with the tact and skill a very accomplished diplomatist to carry a man through the scenes which Catlin has visited; and the observation of a philosophical genius must be joined to the ready skill of a thoroughly furnished artist, to bring back from those scenes of savage life such illustrations as Catlin now presents. This age will send forth no such man; and should such appear at any future period, he will be too late for the performance of this task.

This museum possesses in itself more to amaze and delight than any work to which we can point. The very spirit of savage existence is unsphered before us as we contemplate these graphic sketches. We feel the freedom and enthusiasm which mark the life of the hunter and the warrior of the west, fascinating above all the attractions of civilized being. We are pleased, astonished, charmed by the variety and strangeness of the spectacles brought before us.

No parent should suffer himself to feel that he has done justice to his children until he has taken them to view this gallery, which will never again be open to their inspection. No citizen should suffer it to leave the country until he has fully possessed himself of all that it reveals respecting the aborigines of his country.

THE UNITED STATES GAZETTE.

Mr. Catlin's Views of the Far West.—There can be no mistake or exaggeration in pronouncing the exhibition of these views of the scenery and natural history of the western country the most important and interesting object for public attention which has ever been offered to the eastern division of the United States.

It has been with a fascinating degree of feeling and adventure that Mr. Catlin has gone over the immense plains of the west, and employed himself with pallet and pencil among all the scenes he could select of landscape and natural history, and with the western natives, and to sketch people, views, and objects which have formed so much of its distinctive character, by which he may rescue and retain the almost incredible appearances and habits of a race of men and animals now fast disappearing in the march of civilization, upon the remembrance and record of history.

The collection of Portraits, made of upwards of 300 persons, forms a representation from forty-eight Indian nations, chiefly between the settled part of our country and the Rocky Mountains, among which are the Sacs, Osage, Pawnee, Camanchee, Sioux, Mandans, Blackfeet, Shawnee, Cherokee, Seneca, and Seminoles; and of these, the portraits of Osceola, Micanopeah, Keokuk, Black Hawk, Io-way, Red Jacket, Co-ee-ha-jo, King Philip, John Ross, with several of their wives and children, will always be prominent in the references of American history.

In addition to these important objects of personal consideration, the peculiar and correct representations and appearances of the general western country are prominent, and are all of a highly novel and beautiful character.

The views of rivers, towns, settlements, mountains, prairies, and water-falls, and animals, are generally those which have never been before presented to us. They have been taken in upwards of 200 oil paintings coloured to nature, and consist of the most important localities reaching to the Rocky Mountains, finished on the spot with a fidelity of delineation and picturesque effect which would be creditable to an artist of very high attainments with all the "appliances and means" afforded by the best accommodation and leisure.

THE PHILADELPHIA SATURDAY COURIER.

Catlin's Indian Gallery.—In a late number we took notice of the vast and wonderful assemblage of pictures and curiosities by which Mr. Catlin has contrived to bring before our eyes the fullness of the life of the Western Indians. We would again urge upon our citizens, as Americans, and as valuing curious information and refined pleasure, to give this gallery a visit. There is not in our land, nor in any part of Europe which we have visited, anything of the kind more extraordinary or more interesting. The galleries illustrative of national character and antiquities which are to be found in London, Paris, Florence, and other cities, have been collected by the power of great kings; and the outlay of immense treasure, and the apparatus of negotiations, and special ministers, and resident consuls, and agents innumerable, have been requisite to their completion. This is the work of a single individual, a man without fortune and without patronage, who created it with his own mind and hand, without aid and even against countenance; and who sustained the lonely toils of eight years in a region fearful and forbidding beyond the conceptions of civilized life, in order to present his countrymen with a work which he knew they would one day value as the most remarkable thing they owned, and which he was assured that no spirit and no skill but his own could accomplish. He may point to his magnificent collection, which now receives the admiration of every eye, and may say with honest pride, "Alone I did it!" But without the abatement of a reference to the circumstances of the case and without any qualification of any sort, we declare that if this museum is less gorgeous and less stately than those imperial galleries which give fame even to the capitals of England and France, it is not less instructive or entertaining than the greatest of them. Of the enterprise, the free genius, the noble self-dependence, the stern endurance, and indomitable perseverance which our republican system glories in inspiring and cherishing, there is no nobler, and there will be no more abiding monument, than Catlin's Indian Gallery.

PHILADELPHIA SATURDAY NEWS.

Catlin's Indian Gallery—We have visited it repeatedly, and have studied its contents with close attention, as the best exposition of savage character and life that has ever been given to the world; and the result of our impressions is, that whether we regard the historical and philosophic value of this museum, its strangeness and interest as matter of entertainment, or the wonderful toil and difficulty that must have attended its formation, there is not in our country a work more honourable to its author, or more deserving of the esteem and admiration of the community. The hardships of Indian existence are brought before us with a bold effect; the few refinements by which it is comforted are impressively presented; the labours by which it is sustained are shown; and the romance which makes it charming is brilliantly and copiously exhibited. The gallery is a complete and fascinating panorama of savage life; and all who have the smallest interest in the wild and stirring existence of the Indian hunter should hasten to contemplate this splendid picture. No man has tasted these scenes of daring and peril with half the sympathy and understanding of Mr. Catlin; and neither in the delicate touches of Irving, nor the more vigorous drawings of Hoffman, is there anything like the intelligence and interest of these animated sketches. Whoever would know to what sounds of glee and exultation the northern forests, even at this hour, are echoing, or with what spectacles of merriment or toil the flatness of the prairie is enlivened, must view and ponder over this collection.

Mr. Catlin intends to remove this museum to England very soon, and from that country it will probably never return. This, therefore, is the last opportunity which Americans will have of ever inspecting this most curious assemblage. We exhort every one who is a lover either of rare entertainment or strange knowledge to lose no time in visiting this gallery.

THE AMERICAN DAILY ADVERTISER.

Catlin's Indian Gallery.—The collection embraces a wonderful extent and variety of national history, likewise an exact and discriminating range throughout the different tribes. They are all classed with the method and arrangement of a philosopher, developed and associated with the vivacity of a dramatist, and personated, defined, and coloured with the eye and hand of a painter. Rarely, indeed, would one man be found who could do all this; still more rarely a man, who to these various offices and talents would add the courage, the patience, and the taste to become an eye-witness of his subjects, and above all, would possess the industry and the veracity to represent them to others, and thus to command credibility and admiration.

I hope my fellow-citizens will give this exhibition their repeated attention. They will find in it much more than has ever been combined before. It will greatly abridge their labours in reading, nay, it will tell them what books do not teach; and it will impress upon their senses and upon their memories the living portraits of a race, distinguished by inextinguishable ardour, unbounded ingenuity, and indomitable determination—a race now fast eluding the projects of the politician, the researches of the curious, and soon to cease from demanding even the sympathies of the humane and conscientious.

We learn that Mr. Catlin is soon to embark for England, where encouragement is offered to his remarkable talents and energy, and we sincerely wish him the rewards due to native genius, exemplary diligence, and moral integrity and refinement.

PHILADELPHIA INQUIRER.

Catlin's Gallery.—We called the attention of our readers some days ago to Catlin's Indian Gallery, now exhibiting in this city. This collection is in every respect so remarkable and interesting, that we again bring it before the notice of the community.

Mr. Catlin visited nearly fifty different tribes of Indians, and resided familiarly among them for several years. He made their habits and character his exclusive study. With the eye of a poet, the judgment of a man of rare sagacity, and the hand of an accomplished artist, he saw and scrutinized, and sketched the forms, the feats, the entire style of life of the varied nations with whom he had made his home. The general features of this strange and most interesting people are presented to us in this collection with a copiousness and variety which could only be attained by one who had devoted the enthusiasm of years to a task, to which he had, in the first instance, brought extraordinary talents. Whatever met his watchful glance that was striking or peculiar in the religious ceremonies, the warlike demonstrations, the festive celebrations of peace and leisure, the separate acts and social habits of the wanderers of the distant wilds of the west, was instantly transferred to his canvas, and fixed in living colours on the very spot where the scene was shown. Accordingly we have here illustrations of the mode in which almost every thing, which is common or curious, usual or occasional, among the tribes is performed. The chace, which there has no meaner object than the "stately buffalo," is before us in full and numerous portraiture; the rousing of the herd in the centre of some endless prairie, the reckless vehemence of the pursuit by the wild horse and the wilder hunter, the mad dashing of the fearless sportsman into the midst of the monstrous throng, with nothing but bow and knife; the unhorsing of some, who roll trampled under foot, and of others who are tossed high into the air; the final capture and death of the huge victim of the sport, all these are presented to us in the freshness and freedom of the very scenes themselves of this

magnificent excitement.   Then there are dances of an art and an intricacy
that might instruct Almack's itself; the bear dance, in which, clothed
in skins, they imitate the postures and movements of that animal; the
buffalo dance, in which they are masked in the skulls which they
have taken in the hunt; the eagle dance, which mimics the attitude of
that bird; the dance on the snow in peculiar shoes; and the numerous
dances of war.   Then we have bold and admirable sketches of the scenery
of the prairies and the hills 2000 miles above St. Louis, presenting a
richness and brilliance of verdure of which the Atlantic resident has never
formed a conception.   In short, it would be difficult to point out a single
particular in which the sketches of this ardent and able painter do not
furnish the fullest and most valuable information about the western continent and its inhabitants.   There are portraits, likewise, of all the remarkable persons whom the artist encountered in his rambles, painted on the
spot, in their actual dresses and natural positions, certified as rigidly accurate, in every instance, by officers of the United States, who were present
at the time.

But sketches are not all that this unique collection consists of.   There
is a large number of the dresses of the chiefs and women, rich and curious
to a very great degree, implements of war and of social life—articles by
which friendship is promoted and leisure is amused.

PHILADELPHIA HERALD AND SENTINEL.

Catlin's Indian Gallery is one of the most curious and interesting collections ever brought before the public.   The portraits of the chiefs and
warriors constitute perhaps the least striking portion of the gallery; although the natural freedom and boldness of the attitudes, and the life-like
variety and expression of the countenances, caught with a rare felicity by
the accomplished artist, render them immeasurably superior in attraction
and value to anything of that kind ever before presented to the community.
They were all sketched on the spots of their residence, and in the characteristic attire of their tribes; and the certificates of different United States
officers, attached to the back of each picture, testify to the accuracy and
completeness of each individual portraiture.   The largest and by far the
most engaging and peculiar part of the collection, consists of sketches of
groups occupied in the various games, sports, and diversions, by which the
monotony of savage life is amused.

Mr. Catlin visited forty-eight different tribes, and was domesticated
amongst them for eight years; and whenever any spectacle of merriment,
or business, or religion was got up, the painter drew apart from the company, and producing the canvas which was always in readiness, seized
with an Hogarthian quickness and spirit the outlines and the impression
of the scene before him, and has perpetuated for the gratification of posterity the faithful and vivid likenesses of some of the most extraordinary

acts and incidents which the history of man can exhibit. Sketched with a distinctness and a particularity which indicate an uncommon degree of talent and skill on the part of the artist, we find among these paintings almost everything that is characteristic in the life and conduct of the Indian: the energetic dance, marked by a science and a significance, unknown to the amusements of more cultivated nations,—the hunt of the buffalo, with its impressive incidents of danger and daring—the religious rite—the military council—the game—the fight—the voluntary torture by which the "Stoic of the woods" displays his hardihood of nerve and spirit —and the grotesque gaiety which marks the occasional mirthfulness of a nature usually so much restrained. All these are brought before us with a fidelity of delineation attested by the certificates of the most competent and reputable witnesses, and animation and interest acknowledged by all who have approached them.

This collection is not only unique, as it concerns the particular people whose state and character it illustrates; but, as throwing light upon a grade and condition of the human race of which little has ever been known, it possesses an importance novel and unparticipated: for it has never happened, in the history of the world, that a savage people has been approached and depicted with this intelligent completeness. He who would learn what are the dispositions and the faculties which belong to the mind and heart of man, in the mere rudeness of his natural state, will find more satisfactory sources of information in this Indian gallery than in the fullest descriptions of travellers or the astutest schemes of metaphysicians.

THE PHILADELPHIA GAZETTE.

Catlin's Indian Gallery.—It is a remarkable circumstance, and one very characteristic of the energy of this age, that the same year and almost the same month should have witnessed the completion of three independent collections, each of which, after its way, gives us a complete portraiture of the nation to which it refers. What Mr. Dunn's figures have accomplished for China, and Mr. Wilkinson's drawings have done for Egypt, Mr. Catlin's paintings have performed for the Indian tribes. The first of these has excited the admiration of America, the second has won the applause of Europe; if the last is less brilliant than the one, it is more lively than the other, and it is not less complete than either. It is not merely a minute and thorough description of a nation whose situation and history render everything that relates to it in the highest degree curious and personal to Americans, but it addresses itself to the admiration and instruction of every philosophic mind as an encyclopædia picture of the savage state. While no histories present us with such copious information of the characteristics of those particular tribes, which are intimately and eternally connected with our annals, no speculative treatises contain anything like the knowledge here garnered of the qualities and attributes of that condition which is called the state of nature. The eye of childhood and the mind of age are alike astonished and informed by the spectacles here strikingly presented by this unrivalled work.

Mr. Catlin is a native of Pennsylvania, and has therefore peculiar claims upon the attention of Philadelphians. We know and are persuaded that when this Museum, after the very few days allotted to its continuance here, is closed and removed for ever from our land, it will be a matter of deep and permanent regret to all who now fail to visit it, that they have lost the sight.

THE PHILADELPHIA EVENING STAR.

Catlin's Indian Gallery.—This interesting museum of curiosities, collected by Mr. Catlin, during a residence of more than eight years among forty tribes of Indians, and of sketches painted by him, illustrative of their habits and customs, is now exhibited at the Arcade in this city. It is an eloquent and illustrious witness of the genius, disinterestedness, and toil of the person who brought it together. Those productions of Mr. Catlin's pencil, which were given to the world many years since, evinced his ability to rank, at some day, with the first artists of this country ; but instead of devoting himself to those lucrative branches of his profession, which would have gained him a sure return of wealth, he resolved, at the bidding of an enthusiasm, perhaps inspired by the legends of his native valley of Wyoming, to dedicate his life to the great and generous purpose of presenting to his countrymen a satisfactory portraiture of a nation which had so interesting a connexion with their own history, and whose condition has always produced so strong an impression upon the imagination of Americans. Alone and unsupported, save by a dauntless spirit, he turned towards the western forests to seek the Indian in his boundless home.

> " The general garden, where all steps may roam,
> Whose nature owns a nation for her child,
> Exulting in the enjoyment of the wild."

The perils of more than a Ulyssean voyage were encountered before the artist could feel that his object was accomplished, and before he would permit himself to return to his family and friends.

We have devoted much time and a close attention to the sketches which Mr. Catlin has brought back ; and we are convinced that, severe as were the labours and privations to which he was subject, they were less than the value of this collection. Whoever will study the numerous and varied representations here given of savage life, and will reflect how complete a picture is presented of a most peculiar and unknown race, will be persuaded, we think, that no greater accession has been made to the sum of human knowledge and human entertainment, in this age and country, than is produced by this Museum. The philosophy of Indian character is revealed with curious distinctness by one portion of the paintings, while another class presents the picturesque of that existence with singular spirit. Many striking suggestions for the history of civility, and many valuable metaphysical considerations, are prompted by a survey of these illustrations of the intelligence and the instincts of this people ; and any man who would taste the poetry of this wild life, will find enough to satisfy him in the animated exhibitions of the hunt, the march, and the fight, which are here brought before his eyes. In Mr. Irving's very graphic descriptions of the amusements of the prairie, there is nothing half so bold and stirring as the noble pictures which here bring the adventures of the buffalo-hunt before us, or the terrors of the fight with the grisly bear.

THE PENNSYLVANIAN.

Catlin's Indian Gallery. — We alluded briefly a few days since to Catlin's Indian Gallery, now open in the saloon at the Arcade, and we again call attention to it as one of the most gratifying exhibitions of the day, to all who feel the slightest interest in the aborigines of our country, or desire to become acquainted with the topographical features of the great western wild. This collection is the result of years of toil and privation, sustained by a rare and commendable enthusiasm. Mr. Catlin, who is an artist of much ability, and is likewise in other respects well fitted for the task which he volutarily assumed, devoted himself to a study of the Indian character, and steadily followed out his great object for a considerable length of time. He has visited many of the tribes who yet roam in their native wildness, and he became as it were domesticated among them to study their habits and dispositions, encountering all the perils and privations which necessarily attend an enterprise of this nature. In the course of his rambles, he made paintings of every thing calculated to give a vivid impression to others of the persons, events, and scenes which fell under his notice, and the result is a magnificent collection of portraits and views of the most interesting character, made still more attractive by an immense variety of Indian dresses, arms, and utensils of many kinds, which, with the illustrative scenes, give a clear idea of aboriginal characteristics, and form a pleasing evidence of the results which can be achieved by the untiring perseverance of a single man. Mr. Catlin has in this way made a contribution to American history which must gain for him an enduring fame. It should form the nucleus of a national museum, that posterity may have some relics of a people doomed to speedy destruction, as much by their own inflexible nature as by the rolling tide of civilization.

THE PHILADELPHIA GAZETTE.

Catlin's Indian Gallery.—We could scarcely recommend a more pleasing and instructive collection than this to the notice of the community. It is what only a Catlin, with his enthusiasm and perseverance, could have accomplished. To him the study of nature is most appropriate in her great hall or cathedral :—

> " That vast cathedral, boundless as our wonder,
>   Whose quenchless lamps the sun and moon supply ;
>   Its choir the winds and waves ; its organ thunder ;
>   Its dome the sky."

The boundless woods have been his home, and dwellers of the wilderness the sitters for his art. So far as Indian life is concerned, the reader will find a little of every thing in Catlin's gallery ; not of faces merely, but of grand western life and scene.

THE WORLD.

Catlin's Indian Gallery.—I visited this collection with expectations very highly excited by the strong and renewed expressions of admiration which it had received from the press in New York and Boston ; but my anticipations had fallen below the reality in degree as much as they had differed from it in kind. I had supposed that it was merely an assemblage of the portraits of distinguished Indian chieftains, instead of being, as we find that it is, a very complete and curious tableau of the life and habits of the strange and interesting races which once inhabited the soil we now possess. Mr. Catlin's advertisement does no justice to the character of his collection. He does not state himself. He is a person of lofty genius and disinterested ambition, and he has abhorred to tarnish the purity of his self-respect by even claiming his own.

Mr. Catlin spent eight years in the most intimate intercourse with the tribes which occupy the territory lying 2000 miles above St. Louis. His only purpose in visiting these remote and secluded nations was to transfer to his canvas faithful representations of those scenes of conduct which were most characteristic of that people, and those personal traits which would best transmit the memory of the savage to times which would no longer witness his existence. This design he fulfilled by copying on the spot pictures of the sports, fights, business, and religious ceremonies which passed before his sight ; and the gallery which he now opens to the community, revives before the gaze of refinement, the whole condition and qualities of the wild and far-roaming occupants of the prairies and forests. An attentive examination of his museum has led us to the opinion that this is one of the most striking triumphs that the pencil has ever achieved ; for while the brush of Lawrence preserves the likeness of an individual, that of Catlin has perpetuated the portraits of a nation. Let every American visit this exhibition ; let every one who would be informed or entertained give it his protracted study. The more it is examined the more it will gratify.

FRENCH PRESS.

CONSTITUTIONNEL du 22 Juin.

Le museé Catlin est une des collections les plus curieuses qu'on ait vues à Paris, tant à cause du caractère naïf de la peinture, qu'à cause de l'originalité des sujets qu'elle représente.

M. Catlin a donc rapporté de son voyage aux Montagnes Rocheuses quatre à cinq cents toiles, portraits ou paysages, tous peints d'après nature. Parmi ces portraits, il y a des figures d'une beauté, d'une élégance superbes. Il y a des profils, le croirait-on, qui rappellent le type grec ou l'Antinoüs. Bien plus, dans les scènes de danse ou de combat, dans les fêtes ou les assemblées de tribus, on remarque très souvent des personnages dont la pose, l'attitude, le geste, ressemblent tout-à-fait à l'antique. Cela n'est pas, d'ailleurs, si surprenant pour qui veut réflechir au caractère de la beauté antique. Qu'est-ce donc qui distingue l'art grec entre tous les arts? n'est-ce pas la simplicité et le naturel ? Les artistes grecs avaient le bonheur de trouver d'abord autour d'eux toutes les conditions premières de race, de climat, de civilisation, qui favorisent le développement de la beauté ; et secondement, ils laissaient faire la nature et ne torturaient jamais le mouvement de leur modèle. Il n'y a dans toute la statuaire grecque que cinq ou six poses peut-être qui sont le type de tous les autres mouvemens. Les hommes rapprochés de la nature ne se tortillent pas comme les civilisés. Le calme est d'ordre naturel ; et c'est là un des premiers élémens de la beauté antique qu'on retrouve dans la *beauté sauvage.*

Les paysagistes pourraient bien aussi étudier avec profit la peinture facile et vraie de M. Catlin qui n'est pourtant initié à aucun des procédés scabreux de l'art civilisé. M. Catlin peint tranquillement du premier coup, en mettant un ton juste et franc à côté d'un autre, et il ne paraît pas qu'il revienne jamais ni par glacis ni par empâtement. Mais son sentiment est si vif et en quelque sorte si sincère, son exécution si naïve et si spontanée, que l'effet, vu juste, est rendu juste. Il a fait ainsi des ciels d'une transparence et d'une lumière bien difficile à obtenir, même pour les praticiens les plus habiles des lointains d'une finesse rare et bien balancés entre la terre et le ciel. En présence de cette nature toute nouvelle, de ces formes singulières du pays, de cette couleur du ciel et des arbres, si originale, un peintre de profession se serait bien tourmenté pour exprimer toutes ces belles choses, et il y aurait sans doute mis beaucoup trop de ses préjugés et de sa personnalité civilisée. Il est très heureux que M. Catlin ait été seulement assez peintre pour faire tout bonnement sur la toile ce qu'il voyait, sans parti pris d'avance et sans convention européenne. Nous avons ainsi des steppes dont nous ne nous faisions pas une image, des buffles prodigieux, des chasses fantastiques, et une foule d'aspects et de scènes plus intéressantes l'une que l'autre. Ici, c'est un marais vert tendre, entouré d'arbres sveltes et légers. Là, c'est la plaine infinie avec ses grandes herbes mouvantes comme les vagues d'une mer sans repos, et l'on aperçoit une course diabolique de quelques animaux dont on a peine à distinguer la forme et qui fendent l'immensité.   C'est un buffle poursuivi par un cavalier penché sur la crinière de son cheval sauvage ; mais au-dessus des herbes profondes, on ne voit que les épaules bossues du buffle et les oreilles dressées du cheval.   Quel drame !   Où vont-ils ? où s'arrêteront-ils ?   Quelques autres tableaux présentent les aventures de la navigation et de la guerre, des chasses où les hommes, couverts de peaux de loup, s'avancent à quatre pattes pour surprendre les buffles, où les chevaux sauvages sont enveloppés de lacets perfides, des cérémonies religieuses où de volontaires martyrs se font pendre et torturer en l'honneur du Grand Esprit.

LE CHARIVARI, Paris, 1845.

Il y avait là une magnifique collection, un musée rare, que dis-je ? unique et précieux, amassé à grands frais, à grand' peine, par un artiste passionné et patient, par M. Catlin, voyageur aussi intrépide que peintre naïf et que sincère historien.   Ce musée est à la fois une collection d'objets d'art et un recueil de notes scientifiques sur une classe d'hommes qui diminue de jour en jour devant les empiètemens de la civilisation, et qui dans cinquante ans aura complètement disparu du globe.   C'est le portrait aussi fidèle que possible, le daguerréotype d'un monde qu'on ne retrouvera plus, et le gouvernement l'a laissé partir, l'a laissé perdre ; il n'a pas même senti la nécessité de l'acquérir. Il n'a fait ni une offre ni un prix à l'artiste qu'il eût récompensé ainsi qu'il devait l'être de dix ans d'études et d'efforts. Tout le monde y aurait gagné : le peintre qui craint devoir éparpiller un jour le résultat de tant de peines et de travaux, eût été heureux de le voir conservé, concentré, consacré à jamais, en lieu sûr, à la science et à l'art.

L'OBSERVATEUR, Oct. 9, 1845.

Le Musée-Indien de M. Catlin.—Lorsque la civilisation recule partout les bornes de son horison et resserre dans un étroit espace les peuplades nomades et sauvages qui se refusent au joug de la domination européenne, ce n'est pas sans un certain intérêt qu'on visite le Musée Indien de M. Catlin. En voyant la collection du célèbre touriste, l'esprit se refuse à croire que ce soit là l'œuvre d'un seul homme.   Et cependant, rien n'est plus vrai.   Explorateur hardi, M. Catlin a passé huit années de sa vie à parcourir les Montagnes Rocheuses et les parties les plus reculées de l'Amérique septentrionale ; artiste enthousiaste, il a bravé les dangers, supporté les fatigues et les privations de toutes sortes pour mener à bonne fin son audacieuse entreprise.   Il a visité les Indiens dans leurs wig-wams ; il les a suivis dans leurs chasses ; il a étudié leurs mœurs, leurs coutumes, ne se laissant arrêter par aucun obstacle, tenant quelquefois son pinceau d'une main, tandis qu'il conduisait son canot de l'autre.   Aussi, ne nous montrerons nous pas d'une grande sévérité à l'égard de ses tableaux ; ce n'est, pour la plupart, que des esquisses faites à grands traits et dont le mérite consiste dans la vérité des costumes et des sites et dans la ressemblance parfaite des portraits, ainsi que l'attestent les certificats les plus flatteurs délivrés au hardi voyageur, sur les lieux mêmes, par des personnes dont la véracité et la compétence ne sauraient être mises en doute.

La collection que M. Catlin a rapportée de ses excursions est d'autant plus curieuse qu'elle est unique en son genre. Elle se compose de plus de cinq cents tableaux représentant des portraits, des paysages, et des scènes de mœurs qui sont comme une histoire descriptive de ces races primitives, que la guerre et la chasse déciment chaque jour, et qui disparaîtront sans doute bientôt de la surface du globe.

Quant à M. Catlin, nous devrons à ses explorations et à sa collection de ne pas voir tomber dans l'oubli les mœurs, les costumes, et la physionomie de ces races, qui dans quelques siècles n'existeront peut-être plus qu'à l'état de souvenir.

MONITEUR DE L'ARMÉE.

M. Catlin, c'est le nom de cet artiste plein de résolution et de persévérance, a passé huit années au milieu des villages Indiens et sur la prairie ; il a connu tous les chefs des tribus et les guerriers les plus renommés ; il a assisté aux chasses dangereuses, aux jeux animés et quelquefois sanglans des sauvages ; il a observé leurs coutumes et leurs superstitions ; il a recueilli leurs traditions orales, et tout ce qu'il a vu, sous les yeux des Indiens, ses hôtes, et souvent au péril de sa vie, il l'a représenté sur la toile, écrivant ainsi d'après nature toute l'histoire de populations que la guerre, et surtout les liqueurs fortes et la petite vérole, font décroître d'année en année dans une progression si rapide, que l'on peut prévoir que d'ici à cinquante ans, la civilisation les pressant d'ailleurs et les refoulant vers les montagnes, il ne restera peut-être plus d'elles que de très petits groupes ou des individus isolés destinés à disparaître bientôt de la terre. Les peaux rouges ne pouvant laisser aucune trace durable de leur passage sur le globe,—car si quelques tribus ont des cabanes de terre, aucune n'a élevé de monumens qui puissent témoigner de leur existence auprès des générations à venir—les résultats que M. Catlin a si heureusement obtenus dans une entreprise si hasardeuse ne sauraient être trop appréciés par les amis de la science, les ethnographes et les artistes.

QUOTIDIENNE, Paris.

M. Catlin est un peintre plein de conscience et de talent, et un voyageur aussi intrépide qu'intelligent, qui a passé huit ans de sa vie à explorer les tribus sauvages du nord de l'Amérique et les rives du Missouri. Les efforts et les travaux de cet Américain méritent qu'on les examine avec attention, et qu'on les recommande à l'appréciation des artistes et des savans.

GALIGNANI, 1845.

The Catlin Museum.—The utter strangeness of this remarkable exhibition —displaying, it may be said, a living *tableau* of the customs and habitudes of a race who, while the march of time has been effecting the most extraordinary changes in the great family of mankind, still remain in a primitive state of nature—at first misunderstood by the Parisian public, has now become an object of general and intense curiosity. Mr. Catlin's collection of the arms and utensils of the various tribes, with their wigwams, the identical habitations which have ere now sheltered them from the tempest in the depths of some North American forest, they carry back the mind, as it were, to the infancy of the human species, " when wild in woods the noble savage ran." The illusion, for it nearly amounts to that, is wonderfully aided by an examination of Catlin's sketches, taken upon the spot, and often in the midst of the dangers he has depicted with spirited fidelity. These paintings, boldly and rapidly thrown off, are illustrative of every phase of savage existence. We have to thank Mr. Catlin for an insight into the lives and history of this most interesting race, which has all the charms of the wildest romance, but which books can never supply.

GAZETTE DE FRANCE.

Grace à M. Catlin, l'anéantissement de ces intéressantes peuplades n'est plus possible : leurs mœurs, leurs coutumes, leurs usages, seront sans doute de sa part l'objet d'un travail consciencieux et approfondi, en même temps que ces pinceaux conserveront les traits et la physionomie de ces Peaux Rouges, que déjà le célèbre romancier Américain nous avait fait connaître. Non content d'avoir transporté en Europe les armes, les costumes, les tentes, et tous les instrumens qui servent à l'usage des Indiens, et qui forment un singulier contraste avec notre civilisation, M. Catlin a voulu que des monumens plus durables conservassent le souvenir de ces sauvages de l'Amérique du Nord ; il a dessiné lui-même les portraits des Indiens les plus remarquables, leurs danses, leur manière de fare la chasse, et leurs expéditions guerrières.

On ne peut assez admirer comment un homme a pu tracer tant de figures et de paysages, pris sur les lieux mêmes, dans des courses souvent très longues et très fatigantes. C'est là un prodige de la science. Assis au milieu des sauvages, M. Catlin employait son temps à retracer sur la toile tout ce qu'il voyait. Aussi peut-on être assuré d'avoir sous les yeux la représentation exacte des costumes des sauvages du Nouveau-Monde. Si quelques-uns de ces portraits ne sont pas des œuvres d'art, du moins les savans leur doivent-ils l'histoire d'une tribu sauvage, détruite entièrement par les ravages de la petite-vérole. Sans M. Catlin, on ne saurait plus maintenant si elle a existé, et son pinceau l'a sauvée de l'oubli.

L'ILLUSTRATION.

La présence à Paris des Indiens Y-o-Ways donne de l'àpropos au compte rendu suivant d'un voyage chez les Indiens de l'Amérique du Nord, voyage dû à M. Geo. Catlin, auquel un séjour de huit années parmi ces diverses peuplades a permis de s'initier d'une manière complète à leurs mœurs et à leurs habitudes. Dans un livre plein d'intérêt, de faits curieux, de révélations si extraordinaires qu'on croit rêver en les lisant, il a consigné les résultats de ses investigations et des observations qu'il a recueillies sur une race d'hommes qui va s'éteignant de jour en jour, et dont, sur l'affirmation de l'auteur, il ne restera plus vestiges d'ici à peu d'années. Au charme de ces récits, M. Geo. Catlin a ajouté des dessins d'une scrupuleuse exactitude, des portraits des principaux chefs de tribus, dans leurs riches costumes que nous aurons occasion de décrire, des paysages d'un effet saisissant, des esquisses de jeux, de chasses, de cérémonies religieuses, de combats, etc., etc. On peut donc dire que le livre de M. Catlin est écrit aussi bien pour les hommes sérieux que pour les grands enfants qui aiment tant les images, comme nous avouons les aimer, et qui s'amuseront de la bizarrerie des costumes de tous ces bons sauvages.

REVUE DE PARIS.

Galerie Indienne de M. Catlin.—La salle Valentino, transformée en une sorte de Musée Indien, au moyen des cinq à six cents peintures et esquisses, exécutées toutes, d'après nature, par M. Catlin, cet énergique et courageux voyageur, durant une pérégrination de huit années, à travers l'immense territoire qui s'étend des Montagnes Rocheuses aux derniers établissemens Américains ou Mexicains,—cette salle offrait déjà un spectacle fort intéressant. M. Catlin a visité, en bravant mille obstacles et souvent au péril de sa vie, quarante-huit des tribus qui résident dans la prairie, où elles vivent dans un état de guerre perpétuel. Installé sous le wigwam de l'Indien Corbeau ou du Mandan, dans la cabane du Chérokee ou de l'Ariccara, il a exécuté chacun des tableaux de cette immense collection ayant la nature sous les yeux ; aussi les présente-t-il au public plutôt comme des *fac-similes* identiques de la vie Indienne que comme des œuvres d'art. Ces *fac-similes* sont on ne peut plus expressifs et curieux.

La collection des peintures de M. Catlin se compose de trois cent dix portraits de chefs Indiens et de personnages de distinction, hommes ou femmes de différentes tribus, et de deux cents esquisses représentant les sites les plus remarquables des contrées qu'il a visitées, les danses et les cérémonies des peuplades qui les habitent, et des scènes de guerre et de chasse. C'est donc à la fois une représentation fidèle de la physionomie du pays et des mœurs et coutumes de ses habitans, représentation d'autant plus précieuse qu'elle a pour objet une race qui s'éteint (*dying people*), et qui s'éteint avec une rapidité qui tient du prodige.

MONITEUR INDUSTRIEL, Nov. 16, 1845.

Parmi tous les voyageurs qui ont exploré l'Amérique du Nord, aucun ne s'est occupé des races Indiennes autant que M. Catlin. Presque seul dans un canot d'écorce, il a suivi tout le cours du Missouri, et pendant huit années il en a parcouru en tous sens l'immense bassin, s'en allant de tribu en tribu, comme autrefois Hérodote, le père de l'histoire, s'en allait de ville en ville, de région en région, s'enquérant des mœurs, des traditions et des idées des populations lointaines.

M. Catlin est encore dans la force de l'âge, mais ses traits pâlis portent l'empreinte d'une vie déjà longuement et péniblement éprouvée. Son abord est froidement poli, son visage sévère et pensif, comme celui d'un homme qui a vu beaucoup de choses. Toute sa personne révèle une indomptable énergie. En public, il parle l'Anglais avec une remarquable puissance ; il y a dans son accentuation quelque chose du magnifique enthousiasme d'un poète.

Le grand ouvrage de M. Catlin est un beau monument élevé à la science ; il faut espérer qu'on songera à en donner une traduction Française. Chemin fesant, M. Catlin a dessiné et peint une étrange collection de vues, de scènes naturelles, de portraits d'indigènes et de scènes de mœurs. Cette nombreuse collection de toiles doit nécessairement se sentir de la rapidité forcée du travail, et des circonstances difficiles d'exécution où s'est trouvé l'artiste dans un voyage à travers les déserts de l'Ouest. On demeure, ar contraire, étonné que le courageux explorateur ait pu mettre dans de telles peintures autant de mouvement et de vérité. Ici, c'est un troupeau de bisons surpris par des chasseurs qui se traînent en rampant, couverts de peaux trompeuses ; là, c'est un guerrier à cheval, poursuivant son ennemi dans une course, sans hyperbole, vraiment échevelée ; plus loin, c'est une danse frénétique, excitation à la volupté ou au carnage ; ou bien des scènes de tortures qui semblent copiées dans l'enfer.

INDEPENDANCE, Brussels, Jan. 4, 1846.

Letters and Notes on the Manners, Customs, and Condition of the North American Indians, by G. Catlin (Lettres et Notes sur les Mœurs, les Coutumes, et l'Etat Social des Indiens du Nord de l'Amérique, par George Catlin). 2 vol. ornés de plusieurs centaines de planches.

Fils d'un homme de loi, élevé lui-même pour figurer au barreau, devenu enfin avocat, M. Catlin aimait trop le grand air et les voyages pour se laisser claquemurer dans l'antre de la chicane. Deux passions d'ailleurs se partageaient sa vie : la pêche et la peinture. Quand il n'était pas au bord d'une rivière, il était devant une toile, et vice-versâ. Il apprit la peinture sans maître, y devint habile après trois ou quatre ans d'études, et se demandait à quel but il dévouerait son existence, et l'esprit un peu enthousiaste qui l'animait, lorsqu'arrivèrent à Washington, des pays bien loin à l'Ouest, une douzaine d'Indiens au port noble et majestueux, accoutrés de leurs vêtements bizarres, mais pittoresques, la tête ornée de leur casque, le bras chargé de leur bouclier, le corps ceint de la tunique de peau d'antilope, les épaules couvertes du manteau de buffle.

Ces braves gens firent l'admiration des gamins et du beau monde de Washington et donnèrent beaucoup à réfléchir à notre peintre. Il se dit que les vêtements de la civilisation ne servaient pas seulement à voiler, mais à gâter la grâce et la beauté naturelles, que l'homme non garrotté dans les liens de l'art, devait offrir à l'artiste le plus magnifique modèle, et que l'histoire et les coutumes des peuplades sauvages étaient des sujets dignes d'occuper la vie d'un homme.

Ces réflexions étaient à peine achevées que M. Catlin prit son parti. Il consulta bien pour la forme quelques amis qui essayèrent de le détourner de son projet; ils lui représentèrent les dangers auxquels il allait s'exposer, les fatigues inouies qu'il aurait à supporter et bien d'autres arguments auxquels il fut insensible. M. Catlin fit ses paquets qui n'étaient pas lourds, et qui se composaient de toiles roulées, de brosses, de couleurs, de papier et de crayons; il mit sa carabine en bandoulière; et le bâton blanc à la main il partit pour l'Ouest en quête d'aventures, de Peaux-Rouges, de buffles et de prairies.

Mais au train dont marchent les Yankees, il avait long à aller avant d'atteindre les vastes solitudes où sont encore disséminées les peuplades sauvages. La civilisation le poursuivait partout; là où il espérait voyager en canot, il était forcé de prendre le bateau à vapeur; là où il se croyait au milieu des sauvages, il se trouvait avec des compatriotes; l'Ouest, but de son voyage, semblait le fuir à mesure qu'il en approchait. Il maudissait les pionniers qui avec leur bêche et leur marteau ont implanté la civilisation dans les parties les plus reculées de l'Amérique, et il désespérait de rencontrer les Peaux-Rouges qui devenaient un mythe pour lui, lorsqu'il tomba au milieu d'un village Mandan. Sa joie fut un peu calmée en apercevant que la civilisation avait encore passé par là sous la forme d'un agent de la compagnie des fourrures du Missouri. Mais il restait assez de sauvagerie dans la localité pour le satisfaire provisoirement. Quand il eut bien vu et bien observé, quand il eut bien fumé le calumet de paix; bien vécu sur un quartier de buffle braisé, bien dormi sous le wigwam hospitalier, et " pourtraicté " le chef Mandan, revêtu de son grand costume de guerre, depuis les cornes de buffle dont il s'orne le front jusqu'à ses mocassins brodés de paille, y compris la longue bande de plumes d'aigle qui descend depuis le derrière de la tête jusqu'aux talons, M. Catlin reprit sa course vers les régions inconnues, en s'arrêtant en route chaque fois qu'un site ou quelques aventures ou des figures d'Indiens fournissaient des sujets à son pinceau.

M. Catlin est resté huit ans en voyage; il a visité quarante-huit tribus dont la population totale s'élevaient à plusieurs centaines de mille individus. Il a rapporté chez lui 350 portraits à l'huile d'Indiens, 200 tableaux représentant des vues de leurs villages, leurs wigwams, leurs jeux, et leurs cérémonies religieuses, leurs danses, leurs chasses, des paysages admirables, et

enfin une nombreuse et très-curieuse collection de leurs costumes et vêtements, et d'autres objets de leur fabrique, depuis une de leurs maisons
jusqu'à de petits riens qui leur servent de jouets.

Toute cette collection avec les portraits et les tableaux figurent au Louvre
où le Roi Louis-Philippe leur a fait donner une place.　La galerie Indienne
de l'Amérique du Nord, de M. Catlin, est bien connue et montre le résultat
auquel peut arriver un homme entreprenant, patient et ferme qu'inspirent le
goût de l'art et une certaine dose d'enthousiasme.

C'est l'histoire de cet intéressant voyage que M. Catlin a écrite dans une
série de lettres au nombre de 58, et accompagnées de 310 gravures au trait
et de cartes géographiques.　Ces lettres étaient écrites sur les lieux et en-
voyées par des Indiens jusqu'aux bureaux de postes placés par cette maudite
civilisation jusqu'aux frontières les plus reculées de l'Ouest.

Peu de livres ont plus d'intérêt que celui de M. Catlin.　On lit cet
ouvrage avec le plaisir que l'on prendrait à la lecture d'un bon roman, s'il
y avait encore de bons romans pour servir de point de comparaison.　On
suit M. Catlin dans ses courses vagabondes, on aime avec lui ces Indiens
qu'il a toujours trouvés francs et hospitaliers, généreux et dignes.　Ces
Indiens si méconnus ont, quoique sauvages, toutes les qualités qui distin-
guent l'épicier le plus civilisé de la rue Saint-Denis, caporal de la garde
nationale ; comme celui-ci, ils sont bons pères, bons époux, amis dévoués ;
la seule différence entr'eux, c'est qu'ils ne payent pas très-exactement leurs
contributions par la raison qu'on ne leur en demande pas, et qu'ils ne mon-
tent pas assidûment leur garde, par l'autre raison qu'on ne connaît pas les
guérites dans ce pays.

Une Odyssée de huit ans a fait apprécier à M. Catlin les mérites et les
vertus des sauvages ; et, après avoir lu son livre, j'ai fini par croire avec
Jean-Jacques Rousseau que l'homme, tel que nous avons le malheur de le
connaître, est un animal dépravé par la civilisation.

Rien de plus touchant que l'apologie des Indiens faite par M. Catlin,
dans sa neuvième lettre ; partout où il peut mettre en saillie la noblesse de
leur caractère, M. Catlin le fait avec bonheur ; il se souvient du bon temps
passé au milieu d'eux, des marques d'affection qu'ils lui ont données, et il
les venge du mépris que les civilisés déversent sur ces pauvres et braves
gens, contents de leur sort, sans regret du passé, sans souci de l'avenir, sans
autres lois que celles de l'honneur qui est tout puissant chez eux.

Tous ceux qui ont lu les admirables romans de Cooper retrouvent dans
l'ouvrage de M. Catlin les scènes, mais cette fois vraies, animées, vivantes,
décrites avec tant de talent par le fécond romancier Américain.　M. Catlin
a décrit aussi l'embrâsement des prairies, et pouvait dire : *Quorum pars
magna fui ;* car il ne dut qu'à la vitesse de son " pony " Indien d'échapper
à la flamme immense qui courait sur lui avec plus de rapidité qu'une locomotive lancée à fond de train.　J'étais en sûreté, dit-il, que je tremblais
encore.　Une autre fois, plus de 2000 buffles se jettent à l'eau pour atteindre
le canot dans lequel il nageait, et c'est à grand'peine qu'il se sauve et que
le canot ne chavire pas, soulevé par le dos d'un de ces animaux ; une autre

fois encore, il se rencontre nez à nez avec une ourse grise accompagnée de ses deux petits, bête énorme de la taille d'un rhinocéros et qui vous dépèce un homme en un tour de main, à l'aide de ses ongles longs d'un décimètre et larges à la base de cinq centimètres pour finir par la pointe la plus aiguë.

Un des plus agréables épisodes de ce voyage, c'est la rencontre que fait M. Catlin, dans un immense désert et au détour d'un bois, d'un trappeur Canadien qui sifflait entre ses lèvres un vaudeville Français du temps de Louis XIV. et se mit à entrer en conversation avec M. Catlin, moyennant un langage dans lequel le Français, l'Anglais et l'Indien entraient chacun pour un tiers. L'honnête Baptiste, descendant d'un de ces hommes que les racoleurs allaient *presser* sur le quai de la Ferraille pour en faire des colons *volontaires* destinés à peupler le Canada, devint le compagnon de voyage de M. Catlin, le Vendredi dévoué de ce nouveau Robinson de terre ferme, et n'est pas le personnage le moins intéressant de la relation.

M. Catlin, indépendamment de son mérite d'écrivain et de dessinateur, aura celui d'avoir donné l'histoire la plus complète des mœurs de ces peuplades que la civilisation balaye devant elle et qu'elle tue avec de l'eau-de-vie et la variole. Ces peuplades, autrefois maîtresses du grand continent du nord de l'Amérique, s'éteignent rapidement ; leur mémoire s'éteindrait même si de hardis voyageurs n'allaient pas recueillir parmi elles les renseignements qui peuvent la préserver de l'oubli. Au nombre de ces voyageurs il faut citer au premier rang l'honorable M. Catlin, qui a rectifié bien des idées erronnées et fait connaître bien des faits jusqu'ici ignorés.

APPENDIX—(B).

MUSEUM OF HISTORY.

Established 1844.

THIS institution is intended to illustrate the History of Man by means of popular Lectures, aided and enforced by scenery, maps, and national costumes, adding every scenic attraction to the higher views of instruction, and combining art, history, philology, and geography ; the audience, as it were, being thus transported to the sites themselves.

It is also in contemplation to add *gradually*, as funds shall accumulate—

1. Models and coloured portraits of the races of man.
2. A gallery of architectural models.
3. A cabinet of coins and inscriptions.
4. Collection of views and drawings.
5. Collection of objects illustrative of the arts, sciences, navigation, commerce, agriculture, amusements, and domestic economy of ancient and modern nations.
6. Specimens of manufactures.
7. A library and reading-room, to contain the principal British and foreign periodicals and newspapers, and without distinction of party ; as also the latest publications on subjects connected with the objects of the institution.

The transactions of the institution will be published.

Illustrated lectures will be given on ancient and modern history, as also on New Zealand and Australia, embracing the modern settlements, and their capabilities for the colonist or emigrant.

Amongst the illustrated lectures to be given will be the following :—

On the Grecians.

On the Byzantines.

On the Modern Greeks.

On the Egyptians.

On the Arabians.

On the Romans.

On Russia and Siberia.

On New Zealand.

On Japan.

On the Ruined Cities of America.

With the aid of transparent maps (on a scale never before attempted) the spectator can follow the historian or traveller step by step, and with the advantages and beauties of scenery combined, is enabled to locate, classify, define, and retain the knowledge thus acquired.

The scenery and machinery have been so constructed, that whilst one series is used in London, others may be speedily sent to Edinburgh and elsewhere, where branch societies will be formed.

The management of the institution to be vested in a council elected by the subscribers, two of whom to retire annually, who may however be eligible for re-election.

TERMS.

For permanently reserved places at the lectures, five guineas per annum. Ordinary subscribers, two guineas per annum.

Authors, artists, ladies, members of learned societies, and foreigners, one guinea per annum.

Ambassadors, foreign ministers, consuls, and secretaries of learned societies *only* can become honorary members.

Admission to the public, two shillings for reserved places at the lectures; one shilling for ordinary visitors.

Subscribers to possess the right to be present at all lectures.

Subscribers to meet annually.

Trustees and auditors to be chosen by the subscribers.

All communications may be addressed to W. H. SHIPPARD, Esq., Turnham Green.

Museum of History,
 28th April, 1845.

A DESCRIPTIVE CATALOGUE

OF

CATLIN'S INDIAN COLLECTION;

CONTAINING

PORTRAITS, LANDSCAPES, COSTUMES, ETC.,

AND

REPRESENTATIONS OF THE MANNERS AND CUSTOMS OF THE NORTH AMERICAN INDIANS.

COLLECTED AND PAINTED ENTIRELY BY MR. CATLIN, DURING EIGHT YEARS' TRAVEL AMONGST FORTY-EIGHT TRIBES, MOSTLY SPEAKING DIFFERENT LANGUAGES.

Exhibited three years, with great success, in the Egyptian Hall, Piccadilly, London.

I WISH to inform the visitors to my Collection that, having some years since become fully convinced of the rapid decline and certain extinction of the numerous tribes of the North American Indians ; and seeing also the vast importance and value which a full *pictorial history* of these interesting but dying people might be to future ages—I sat out alone, unaided and unadvised, resolved (if my life should be spared), by the aid of my brush and my pen, to rescue from oblivion so much of their primitive looks and customs as the industry and ardent enthusiasm of one lifetime could accomplish, and set them up in a *Gallery unique and imperishable*, for the use and benefit of future ages.

I devoted eight years of my life exclusively to the accomplishment of my design, and that with more than expected success.

I visited with great difficulty, and some hazard to life, forty-eight tribes (residing within the United States, British, and Mexican Territories), containing about half a million of souls. I have seen them in their own villages, have carried my canvas and colours the whole way, and painted my portraits, &c., from the life, as they now stand and are seen in the Gallery.

The collection contains (besides an immense number of costumes and other manufactures) near six hundred paintings, 350 of which are *Portraits* of distinguished men and women of the different tribes, and 250 *other Paintings*, descriptive of *Indian Countries,* their *Villages, Games,* and *Customs ;* containing in all above 3000 figures.

As this immense collection has been gathered, and *every painting has been made from nature,* BY MY OWN HAND—and that too when I have been paddling my canoe, or leading my pack-horse over and through trackless wilds, at the hazard of my life—the world will surely be kind and indulgent enough to receive and estimate them, as they have been intended, as *true and fac-simile traces of individual life and historical facts,* and forgive me for their present unfinished and unstudied condition as works of art.

GEO. CATLIN.

INDIAN PORTRAITS.

CERTIFICATES.

I hereby certify that the persons whose signatures are affixed to the certificates used below, by Mr. Catlin, are officers in the service of the United States, as herein set forth : and that their opinions of the accuracy of the likenesses, and correctness of the views, &c., exhibited by him in his " Indian Gallery," are entitled to full credit.

J. R. POINSETT, Secretary of War, Washington.

With regard to the gentlemen whose names are affixed to certificates below, I am fully warranted in saying, that no individuals have had better opportunities of acquiring a knowledge of the persons, habits, costumes, and sports of the Indian tribes, or possess stronger claims upon the public confidence in the statements they make respecting the correctness of delineations, &c., of Mr. Catlin's " Indian Gallery ;" and I may add my own testimony, with regard to many of those Indians whom I have seen, and whose likenesses are in the collection, and sketched with fidelity and correctness.

C. A. HARRIS, Commissioner of Indian Affairs, Washington.

I have seen Mr. Catlin's collection of Portraits of Indians, many of which were familiar to me, and painted in my presence; and, as far as they have included Indians of my acquaintance, the *likenesses* are easily recognised, bearing the most striking resemblance to the originals, as well as faithful representations of their costumes.

W. CLARK, Superintendent of Indian Affairs, St. Louis.

I have examined Mr. Catlin's collection of the Upper Missouri Indians to the Rocky Mountains, all of which I am acquainted with, and indeed most of them were painted when I was present, and I do not hesitate to pronounce them correct likenesses, and readily to be recognised. And I consider the *costumes*, as painted by him, to be the *only correct representations* I have ever seen.

JOHN F. A. SANFORD,
U. SS. Indian Agent for Mandans, Rickarees, Minatarees,
Crows, Knisteneaux, Assinneboins, Blackfeet, &c.

Having examined Mr. Catlin's collection of Portraits of Indians of the Missouri and Rocky Mountains, I have no hesitation in pronouncing them, so far as I am acquainted with the individuals, to be the best I have ever seen, both as regards the expression of countenance and the exact and complete manner in which the costume has been painted by him.

J. L. BEAN, S. Agent for Indian Affairs.

I have been for many years past in familiar acquaintance with the Indian tribes of the Upper Missouri and the Rocky Mountains, and also with the landscape and other scenes represented in Mr. Catlin's collection, and it gives me great pleasure to assure the world that, on looking them over, I found the likenesses of my old friends easily to be recognised, and his sketches of Manners and Customs to be portrayed with singular truth and correctness.

J. PILCHER, Agent for Upper Missouri Indians.

It gives me great pleasure in being enabled to add my name to the list of those who have spontaneously expressed their approbation of Mr. Catlin's collection of Indian Paintings. His collection of materials places it in his power to throw much light on the Indian character; and his portraits, so far as I have seen them, are drawn with great fidelity as to character and likeness.

H. SCHOOLCRAFT, Indian Agent for Wisconsin Territory.

Having lived and dealt with the Blackfeet Indians for five years past, I was enabled to recognise *every one* of the portraits of those people, and of the Crows also, which Mr. Catlin has in his collection, from the faithful likenesses they bore to the originals.

St. Louis, 1835.   J. E. BRAZEAU.

Having spent sixteen years in the continual acquaintance with the Indians of the several tribes of the Missouri represented in Mr. Catlin's Gallery of Indian Paintings, I was enabled to judge of the correctness of the likenesses, and I *instantly recognised every one of them,* when I looked them over, from the striking resemblance they bore to the originals; so also of the landscapes on the Missouri.   HONORE PICOTTE.

The portraits in the possession of Mr. Catlin of Pawnee Picts, Kioways, Camanches, Wecos, and Osages, were painted by him *from life,* when on a tour to their country with the United States Dragoons. The *likenesses* are good, very easily to be recognised, and the *costumes* faithfully represented.

HENRY DODGE, Col. of Drag.	D. PERKINS, Capt. of Drag.
R. H. MASON, Major of ditto.	M. DUNCAN, ditto.
D. HUNTER, Capt. of ditto.	T. B. WHEELOCK, Lieut. ditto.

We have seen Mr. Catlin's Portraits of Indians east of the Rocky Mountains, many of which are familiar to us : the likenesses are easily recognised, bearing a strong resemblance to the originals, as well as a faithful representation of their costumes.   J. DOUGHERTY, Indian Agent.
November 27th, 1837.   J. GANTT.

We hereby certify that the portraits of the Grand Pawnees, Republican Pawnees, Pawnee Loups, Tappage Pawnees, Otoes, Omahaws, and Missouries, which are in Mr. Catlin's Indian Gallery, were painted from life by Mr. George Catlin, and that the individuals sat to him in the costumes precisely in which they are painted.   J. DOUGHERTY, I. A. for Pawnees, Omahaws, and Otoes.
New York, 1837.   J. GANTT.

I have seen Mr. Catlin's collection of Indian Portraits, many of which were familiar to me, and painted in my presence at their own villages. I have spent the greater part of my life amongst the tribes and individuals he has represented, and I do not hesitate to pronounce them correct likenesses, and easily recognised ; also his sketches of their *manners* and *customs*, I think, are excellent ; and the *landscape views* on the Missouri and Mississippi are correct representations.
     K. M'KENZIE, of the Am. Fur Co., Mouth of Yellow Stone.

We hereby certify that the portraits of Seminoles and Euchees, named in this catalogue, were painted by George Catlin, from the life, at Fort Moultrie ; that the Indians sat or stood in the costumes precisely in which they are painted, and that the likenesses are remarkably good.

        P. MORRISON, Capt. 4th Inft.
        J. S. HATHAWAY, 2nd Lieut. 1st Art.
        H. WHARTON, 2nd Lieut. 6th Inft.
Fort Moultrie, Jan. 26, 1838.   F. WEEDON, Assistant-Surgeon.

In addition to the above certificates, nearly every portrait has inseparably attached to its back an *individual* certificate, signed by Indian agents, officers of the army, or other persons, who were present when the picture was painted. The form of these certificates is as follows :—

No. 131, BLACKFOOT, PE-TOH-PE-KISS (THE EAGLE-RIBS).

I hereby certify that this portrait was painted from the life, at Fort Union, mouth of Yellow Stone, in the year 1832, by George Catlin, and that the Indian sat in the costume in which it is painted.
      JOHN F. A. SANFORD, United States Indian Agent.

DEAR SIR,   *Légation des Etats Unis, Paris, Dec.* 8, 1841.

No man can appreciate better than myself the admirable fidelity of your drawings and book which I have lately received. They are equally spirited and accurate—they are true to nature. Things that *are* are not sacrificed, as they too often are by the painter, to things as in his judgment they should be.

During eighteen years of my life I was Superintendent of Indian Affairs in the north-western territory of the United States; and during more than five I was Secretary of War, to which department belongs the general control of Indian concerns. I know the Indians thoroughly—I have spent many a month in their camps, council-houses, villages, and hunting-grounds—I have fought with them and against them—and I have negotiated seventeen treaties of peace or of cession with them. I mention these circumstances to show you that I have a good right to speak confidently upon the subject of your drawings. Among them I recognise many of my old acquaintances, and everywhere I am struck with the vivid representations of them and their customs, of their peculiar features, and of their costumes. Unfortunately they are receding before the advancing tide of our population, and are probably destined, at no distant day, wholly to disappear; but your collection will preserve them, as far as human art can do, and will form the most perfect monument of an extinguished race that the world has ever seen.

LEWIS CASS.

To George Catlin.

———————

DEAR SIR,   *Cottage, Haddington, 15th April,* 1843.

I have enjoyed much pleasure in attending your lectures at the Waterloo Rooms in Edinburgh. Your delineations of the Indian character, the display of beautiful costumes, and the native Indian manners, true to the life, realised to my mind and view scenes I had so often witnessed in the parts of the Indian countries where I had been; and for twenty years' peregrinations in those parts, from Montreal to the Great Slave River north, and from the shores of the Atlantic, crossing the Rocky Mountains, to the mouth of the Columbia River, on the Pacific Ocean, west, I had opportunities of seeing much. Your lectures and exhibition have afforded me great pleasure and satisfaction, and I shall wish you all that success which you so eminently deserve for the rich treat which you have afforded in our enlightened, literary, and scientific metropolis.

I remain, dear Sir, yours very truly,

To George Catlin, Esq.   JOHN HALDANE.

———————

The following is an extract of a letter received some days since by a gentleman in Edinburgh, from Mr. James Hargrave, of the Hudson's Bay Company, dated York Factory, Hudson's Bay, 10th December, 1842:—

"Should you happen to fall in with Catlin's Letters on the North American Indians, I would strongly recommend a perusal of them for the purpose of acquiring a knowledge of the habits and customs of those tribes among whom he was placed. Catlin's sketches are true to life, and are powerfully descriptive of their appearance and character."

———————

CATLIN'S INDIAN COLLECTION

INDIAN PORTRAITS.

SACS (SÁU-KIES).

A TRIBE OF INDIANS residing on the Upper Mississippi and Desmoines rivers. Present number (in 1840) about 5000. The smallpox carried off half their population a few years since; and a considerable number were destroyed in the "Black Hawk War" in 1832-3. This tribe shave the head, leaving only a small tuft of hair on the top, which is called the "scalplock."

[The *acute accent* is used in the spelling of the Indian names merely to denote the emphasis.]

1. *Kee-o-kúk*, the Running Fox ; present Chief of the Tribe. Shield on his arm and staff of office (sceptre) in his hand ; necklace of grisly bear's claws, over the skin of a white wolf, on his neck.

   This man, during the Black Hawk War, kept two-thirds of the warriors of the tribe neutral, and was therefore appointed chief by General Scott, in treaty, with the consent of the nation.

2. *Múk-a-tah-mish-o-káh-kaik*, the Black Hawk ; in his war dress and paint. Strings of wampum in his ears and on his neck, and his *medicine-bag* (the skin of the black hawk) on his arm.

   This is the man famed as the conductor of the Black Hawk War. Painted at the close of the war, while he was a prisoner at Jefferson Barracks, in 1832.

3. *Náh-se-ús-kuk*, the Whirling Thunder ; eldest son of Black Hawk.

   A very handsome man. He distinguished himself in the Black Hawk War.

4. *Wa-sáw-me-saw*, the Roaring Thunder ; youngest son of Black Hawk.

   Painted while a prisoner of war.

5. (   ), wife of Kee-o-kúk (No. 1) ; in a dress of civilized manufacture, ornamented with silver brooches.

   This woman is the eldest of seven wives whom I saw in his lodge, and, being the mother of his favourite son, the most valued one. To her alone would he allow the distinguished honour of being painted and hung up with the chiefs.

6. *Me-sóu-wahk,* the Deer's Hair; the favourite son of Kee-o-kúk, and by him designated to be his successor.

7. *Wah-pe-kée-suck,* White Cloud, called the "Prophet;" one of Black Hawk's principal warriors and advisers.
    Was a prisoner of war with Black Hawk, and travelled with him through the Eastern States.

8. *Náh-pope,* the Soup; another of Black Hawk's principal advisers; and travelled with him, when he was a prisoner of war, to the Eastern cities.
    He desired to be painted with a white flag in his hand.

9. *Ah-móu-a,* the Whale, one of Kee-o-kúk's principal braves; holding a handsome war-club in his hand.

10. *Wa-quóth-e-qua,* the Buck's Wife, or Female Deer; the wife of Ah-móu-a.

11. *Pash-ee-pa-hó,* the Little Stabbing Chief; holding his staff of office in his hand, shield and pipe.
    A very venerable old man, who has been for many years the first civil chief of the Sacs and Foxes.

12. *I-o-wáy,* the Ioway; one of Black Hawk's principal warriors; his body curiously ornamented with his "war-paint."

13. *Pam-a-hó,* the Swimmer; one of Black Hawk's warriors.
    Very distinguished.

14. *No-kúk-qua,* the Bear's Fat.

15. *Pash-ee-pa-hó,* the Little Stabbing Chief (the younger); one of Black Hawk's braves.

16. *Wáh-pa-ko-lás-kuk,* the Bear's Track.

FOXES.

On the Desmoines River; present number (in 1840), 1500.

17. *Aíh-no-wa,* the Fire; a doctor or "*medicine*" *man*; one half of his body painted red, and the other yellow.

18. *Wée-sheet,* the Sturgeon's Head; one of Black Hawk's principal warriors; his body most singularly ornamented with his *war-paint.*
    This man held a spear in his hand, with which, he assured me, he killed four white men during the war.

19, 20, 21. Three in a group; names not known.

KON-ZAS.

A tribe of 1560 souls, residing on the Konza river, sixty or eighty miles west of the Missouri. Uncivilized remains of a powerful and warlike tribe. One-half died with the smallpox a few years since. This tribe shave the head like the Osages, Sacs, and Foxes.

22. *Shó-me-kós-see*, the Wolf; one of the Chiefs; his head curiously ornamented, and numerous strings of wampum on his neck.

23. *Jee-hé-o-hó-shah*, He who cannot be thrown down; a warrior.

24. *Wá-hón-ga-shee*, No Fool; a very great fop.

Used half the day in painting his face, preparing to sit for his picture.

25. *Meach-o-shín-gaw*, Little White Bear; a spirited and distinguished brave, with a scalping-knife grasped in his hand.

26. *O-rón-gás-see*, the Bear-catcher; a celebrated warrior.

27. *Chésh-oo-hong-ha*, the Man of Good Sense; a handsome young warrior; style of his head-dress like the Grecian helmet.

28. *Hón-je-a-pút-o*, a woman; wife of O-rón-gás-see.

O-SÁGE, or WA-SÁW-SEE.

A tribe in their primitive state, inhabiting the head-waters of the Arkansas and Neosho or Grand Rivers, 700 miles west of the Mississipi. ¡Present number of the tribe, 5200; residing in three villages; wigwams built of barks and flags, or reeds. The Osages are the tallest men on the continent, the most of them being over six feet in stature, and many of them seven. This tribe shave the head, leaving a small tuft on the top, called the "scalp-lock."

29. *Cler-mónt*, ———— ; first Chief of the tribe; with his warclub in his hand, and his leggins fringed with scalp-locks taken from his enemies' heads.

This man is the son of an old and celebrated chief of that name, who died a few years since.

30. *Wáh-chee-te*, ———— ; woman and child; wife of Cler-mónt.

31. *Tchong-tas-sáb-bee*, the Black Dog; second Chief of the Osages; with his pipe in one hand and tomahawk in the other; head shaved, and ornamented with a crest made of the deer's tail, coloured red.

This is the largest man in the Osage nation, and blind in his left eye.

32. *Tál-lee*, ———— ; an Osage warrior of distinction; with his shield, bow, and quiver.

33. *Wa-ho-béck-ee*, ———— ; a brave; said to be the hand-

somest man in the nation ; with a profusion of wampum on his neck, and a fan in his hand made of the eagle's tail.

34. *Mun-ne-pús-kee*, He who is not afraid.⎫
35. *Ko-ha-túnk-a*, the Big Crow. ⎬ group.
36. *Nah-cóm-ee-shee*, Man of the Bed. ⎭

    Three distinguished young warriors, who desired to be painted on one canvas.

37. *Moi-eén-e-shee*, the Constant Walker.
38. *Wa-másh-ee-sheek*, He who takes away.⎫
39. *Wa-chésh-uk*, War. ⎬ group.
40. *Mink-chésk*, ————. ⎭

    Three distinguished young men, full length.

41. *Tcha-tó-ga*, Mad Buffalo ; bow and quiver on his back.

    This man was tried and convicted for the murder of two white men, under Mr. Adams's administration, and was afterwards pardoned, but is held in disgrace in his tribe since.

42. *Wash-ím-pe-shee*, the Madman ; a distinguished warrior ; full length.
43. *Pa-hú-sha*, White Hair ; the younger ; with lance and quiver. Chief of a band, and rival of Cler-mónt.
44. *Shin-ga-wás-sa*, the Handsome Bird ; a splendid-looking fellow, six feet eight inches high ; with war-club and quiver.
45. *Cáh-he-ga-shín-ga*, the Little Chief ; full-length, with bow and quiver.

————◆————

CA-MÁN-CHEES.

    One of the most powerful and hostile tribes in North America, inhabiting the western parts of Texas and the Mexican provinces, and the south-western part of the territory of the United States near the Rocky Mountains : entirely wild and predatory in their habits ; the most expert and effective lancers and horsemen on the continent. Numbering some 25,000 or 30,000 ; living in skin lodges or wigwams ; well mounted on wild horses ; continually at war with the Mexicans, Texians, and Indian tribes of the north-west.

46. *Eé-shah-kó-nee*, the Bow and Quiver ; first Chief of the tribe. Boar's tusk on his breast, and rich shells in his ears.
47. *Ta-wáh-que-nah*, the Mountain of Rocks ; second Chief of the tribe, and largest man in the nation.

    This man received the United States Regiment of Dragoons with great kindness at his village, which was beautifully situated at the base of a huge spur of the Rocky Mountains : he has decidedly African features, and a beard of two inches in length on his chin.

48. *Ish-a-ró-yeh*, He who carries a Wolf ; a distinguished brave ;

so called from the circumstance of his carrying a *medicine-bag* made of the skin of a wolf: he holds a whip in his hand.

This man piloted the dragoons to the Camanchee village, and received a handsome rifle from Colonel Dodge for so doing.

49. *Kots-o-kó-ro-kó,* the Hair of the Bull's Neck; third grade Chief; shield on his arm and gun in his hand.

50. *Is-sa·wáh-tám-ah,* the Wolf tied with Hair; a Chief, third rate: pipe in his hand.

51. *His-oo-sán-chees,* the Little Spaniard; a brave of the highest order in his tribe; armed as a warrior, with shield, bow and quiver, lance fourteen feet long, and war-knife.

This was the first of the Camanchees who daringly left his own war-party and came to the regiment of dragoons, and spoke with our interpreter, inviting us to go to their village. A man of low stature, but of the most remarkable strength and daring courage.—See him approaching the dragoons on horseback, No. 489.

52. *Háh-nee,* the Beaver; a warrior of terrible aspect.

53-54. Two Camanchee Girls (sisters), showing the wigwam of the Chief, his dogs, and his five children.

PAW-NEE PÍCTS (TOW-EE-AHGE).

A wild and hostile tribe, numbering about 6000, adjoining the Camanchees on the north. This tribe and the Camanchees are in league with each other, joining in war and in the chase.

55. *Wee-tá-ra-shá-ro,* —————; head Chief; an old and very venerable man.

This man embraced Colonel Dodge, and others of the dragoon officers in council, in his village, and otherwise treated them with great kindness, theirs being the first visit ever made to them by white people.

56. *Sky-se-ró-ka,* —————; second Chief of the tribe.

A fine-looking and remarkably shrewd and intelligent man.

57. *Kid-á-day,* ————— ; a brave of distinction.

58. *Káh-kée-tsee,* the Thighs. ⎫
59. *Shé-de-ah,* Wild Sage.   ⎭

Both of these women were prisoners amongst the Osages; they were purchased by the Indian Commissioner, and sent home to the nation by the dragoons.

60. *Ah'-sho-cole,* Rotten Foot; a noted warrior.

61. *Ah'-re-kah'-na-có-chee,* the Mad Elk; a great warrior.

KÍ-O-WA.

Also a wild and predatory tribe of 5000 or 6000, living on the west of the Pawnee Picts and Camanchees, and also in alliance with those warlike and powerful tribes.   They inhabit the base of, and extend their wars and hunts through a great extent of the Rocky Mountains: and, like the Camanchees, are expert and wonderful horsemen.

62. *Téh-tóot-sah*, ————————, first Chief.

This man treated the dragoons with great kindness in his country, and came in with us to Fort Gibson; his hair was very long. extending down as low as his knees, and put up in clubs, and ornamented with silver brooches.

63. *Kotz-a-tó-ah*, the Smoked Shield; a distinguished warrior; full-length.

64. *Bón-són-gee*, New Fire; Chief of a band; boar's tusk and war-whistle on his breast.

65. *Quáy-hám-kay*, the Stone Shell; a brave, and a good specimen of the wild untutored savage.

66. *Túnk-aht-óh-ye*, the Thunderer (boy).

67. *Wun-pán-to-mee*, the White Weasel (girl).

This boy and girl, who had been for several years prisoners amongst the Osages, were purchased by the Indian Commissioner; the girl was sent home to her nation by the dragoons, and the boy was killed by a ram the day before we started.   They were brother and sister.

WÉE-CO.

A small tribe, living near to, and under the protection of, the Pawnee Picts, speaking an unknown language; probably the remnant of a tribe conquered and enslaved by the Pawnee Picts.

68. *U'sh-ee-kitz*, He who fights with a Feather.   Chief of the tribe.

This man came into Fort Gibson with the dragoons; he was famous for a custom he observed after all his speeches, of *embracing* the officers and chiefs in council.

SIÓUX (DAH-CÓ-TA).

This is one of the most numerous and powerful tribes at present existing on the continent, numbering, undoubtedly, some 40,000, occupying a vast tract of country on the upper waters of the Mississippi and Missouri rivers, and extending quite to the base of the Rocky Mountains.   They live in skin lodges, and move them about the prairies, without any permanent residence.   This tribe lost about 8000 by smallpox a few years since.

69. *Ha-wón-je-tah*, the One Horn; first Chief of the tribe; *Mee-ne-cow-e-gee* band, Upper Missouri; hair tied on his head in form of a turban, and filled with glue and red earth, or vermilion.

The Sioux have forty-one bands; every band has a chief, and this man was head of all: he has been recently killed by a buffalo-bull.

70. *Wá-nah-de-túnk-ah*, the Big Eagle, or Black Dog; at the Falls of St. Anthony. Chief of the *O-hah-kas-ka-toh-y-an-te*, or *Long Avenue* band.

71. *Tchán-dee*, Tobacco; second Chief of the nation, of the *O-gla-la* band, Upper Missouri.

72. *Wán-ee-ton*, ————; Chief of the *Sus-se-ton* band, Upper Missouri; full-length, in a splendid dress; head-dress of war-eagle's quills and ermine, and painted robe.

One of the most noted and dignified, as well as graceful chiefs of the Sioux tribe.

73. *Tóh-to-wah-kón-da-pee*, the Blue Medicine; a noted " medicine-man," or doctor, at the St. Peter's, of the *Ting-ta-to-ah* band; with his *medicine* or mystery drum and rattle in his hands, his looking-glass on his breast, his rattle of antelope's hoofs, and drum of deer-skins.

These " *medicine-men*" are conjurers as well as physicians, paying their dernier visits to the sick, with their *mysteries*, endeavouring and pretending to cure by a charm.

74. *Ah-nó-je-nahge*, He who stands on both Sides; and

75. *We-chúsh-ta-dóo-ta*, the Red Man; the two most distinguished ball-players of the Sioux tribe, in their ball-play dress, with their ball-sticks in their hands.

In this beautiful and favourite game, each player is adorned with an embroidered belt, and a tail of beautiful quills or horse-hair; the arms, legs, and feet are always naked, and curiously painted. (See two paintings of ball-plays, and further description of the game, under *Amusements*, Nos. 428, 429, 430, and the ball-sticks among the manufactures.)

76. *Ka-pés-ka-da*, the Shell; a brave of the *O-gla-la* band.

77. *Táh-zee-keh-dá-cha*, the Torn Belly; a very distinguished brave of the *Yank-ton* band, Upper Missouri.

78. *Wúk-mi-ser*, Corn; a warrior of distinction, of the *Ne-caw-ee-gee* band.

79. *Chá-tee-wah-née-che*, No Heart; a very noted Indian. Chief of the *Wah-ne-watch-to-nee-nah* band.

80. *Ee-áh-sá-pa*, the Black Rock; Chief of the *Nee-caw-wee-gee* band; a very dignified chief, in a beautiful dress, full length, head-dress of eagles' quills and ermine, and horns of the buffalo; lance in his hand, and battles of his life emblazoned on his robe.

s 2

81. *Wi-lóoh-tah-eeh-tcháh-ta-máh-nee,* the Red Thing that touches in Marching; a young girl; and the daughter of *Black Rock* (No. 80), by her side—her dress of deer-skin, and ornamented with brass buttons and beads.

82. *Toh-kí-e-to,* the Stone with Horns. Chief of the Yank-ton band, and principal orator of the nation; his body curiously tattooed.

83. *Mah-tó-rah-rísh-nee-eéh-ée-rah,* the Grisly Bear that runs without Regard; a brave of the *Onc-pah-pa* band.

84. *Mah-tó-che-ga,* the Little Bear; a distinguished brave.

85. *Shón-ka,* the Dog; Chief of the *Bad Arrow Points* band.

86. *Táh-téck-a-da-háir,* the Steep Wind; a Brave of the *Ca-za-zhee-ta* (or Bad Arrow Points) band.

These three distinguished men were all killed in a private quarrel (while I was in the country), occasioned by my painting only *one-half* of the face of the first (No. 84); ridicule followed, and resort to fire-arms, in which that side of the face which I had left out was blown off in a few moments after I had finished the portrait; and sudden and violent revenge for the offence soon laid the other two in the dust, and imminently endangered my own life. (For a full account of this strange transaction, see Catlin's ' Letters and Notes on North American Indians.')

87. *Heh-háh-ra-pah,* the Elk's Head; Chief of the *Ee-ta-sip-shov* band, Upper Missouri.

88. *Máh-to-een-náh-pa,* the White Bear that goes out; Chief of the *Black Foot Sioux* band.

89. *Tchón-su-móns-ka,* the Sand Bar; woman of the *Te-ton* band, with a beautiful head of hair; her dress almost literally covered with brass buttons, which are highly valued by the women, to adorn their dresses.

90. *Wá-be-shaw,* the Leaf; Upper Mississippi, Chief of a band, blind in one eye; a very distinguished man, since dead.

91. *Shón-ga-tón-ga-chésh-en-day,* the Horse-dung; Chief of a band; a great conjurer and magician.

92. *Tah-tón-ga-mó-nee,* the Walking Buffalo; Red Wing's son.

93. *Múz-za,* the Iron; St. Peters; a brave of distinction, and a very handsome fellow.

94. *Te-o-kún-ko,* the Swift.

An ill-visaged and ill-natured fellow, though reputed a desperate warrior.

PÚN-CAH.

A small tribe residing on the west bank of the Missouri River, 900 in number, reduced one-half by the smallpox in 1824-5.

95. *Shoo-de-gá-cha*, the Smoke ; Chief of the Tribe.

A very philosophical and dignified man.

96. *Hee-láh-dee*, the Pure Fountain; wife of Shoo-de-gá-cha (No. 95).

97. *Hongs-káy-dee*, the Great Chief; son of the Chief.

This young fellow, about 18 years of age, glowing red with vermilion, signalised himself by marrying *four wives in one day*, whilst I was in his village! He took them all at once to his wigwam, where I saw them, and painted one of them.

98. *Mong-shóng-sha*, the Bending Willow ; one of the four wives of Hongs-káy-dee (No. 97), about 13 years old, and wrapped in a buffalo robe, prettily garnished.

--------◆--------

PÁW-NEES,—OF THE PLATTE.

A wild and very warlike tribe of 12,000, occupying the country watered by the river Platte, from the Missouri to the Rocky Mountains. This once very powerful tribe lost one-half of their numbers by the small-pox in 1823: they are entirely distinct from the Pawnee Picts, both in language and customs, and live 1000 miles from them. This tribe shave the head like the Sacs and Foxes.

FIRST BAND.—GRAND PA'WNEES.

99. *Shón-ka-ki-he-ga*, the Horse Chief ; head Chief of the tribe.

This chief, and a number of his braves, visited Washington in 1837.

100. *La-dóo-ke-a*, the Buffalo Bull ; his *medicine* or *totem* (the head of a buffalo bull) painted on his face and breast, his bow and arrow in his hands.

101. *Ah-sháw-wah-róoks-te*, the Medicine Horse; a brave, or soldier.

SECOND BAND.—TAP-PA'HGE PA'WNEES.

102. *La-kée-too-wi-rá-sha*, the Little Chief; a great warrior.

103. *Loo-rá-wée-re-coo*, the Bird that goes to War.

THIRD BAND.—REPUBLICAN PA'WNEES.

104. *A'h-sha-la-cóots-ah*, the Mole in the Forehead ; Chief of his band ; a very distinguished warrior.

105. *Lá-shah-le-stáw-hix*, the Man Chief.

106. *La-wée-re-coo-re-shaw-wee*, the War Chief.
107. *Te-ah´-ke-ra-lée-re-coo*, the Chayenne; a fine-looking fellow, with a pipe in one hand and his whip in the other.

FOURTH BAND.—WOLF PA'WNEES.

108. *Le-sháw-loo-láh-le-hoo*, the Big Elk; Chief of the band.
109. *Lo-lòch-to-hóo-lah*, the Big Chief; a very celebrated man.
110. *La-wáh-he-coots-la-sháw-no*, the Brave Chief; impressions of hands painted on his breast.
111. *L'har-e-tar-rúshe*, the Ill-natured Man; a great warrior.

O-MÁ-HAS.

The remains of a numerous tribe, nearly destroyed by the small-pox in 1823, now living under the protection of the Pawnees: their numbers, about 1500.

112. *Man-sha-qúi-ta*, the Little Soldier; a brave.
113. *Ki-hó-ga-waw-shú-shee*, the Brave Chief; Chief of the tribe.
114. *Om-pah-tón-ga*, the Big Elk; a famous warrior, his tomahawk in his hand, and face painted black, for war.
115. *Sháw-da-mon-nee*, There he goes; a brave.
116. *Nóm-ba-mon-nee*, the Double Walker; a brave.

OTE-TOES.

These are also the remains of a large tribe, two-thirds of which were destroyed by small-pox in 1823: they are neighbours and friends of the Pawnees, numbering about 600.

117. *Wah-ro-née-sah*, the Surrounder; Chief of the tribe, quite an old man; his shirt made of the skin of a grisly bear, with the claws on.
118. *Nón-je-níng-a*, No Heart; a distinguished brave.
119. *No-wáy-ke-súg-gah*, He who Strikes Two at Once. Sketch quite unfinished; beautiful dress, trimmed with a profusion of scalp-locks and eagles' quills; pipe in his hand, and necklace of grisly bears' claws.
120. *Ráw-no-way-wóh-krah*, the Loose Pipe-stem; a brave (full length); eagle head-dress, shirt of grisly bear's skin.
121. *Wée-ke-rú-law*, He who Exchanges; beautiful pipe in his hand.

MIS-SÓU-RIES.

Once a very numerous and powerful nation, occupying the States of Illinois and Indiana. Reduced in wars with Sacs and Foxes, and lastly by the small-pox in 1823; now merged into the Pawnee tribe. Numbers at present, 400; twenty years ago, 18,000.

122. *Háw-che-ke-súg-ga*, He who kills the Osages; Chief of the tribe; an old man, necklace of grisly bears' claws, and a handsome carved pipe in his hand.

RÍC-CA-REES.

A small but very hostile tribe of 2500, on the west bank of the Missouri, 1600 miles above its junction with the Mississippi; living in one village of earth-covered lodges.

123. *Stán-au-pat*, the Bloody Hand; Chief of the tribe. His face painted red with vermilion, scalping-knife in his hand; wearing a beautiful dress.

124. *Kah-béch-a*, the Twin; wife of the Chief (No. 123).

125. *Pshán-shaw*, the Sweet-scented Grass; a girl of twelve years old, daughter of the Chief (No. 123), full length, in a beautiful dress of the mountain-sheep skin, neatly garnished, and robe of the young buffalo.

126. *Páh-too-cá-ra*, He who Strikes; a distinguished brave.

MÁN-DANS,

(SEE-PO′HS-KA-NU-MA′H-KA′-KEE,) PEOPLE OF THE PHEASANTS.

A small tribe of 2000 souls, living in two permanent villages on the Missouri, 1800 miles above its junction with the Mississippi. Earth-covered lodges; villages fortified by strong piquets, eighteen feet high, and a ditch. [*This friendly and interesting tribe all perished by the small-pox and suicide in 1837 (three years after I lived amongst them), excepting about forty, who have since been destroyed by their enemy, rendering the tribe entirely extinct, and their language lost, in the short space of a few months!* The disease was carried amongst them by the traders, which destroyed in six months, of different tribes, 25,000!]

127. *Ha-na-tá-nu-maúk*, the Wolf Chief; head of the tribe, in a splendid dress, head-dress of raven-quills, and two *calumets* or pipes of peace in his hand.

128. *Máh-to-tóh-pa*, the Four Bears; second Chief, but the favourite and popular man of the nation; costume splendid, head-dress of war-eagles' quills and ermine, extending quite to the ground, surmounted by the horns of the buffalo and skin of the magpie.

129. *Mah-tó-he-ha*, the Old Bear; a very distinguished brave; but here represented in the character of a *Medicine Man* or Doctor, with his *medicine* or *mystery* pipes in his hands, and foxes' tails tied to his heels, prepared to make his last visit to his patient, to cure him, if possible, by *hocus pocus* and magic.

130. *Mah-táhp-ta-u*, He who rushes through the Middle; a brave, son of the former Chief, called " the Four Men." Necklace of bears' claws.

131. *Máh-to-tóh-pa*, the Four Bears; in *undress*, being in mourning, with a few locks of his hair cut off. His hair put up in plaits or slabs, with glue and red paint, a custom of the tribe.

The scars on his breast, arms, and legs, show that he has several times in his life submitted to the propitiatory tortures represented in four paintings, Nos. 505, 506, 507, 508.

132. *Seehk-hée-da*, the Mouse-coloured Feather, or " *White Eyebrows;*" a very noted brave, with a beautiful pipe in his hand; his hair quite yellow.

This man was killed by the Sioux, and scalped, two years after I painted his portrait: his scalp lies on the table, No. 10.

133. *Mi-néek-ee-súnk-te-ka*, the Mink; a beautiful Mandan girl, in mountain-sheep skin dress, ornamented with porcupine-quills, beads, and elk's teeth.

134. *Sha-kó-ka*, Mint.

A very pretty and modest girl, twelve years of age, with *grey hair!* peculiar to the *Mandans.* This unaccountable peculiarity belongs to the Mandans alone, and about one in twelve, of both sexes and of all ages, have the hair of a bright silvery grey, and exceedingly coarse and harsh, somewhat like a horse's mane.

135. *U'n-ka-hah-hón-shee-kow*, the Long Finger-nails; a brave.

136. *Máh-tah'p-ta-hah*, the One who rushes through the Middle.

137, 138, 139, 140, 141, 142. *San-ja-ka-kó-koh*, the Deceiving Wolf; and five others, in a group; names not preserved.

SHI-ENNE.

A small but very valiant tribe of 3000, neighbours of the Sioux, on the west, between the Black Hills and the Rocky Mountains: a very tall race of men, second in stature to the Osages.

143. *Né-hee-ó-ee-wóo-tis*, the Wolf on the Hill; Chief of the

tribe ; a noble and fine-looking fellow : this man has been known to own 100 horses at one time.

144. *Tis-se-wóo-na-tís*, She who bathes her Knees ; Wife of the Chief (No. 143) ; her hair in braid.

FLAT HEADS, or NEZ PERCÉS.

On the head-waters of the Columbia, west of the Rocky Mountains.

145. *Hee-oh'ks-te-kin*, the Rabbit's Skin Leggins ; a brave, in a very beautiful dress.

146. *H'co-a-h'co-a-h'cotes-min*, No Horns on his Head ; a brave, a very handsome man, in a beautiful dress.

147. ( ) Woman and Child ; showing the manner in which the heads of the children are flattened.

CHIN-OOK.

On the lower parts of the Columbia, near the Pacific Ocean.

148. *Hee-doh'ge-ats*, ———— ; a young man, eighteen years of age.

BLACK FEET.

A very warlike and hostile tribe of 50,000, including the *Peagans Cotonnés* and *Gros-ventres de Prairies*, occupying the head-waters of the Missouri, extending a great way into the British territory on the north, and into the Rocky Mountains on the west. Rather low in stature, broad chested, square shouldered, richly clad, and well armed, living in skin lodges. 12,000 of them destroyed by smallpox within the year 1838 !

149. *Stu-mick-o-súcks*, the Buffalo's Black Fat ; Chief of the tribe, in a splendid costume, richly garnished with porcupine-quills, and fringed with scalp-locks.

150. *Eeh-nís-kim*, the Crystal Stone ; wife of the Chief (No. 149).

151. *In-ne-ó-cose*, the Buffalo's Child ; a warrior, full-length, with *medicine-bag* of otter-skin.

152. *Peh-tó-pe-kiss*, the Eagle's Ribs ; Chief of the " *Blood Band*," full-length, in splendid dress ; head-dress of horns of the buffalo and ermines' tails ; lance in his hand and two *medicine-bags*.

153. *Mix-ke-móte-skin-na*, the Iron Horn ; warrior, in a splendid dress.

154. *Peh-no-máh-kan*, He who runs down the Hill.

155. *Ah'-kay-ee-píx-en,* the Woman who Strikes Many; full-length; dress of mountain-sheep skin.

156. *Méh-tóom,* the Hill.

157. *Tcha-dés-sa-ko-máh-pee,* the Bear's Child, with war-club.

158. *Wún-nes-tou,* the White Buffalo; a *medicine-man* or *doctor,* with his *medicine* or *mystery* shield.

159. *Tcha-aés-ka-ding,* ——— ——— ; boy, four years old, wearing his robe made of the skin of a racoon : this boy is grandson of the Chief , and is expected to be his successor.

160. *Peh-tó-pe-kiss,* the Eagle's Ribs ; Chief of the Blood Band ; splendid dress.

> This man boasted to me that he had killed eight white men (trappers) in his country ; he said that they had repeatedly told the traders that they should not catch the beaver in their country, and if they continued to do it they would kill them.

161. (   ) ——————, a *medicine-man,* or *doctor,* performing his *medicines* or *mysteries* over a dying man, with the skin of a yellow bear and other curious articles of dress thrown over him ; with his mystery rattle and mystery spear, which, he supposes, possess a supernatural power in the art of healing and curing the sick.

CROWS (BEL-ANT-SE-A.)

> A tribe of 7000, on the head-waters of the Yellow Stone River, extending their hunts and their wars into the Rocky Mountains—inveterate enemies of the Black Feet ; tall, fine-limbed men, graceful and gentlemanly in deportment, and the most richly and tastefully clad of any Indians on the continent. Skin lodges, many of which are tastefully ornamented and painted like the one standing in the room.

162. *Cháh-ee-chópes,* the Four Wolves; a Chief, a fine-looking fellow ; his hair reaching the ground ; his *medicine* (mystery) *bag* of the skin of the ermine.

> This man was in mourning, having some of his locks cut off.

163. *Eé-hée-a-duck-cée-a,* He who ties his Hair before ; a man of six feet stature, whose natural hair drags on the ground as he walks.

164. *Pa-rís-ka-róo-pa,* the Two Crows; Chief of a band ; his hair sweeps the ground ; his head-dress made of the eagle's skin entire ; he holds in his hand his lance and two *medicine*-bags, the one of his own instituting, the other taken from his enemy, whom he had killed in battle.

165. *Hó-ra-tó-a,* ——————; a brave, wrapped in his robe, and his hair reaching to the ground ; his spear in his hand, and bow and quiver slung.

166. *Oó-je-en-á-he-a,* the Woman who lives in the Bear's Den ; her hair cut off, she being in mourning.

167. *Duhk-gits-o-ó-see,* the Red Bear.

168. *Pa-ris-ka-róo-pa,* the Two Crows (the younger), called the "Philosopher."

    A young man distinguished as an orator and wise man, though the character of his face and head would almost appear like a deformity.

169. *Bi-éets-ee-cure,* the Very Sweet Man.

170. *Ba-da-ah-chón-du,* He who jumps over Every One ; on a wild horse, with war-eagle head-dress on his horse's and his own head ; with shield, bow, quiver, and lance ; his long hair floating in the wind.

————•————

GROS-VENTRES
(MIN-A-TAR-REES), People of the Willows.

    A small tribe, near neighbours and friends of the Mandans, speaking the Crow language, and probably have, at a former period, strayed away from them ; numbering about 1100.

171. *Eh-toh'k-pah-she-pée-shah,* the Black Mocassin ; Chief; over a hundred years old ; sits in his lodge, smoking a handsome pipe ; his arms and ornaments hanging on a post by the side of his bed.   (Since dead.)

172. *E'e-a-chín-che-a,* the Red Thunder ; the son of the Black Mocassin (No. 171), represented in the costume of a warrior.

173. *Pa-ris-ka-róo-pa,* the Two Crows ; with a handsome shirt, ornamented with ermine, and necklace of grisly bears' claws.

    This man is now the head Chief of the tribe.

174. (   ), ——————; woman, the wife of the Two Crows (No. 173).

175. *Seet-sé-be-a,* the Mid-day Sun ; a pretty girl, in mountain-sheep skin dress, and fan of the eagle's tail in her hand.

————•————

CREES (KNIS-TE-NEUX).

A small tribe of 4000, in *Her Majesty's dominions*, neighbours of the Black Feet, and always at war with them ; desperate warriors ; small and light in stature. Half of them have recently died of the smallpox since I was amongst them.

176. *Eeh-tow-wées-ka-zeet*, He who has Eyes behind him ; one of the foremost braves of the tribe, in a handsome dress.

This man visited Washington with the Indian agent, Major Sanford, a few years since.

177. *Tsee-moúnt*, a Great Wonder ; woman carrying her Infant in her robe.

178. *Tow-ée-ka-wet*, ————— ; woman.

AS-SIN-NE-BOINS (STONE BOILERS).

A tribe of 8000, occupying the country from the mouth of the Yellow Stone River to Lake Winnepeg, in her *British Majesty's dominions*, speaking the Sioux or Dahcota language, ranging about, like them, in skin lodges, and no doubt a severed band of that great nation. 4000 of these people destroyed by the smallpox in 1838, since I was amongst them.

179. *Wi-jún-jon*, the Pigeon's Egg Head ; one of the most distinguished young warriors of the tribe.

He was taken to Washington in 1832 by Major Sanford, the Indian agent ; after he went home he was condemned as a liar, and killed, in consequence of the *incredible* stories which he told of the whites.—(See him on *his way to, and returning from*, Washington, No. 475.)

180. *Chin-cha-pee*, the Fire Bug that creeps ; wife of Wi-jún-jon (No. 179) ; her face painted red, and in her hand a stick, used by the women in those regions for digging the " pomme blanche," or prairie turnip.

181. (   ) ; woman and child, in beautiful skin dresses.

CHIP-PE-WAYS (OJIBBEWAYS).

A very numerous tribe, of some 15,000 or 20,000, inhabiting a vast tract of country on the southern shores of Lake Superior, Lake of the Woods, and the Athabasca, extending a great way into the British territory ; residing in skin and bark lodges.

182. *Sha-có-pay*, the Six ; Chief of the Ojibbeways living north of the mouth of Yellow Stone River ; in a rich dress, with his battles emblazoned on it.

183. *Kay-a-gís-gis*, ————— ; a beautiful young woman pulling her hair out of braid.

184. *Háh-je-day-ah'-shee*, the Meeting Birds; a brave, with his war-club in his hand.

185. *Kay-ée-qua-da-kúm-ee-gísh-kum*, He who tries the Ground with his Foot.

186. *Jú-ah-kís-gaw*, —————; woman, with her child in a cradle or "crib."

187. *Cáh-be-múb-bee*, He who sits everywhere; a brave.

188. *O-tá-wah*, the Ottaway; a distinguished warrior.

189. *Ka-bés-hunk*, He who travels everywhere; a desperate warrior; his war-club in his left hand and a handsome pipe in his right; strikes with his left hand; eight quills in his head stand for eight scalps he had taken from the heads of the Sioux, his enemies.

190. *Ohj-ká-tchee-kum*, He who walks on the Sea.

191. *Gitch-ee-gáw-ga-oosh*, the Point that remains for ever; a very old and respectable Chief. (Since dead.)

192. *Gaw-záw que-dung*, He who halloos. Civilized.

193. *O'n-daig*, the Crow; a beau or dandy in full array, called by the Ojibbeways, *sha-wiz-zee-shah-go-tay-a*, a *harmless man*.

194. *I-an-be-w'ah-dick*, the Male Carabou; a brave, with a war-club in his hand.

195. (   ), —————; woman.

I-RO-QUOIS.

A small remnant of a tribe who were once very numerous and warlike, inhabiting the northern part of New York; only a few scattered individuals now living, who are merged in the neighbouring tribes.

196. *Nót-to-way*, a Chief, a temperate and excellent man, with a beautiful head-dress on.

197. *Chée-ah-ká-tchée*, —————; woman, wife of Nót-to-way (No. 196).

ÓT-TA-WAS.

A subdued and half-civilized tribe of 5500, speaking the Ojibbeway language, on the eastern shore of Lake Michigan. Agricultural and dissipated.

198. *Shin-gós-se-moon*, the Big Sail; a Chief, blind in one eye.

The effects of whisky and civilization are plainly discernible in this instance.

WIN-NE-BÁ-GOES.

A very fierce and warlike tribe, on the western shores of Lake Michigan, greatly reduced of late years by repeated attacks of the smallpox and the dissipated vices of civilized neighbours; number at this time 4400.

199, 200, 201, 202, 203, 204, 205, 206. *Du-cór-re-a,* ——; Chief of the tribe, and his family; a group of eight.

207. *Wah-chee-háhs-ka,* the Man who puts all out of Doors, called the "Boxer;" the largest man of the Winnebagoes; war-club in his hand, and rattle-snake skins on his arms.

208. *Won-de-tów-a,* the Wonder.

209. *Náw-káw,* Wood; formerly the head Chief, with his war-club on his arm.   (Dead.)

210. *Káw-kaw-ne-chóo-a,* —————; a brave.

211. *Wa-kon-chásh-kaw,* He who comes on the Thunder.

212. *Naw-naw-páy-ee,* the Soldier.

213. *Wah-kón-ze-kaw,* the Snake.

214. *Span-e-o-née-haw,* the Spaniard.

215. *Hoo-w'a-ne-kaw,* the Little Elk.

216. *No-ak-chóo-she-kaw,* He who breaks the Bushes.

217. *Naugh-háigh-hee-kaw,* He who moistens the Wood.

ME-NÓM-O-NIES.

Like the Winnebagoes, mostly destroyed by whisky and smallpox, and now numbering about 3500, and in a miserable state of dependence; on the western side of Lake Michigan.

218. *Mah-kée-mee-teuv,* the Grisly Bear; Chief of the nation, and chief of a delegation to Washington city in 1829 (since dead); handsome pipe in his hand, and wampum on his neck.

219. *Mee-chéet-e-neuh,* the Wounded Bear's Shoulder; wife of the Chief (No. 218).

220. *Chee-me-náh-na-quet,* the Great Cloud; son of the Chief (No. 218), a great rascal.

221. *Ko-mán-i-kin-o-haw,* the Little Whale; a brave, with his *medicine-wand,* his looking-glass, and scissors.

222. *Sha-wá-no,* the South; a noted warrior.

223. *Másh-kee-wet,* —————; a great beau, or dandy.

224. *Pah-shee-náu-shaw,* —————; a warrior.

225. *Tcha-káuks-o-ko-máugh,* the Great Chief (boy).

226. *Aú nah-kwet-to-hau-páy-o,* the One sitting in the Clouds ; a fine boy.

227. *Aúh-ka-nah-paw-wáh,* Earth Standing ; an old and very valiant warrior.

228. *Ko-mán-i-kin,* the Big Wave, called the "Philosopher ;" a very old and distinguished Chief.

229. *O-ho-páh-sha,* the Small Whoop ; a hard-visaged warrior, of most remarkable distinction.

230. *Ah-yaw-ne-tah-cár-ron,* ————— ; a warrior.

231. *Au-wáh-shew-kew,* the Female Bear ; wife of the above (No. 230).

232. *Coo-coo-coo,* the Owl ; a very old and emaciated Chief ; sits smoking a handsome pipe.

233. *Wáh-chees,* ————— ; a brave.

234. *Chésh-ko-tong,* He who sings the War-Song.

235, 236. Two in a group, names not known ; one with his war-club, and the other with his lute at his mouth.

POT-O-WÁT-O-MIE.

Once a numerous tribe, now numbering about 2700, reduced by small-pox and whisky—recently removed from the state of Indiana to the west-ern shores of the Missouri : semi-civilized.

237. *On-sáw-kie,* the Sac ; in the act of praying ; his prayer written in characters on a maple stick.

238. *Na-pów-sa,* the Bear Travelling in the Night ; one of the most influential Chiefs of the tribe.

239. *Kée-se,* ————— ; a woman.

KÍCK-A-POO.

On the frontier settlements ; semi-civilized ; number about 600 ; greatly reduced by smallpox and whisky.

240. *Kee-án-ne-kuk,* the Foremost Man, called the "*Prophet.*" Chief of the tribe, in the attitude of prayer.

This very shrewd fellow engraved on a maple stick, in characters, a prayer which was taught him by a Methodist Missionary ; and by intro-ducing it into the hands of every one of his tribe, who are enjoined to read it over every morning and evening as service, has acquired great celebrity and respect in his tribe, as well as a good store of their worldly goods, as he manufactures them all, and gets well paid for them.

241. *Ah-tón-we-tuck*, the Cock Turkey ; repeating his prayer from the stick in his hand, described above.

242. *Ma-shée-na*, the Elk's Horns ; a Sub-Chief, in the act of prayer, as above described.

243. *Ke-chím-qua*, the Big Bear ; wampum on his neck, and red flag in his hand, the symbol of war or " blood."

244. *A'h-tee-wát-o-mee*, —————; woman, with wampum and silver brooches in profusion on her neck.

245. *Shee-náh-wee*, —————.

KAS-KAS-KIA.

Once famed, numerous, and warlike, on the frontier, but now reduced to a few individuals by smallpox and whisky.

246. *Kee-món-saw*, the Little Chief; Chief; Semi-civilized.

247. *Wah-pe-séh-see*, —————; a very aged woman, mother of the above.

WÉE-AH.

Remnant of a tribe on the frontier; semi-civilized; reduced by whisky and disease; present number 200.

248. *Go-to-ków-páh-ah*, He who Stands by Himself; a brave of distinction, with his hatchet in his hand.

249. *Wah-pón-jee-a*, the Swan ; a warrior ; fine-looking fellow, with an European countenance.

250. *Wáh-pe-say*, the White.

PE-O-RI-A.

Also a small remnant of a tribe on the frontier, reduced by the same causes as *above*; present number about 200.

251. *Pah-mee-ców-ee-tah*, the Man who tracks ; a Chief ; remarkably fine head.

This man would never drink whisky.

252. *Wap-sha-ka-náh*, —————; a brave.

253. *Kee-mo-rá-nia*, No English ; a beau ; his face curiously painted, and looking-glass in his hand.

PI-AN-KE-SHAW.

A frontier tribe, reduced, as *above*; present number 170.

254. *Ni-a-có-mo*, to Fix with the Foot; a brave.
255. *Men-són-se-ah*, the Left Hand; a fierce-looking warrior, with a stone hatchet in his hand.

Í-O-WAY.

A small tribe on the frontier, reduced by smallpox and their enemies; living on the Missouri; number about 1400. Uncivilized fine-looking men.

256. *Notch-ee-níng-a*, No Heart, called "White Cloud;" Chief of the tribe; necklace of grisly bears' claws, and shield, bow and arrows in his hand.
257. *Pah-ta-cóo-chee*, the Shooting Cedar; a brave, with war-club on his arm.
258. *No-o-mún-nee*, He who walks in the Rain; warrior, with his pipe and tobacco-pouch in his hand.
259. *W'y-ee-yogh*, the Man of Sense; a brave, with a handsome pipe in his hand, and bears' claw necklace on his neck.
260. *Wos-cóm-mun*, the Busy Man; a brave.
262. *Mún-ne-o-ye*, ——————; woman.

SEN-E-CAS.

Near Lake Erie, State of New York. 1200, semi-civilized and agricultural. One of the tribes composing the great compact called the "Six Nations."

263. *Red Jacket*, Head Chief of the tribe; full-length, life size, standing on the "Table Rock," Niagara Falls.

This man was chief for many years, and so remained until his death, in 1831. Perhaps no Indian Sachem has ever lived on our frontier whose name and history are better known, or whose talents have been more generally admitted, than those of Red Jacket: he was, as a savage, very great in *council* and in *war*.

264. ( ), Deep Lake; an old Chief.
265. ( ), Round Island; warrior, half-blood.

A very handsome fellow.

266. ( ), Hard Hickory; a very ferocious-looking, but a mild and amiable man.
267. ( ), Good Hunter; a warrior.

268. (   ), —— String; a warrior, renowned.
269. (   ), Seneca Steele; a great libertine.   Hatchet in
     his hand.

O-NEI-DA.

Remnant of a tribe, State of New York, one of the "Six Nations;"
present number, 600.

270. (   ), Bread; the Chief, half-blood, civilized.
     A fine-looking and an excellent man.

TUS-KA-RÓ-RA.

New York, remnant of a numerous tribe, one of the confederacy of the
"Six Nations;" present number, 500; semi-civilized.

271. *Cú-sick*, ————————; son of the Chief.   Civilized and Chris-
     tianized.
     This man is a Baptist preacher, and quite an eloquent man.

MO-HEE-CON-NEU, or "MO-HE-GAN," the Good
Canoemen.

Now living near Green Bay; numbers, 400 or 500; formerly of Mas-
sachusetts; a band of the famous tribe of Pequots; now semi-civilized.

272. *Ee-tów-o-kaum*, Both Sides of the River;   Chief of the tribe,
     with a psalm-book in one hand, and a cane in the other.
     Christianized.
273. *Waun-naw-con*, the Dish (John W. Quinney); missionary
     preacher.   *Civilized.*

DEL-A-WARES.

Remains of a bold, daring, and numerous tribe, formerly of the States
of Pennsylvania and Delaware, and the terror of all the eastern tribes.
Gradually wasted away by wars, removals, small-pox, and whisky; now
living on the western borders of Missouri, and number only 824; lost by
small-pox, at different times, 10,000.

274. *Bód-a-sin*, ————————; the Chief; a distinguished man.
275. *Ni-có-man*, the Answer;   the second Chief, with bow and
     arrows in his hand.
276. *Non-on-dá-gon*, ————————; a Chief, with a ring in his nose.

SHA-WÁ-NO (SHAW-NEE).

Remains of a numerous tribe, formerly inhabiting part of Pennsylvania, afterwards Ohio, and recently removed west of the Mississippi River. Number at present about 1200; lost one-half by small-pox at different times. Semi-civilized; intemperate.

277. *Lay-láw-she-kaw*, He who goes up the River; a very aged man, Chief of the tribe; his ears slit and elongated by wearing weights in them, according to the custom of the tribe, and his hair whitened with age.

278. *Ká-te-quaw*, the Female Eagle; a fine-looking girl, daughter of the above Chief.

279. *Ten-squat-a-way*, the Open Door; called the "Shawnee Prophet," brother of Tecumsch; blind in one eye, holding his *medicine* or mystery fire in one hand, and his "*sacred string of beans*" in the other; a great *mystery-man*.

280. *Pah-te-cóo-saw*, the Straight Man. Semi-civilized.

281. *Lay-lóo-ah-pee-ái-shee-kaw*, Grass, Bush, and Blossom. Half civil, and *more than half* drunk.

282. *Cóo-ps-saw-qúay-te*, ———; woman (the Indescribable).

CHER-O-KEES.

Formerly of the State of Georgia, recently removed west of the Mississippi to the head-waters of the Arkansas. This tribe are mostly civilized and agriculturists; number, 22,000.

283. *John Ross*, a civilized and well-educated man, head Chief of the nation.

284. *Túch-ee*, called "Dutch;" first War-chief of the Cherokees; a fine-looking fellow, with a turbaned head.

I travelled and hunted with this man some months, when he guided the regiment of dragoons to the Camanchee and Pawnee villages: he is a great warrior and a remarkable hunter.

285. *Cól-lee*, ———; Chief of a band of the Cherokees. (Since dead.)

286. *Téh-ke-néh-kee*, the Black Coat; a Chief, also of considerable standing.

287. *Ah-hee-te-wáh-chee*, ———; a very pretty woman, in civilized dress, her hair falling over her shoulders.

T 2

MUS-KÓ-GEE (CREEK).

Recently removed from Georgia and Alabama to the Arkansas, 700 miles west of the Mississippi. Present number, 21,000; semi-civilized and agricultural.

288. *Steeh-tcha-kó-me-co*, the Great King, called, "Ben Perryman;" one of the Chiefs of the tribe.

289. *Hól-te-mál-te-téz-te-néek-ee*, —————, "Sam Perryman;" brother of the Chief above, and a jolly companionable man.

290. *Wat-ál-le-go*, —————, a brave.

291. *Hose-put-o-káw-gee*, —————; a brave.

292. *Tchow-ee-pút-o-kaw*, —————; woman.

293. *Tel-maz-há-za*, —————; a warrior of great distinction.

———◆———

CHOC-TAW.

Recently removed by Government from the States of Georgia and Alabama to the Arkansas, 700 miles west of the Mississippi. Present number, 15,000; semi-civilized.

294. *Mó-sho-la-túb-bee*, He who puts out and kills; first Chief of the tribe.

A gentlemanly-looking man (died recently of small-pox).

295. *Kút-tee-o-túb-bee*, How did he kill? A noted brave.

296. *Há-tchoo-túc-knee*, the Snapping Turtle; half-bred and well-educated man.

297. —————, woman; hair in braid; remarkable expression.

298. *Tul-lock-chísh-ko*, He who drinks the Juice of the Stone.

299. *Tul-lock-chísh-ko*, Full-length, in the dress and attitude of a ball-player, with ball-sticks in his hand, and tail, made of while horse-hair, attached to his belt.

———◆———

SEM-I-NÓ-LEE (RUNAWAY); 3000.

Occupying the peninsula of Florida; semi-civilized, partly agricultural. The Government have succeeded in removing about one-half of them to the Arkansas, during the last four years, at the expense of 32,000,000 dollars, the lives of 28 or 30 officers, and 600 soldiers.

300. *Mick-e-no-páh*, —————; first Chief of the tribe; full-length, sitting cross-legged.

This man owned 100 negroes when the war broke out, and was raising large and valuable crops of corn and cotton.

301. *Os-ce-o-lá*, the Black Drink; a warrior of very great distinction.

> Painted only five days before his death, while he was a prisoner of war at Fort Moultrie. This remarkable man, though not a chief, took the lead in the war, and was evidently (at the time he was captured) followed by the chiefs, and looked upon as the *master-spirit* of the war.

302. *Ee-mat-lá*, King Philip; an old man, second Chief.

> Like Osceola, he died while a prisoner, soon after I painted him.

303. *Ye-hów-lo-gee*, the Cloud; a Chief who distinguished himself in the war.

304. *Co-ee-há-jo*, ————; a Chief, very conspicuous in the present war.

305. *Láh-shee*, the Licker; a half-breed warrior, called "Creek Billey."

306. *How-ee-dá-hee*, ————. a Seminolee woman.

307. ( ) ————; a Seminolee woman.

308. *Os-ce-o-lá*, the Black Drink. Full-length, with his rifle in his hand, calico dress, and trinkets, exactly as he was dressed and stood to be painted five days before his death.

————◆————

EU-CHEE.

> Remnant of a powerful tribe who once occupied the southern part of the peninsula of Florida, were overrun by the Creeks and Seminolees, the remnant of them merging into the Seminolee tribe, and living with them now as a part of their nation. Present number, 150.

309. *Etch-ée-fix-e-co*, the Deer without a Heart, called "*Euchee Jack;*" a Chief of considerable renown.

310. *Chee-a-ex-e-co*, ————; quite a modest and pretty girl, daughter of the above Chief.

LANDSCAPES, SPORTING SCENES, MANNERS, AND CUSTOMS.

————◆————

CERTIFICATES.

The Landscapes, Buffalo-hunting Scenes, &c., above mentioned, I have seen, and, although it has been thirty years since I travelled over that country, yet a considerable number of them I recognised as faithful representations, and the remainder of them are so much in the peculiar character of that country as to seem entirely familiar to me.

WM. CLARK, Superintendent of Indian Affairs.

The Landscape Views on the Missouri, Buffalo Hunts, and other scenes, taken by my friend Mr. Catlin, are correct delineations of the scenes they profess to represent, as I am perfectly well acquainted with the country, having passed through it more than a dozen times. And further I know that they were taken on the spot, from nature, as I was present when Mr. Catlin visited that country.

JOHN F. A. SANFORD, U. SS. Indian Agent.

It gives me great pleasure to be able to pronounce the Landscape Views, Views of Hunting, and other scenes taken on the Upper Missouri, by Mr. Catlin, to be correct delineations of the scenery they profess to represent; and although I was not present when they were taken in the field, I was able to identify almost every one between St. Louis and the grand bend of the Missouri.

J. L. BEAN, S. Agent of Indian Affairs.

I have seen Mr. Catlin's collection of *Indian Portraits*, many of which were familiar to me, and painted in my presence in their villages. I have spent the greater part of my life amongst the tribes and individuals he has represented, and I do not hesitate to pronounce them correct liknesses and easily recognised; also the sketches of their *Manners* and *Customs* I think are excellent, and the *Landscape Views* on the *Missouri* and *Mississippi* are correct representations.

K. M'KENZIE, of the Am. Fur Company, Mouth of Yellow Stone.

I have examined a series of paintings by Mr. Catlin, representing *Indian Buffalo Hunts, Landscapes,* &c.; and from an acquaintance of twenty-seven years with such scenes as are represented, I feel qualified to judge them, and do unhesitatingly pronounce them good and unexaggerated representations.

JNO. DOUGHERTY, Indian Agent for Pawnees, Omahas, and Otoes.

LANDSCAPES.

311. St. Louis (from the river below, in 1836), a town on the Mississippi, with 25,000 inhabitants.

312. View on Upper Mississippi, beautiful prairie bluffs, everywhere covered with a green turf.

313. "Bad Axe" battle-ground, where Black Hawk was defeated by General Atkinson, above Prairie du Chien. Indians making defence and swimming the river.

314. Chippeways gathering wild rice near the source of St. Peter's; shelling their rice into their bark canoes, by bending it over, and whipping it with sticks.

315. View near "Prairie la Crosse," beautiful prairie bluffs, above Prairie du Chien, Upper Mississippi.

316. "Cap o'lail" (garlic cape), a bold and picturesque promontory on Upper Mississippi.

317. Picturesque Bluffs above Prairie du Chien, Upper Mississippi.

318. "Pike's Tent," the highest bluff on the river, Upper Mississippi.

319. View of the "Cornice Rocks," and "Pike's Tent," in distance, 750 miles above St. Louis, on Upper Mississippi.

320. "Lover's Leap," on Lake Pepin, Upper Mississippi, a rock 500 feet high, where an Indian girl threw herself off a few years since, to avoid marrying the man to whom she was given by her father.

321. Falls of St. Anthony, 900 miles above St. Louis; perpendicular fall eighteen feet : Upper Mississippi.

322. Madame Ferrebault's Prairie from the river above; the author and his companion descending the river in a bark canoe, above Prairie du Chien, Upper Mississippi ; beautiful grass-covered bluffs.

323. "Little Falls," near the Falls of St. Anthony, on a small stream.

324. "La Montaigne que tremps l'Eau," Mississippi, above Prairie du Chien.

325. Cassville, below Prairie du Chien, Upper Mississippi ; a small village just commenced, in 1835.

326. Dubuque, a town in the lead-mining country.

327. Galena, a small town on Upper Mississippi, in the lead-mining district.

528. Rock Island, United States Garrison, Upper Mississippi.

329. Beautiful Prairie Bluffs, ditto.

330. Dubuque's Grave, ditto.

Dubuque was the first miner in the lead-mines under the Spanish grant. He built his own sepulchre, and raised a cross over it, on a beautiful bluff, overlooking the river, forty years ago, where it now stands.

331. River Bluffs, magnificent view, Upper Mississippi.

332. Fort Snelling, at the mouth of St. Peter's, U. S. Garrison, seven miles below the Falls of St. Anthony, Upper Mississippi.

333. Prairie du Chien, 500 miles above St. Louis, Upper Mississippi, United States Garrison.

334. Chippeway Village and Dog Feast at the Falls of St. Anthony ; lodges built with birch-bark : Upper Mississippi.

335. Sioux Village, Lake Calhoun, near Fort Snelling; lodges built with poles.

336. "Coteau des Prairies," head-waters of St. Peter's. My companion, Indian guide, and myself encamping at sunset, cooking by our fire, made of buffalo-dung.

337. "Pipestone Quarry," on the Coteau des Prairies, 300 miles N. W. from the Falls of St. Anthony, on the divide between the St. Peter's and Missouri.

> The place where the Indians get the stone for all their red pipes. The mineral, *red steatite*, variety differing from any other known locality — wall of solid, compact quartz, grey and rose colour, highly polished as if vitrified; the wall is two miles in length and thirty feet high, with a beautiful cascade leaping from its top into a basin. On the prairie, at the base of the wall, the pipeclay (steatite) is dug up at two and three feet depth. There are seen five immense granite boulders, under which there are two squaws, according to their tradition, who eternally dwell there—the guardian spirits of the place—and must be consulted before the pipestone can be dug up.

338. Sault de St. Mary's—Indians catching white fish in the rapids at the outlet of Lake Superior, by dipping their scoop nets.

339. Sault de St. Mary's from the Canadian Shore, Lake Superior, showing the United States Garrison in the distance.

340. View on the St. Peter's River, twenty miles above Fort Snelling.

341. View on the St. Peter's—Sioux Indians pursuing a Stag in their canoes.

342. Salt Meadows on the Upper Missouri, and great herds of buffalo—incrustation of salt, which looks like snow.

> Salt water flows over the prairie in the spring, and, evaporating during the summer, leaves the ground covered with muriate as white as snow.

343. Pawnee Village in Texas, at the base of a spur of the Rocky Mountains—lodges thatched with prairie-grass.

344. View on the Canadian, in Texas.

345. View of the junction of Red River with the False Washitta, in Texas.

346. Camanchee Village, in Texas, showing a spur of the Rocky Mountains in the distance—lodges made of buffalo-skins. Women dressing robes and drying meat.

347. View on the Wisconsin—Winnebagoes shooting ducks, in bark canoe.

348. Lac du Cygne (Swan Lake), near the Coteau des Prairies.

> A famous place, where myriads of white swans lay their eggs and hatch their young.

349. Beautiful Savannah in the pine-woods of Florida.

One of thousands of small lakes which have been gradually filled in with vegetation.

350. View on Lake St. Croix, Upper Mississippi.

351. View on the Canadian—Dragoons crossing, 1834.

352. Ta-wa-que-nah, or Rocky Mountain, near the Camanchee Village, Texas.

353. Camanchee Village, and Dragoons approaching it, showing the hospitable manner in which they were received by the Camanchees. Camanchee warriors all riding out and forming in a line, with a white flag, to receive the Dragoons.

354. White Sand Bluffs, on Santa Rosa Island; and Seminoles drying fish, near Pensacola, on the Gulf of Florida.

355. View of the " Stone Man Medicine," Coteau des Prairies.

A human figure of some rods in length, made on the top of a high bluff, by laying flat stones on the grass. A great *mystery* or *medicine* place of the Sioux.

356. Fort Winnebago, on the head of Fox River, an United States outpost.

357. Fort Howard, Green Bay, an U. S. outpost.

358. Fort Gibson, Arkansas, an U. S. outpost, 700 miles west of Mississippi river.

359. The " Short Tower," Wisconsin.

360. Passing the " Grand Chute " with bark canoe, Fox River.

361. View of Mackinaw, Lake Michigan, an U. S. outpost.

362. View in the " Cross Timbers," where General Leavenworth died on the Mexican borders.

363. View on Lower Missouri—alluvial banks falling in, with their huge cotton-woods, forming raft and snags, 600 miles above St. Louis.

364. View on Upper Missouri—the " Blackbird's Grave."

Where " Blackbird," Chief of the Omahas, was buried on his favourite war-horse, which was alive; 1100 miles above St. Louis.

365. View on Upper Missouri—"Blackbird's Grave," a back view; prairies enamelled with wild flowers.

366. View on Upper Missouri—" Brick Kilns," volcanic remains, clay bluffs, 200 feet, supporting large masses of red pumice, 1900 miles above St. Louis.

367. View on Upper Missouri—Foot war-party on the march, beautiful prairie—spies and scouts in advance.

368 View on Upper Missouri—Prairie Bluffs at sunrising, near mouth of Yellow Stone.

369. View on Upper Missouri—Mouth of the Platte; its junction with the Missouri, 900 miles above St. Louis.

370. View on Upper Missouri—Magnificent Clay Bluffs, 1800 miles above St. Louis; stupendous domes and ramparts, resembling some ancient ruins; streak of coal near the water's edge; and my little canoe, with myself and two men, Bogard and Bàtiste, descending the river.

371. View on Upper Missouri—Cabane's trading-house; Fur Company's establishment : 930 miles above St. Louis, showing a great avalanche of the bluffs.

372. View on Upper Missouri—View in the Grand Détour, 1900 miles above St. Louis. Magnificent clay bluffs, with red pumice-stone resting on their tops, and a party of Indians approaching buffalo.

373. View on Upper Missouri—Beautiful Grassy Bluffs, 110 miles above St Louis.

374. View on Upper Missouri—Prairie Meadows burning, and a party of Indians running from it in grass eight or ten feet high.
These scenes are terrific and hazardous in the extreme when the wind is blowing a gale.

375. View on Upper Missouri—Prairie Bluffs burning.

376. View on Upper Missouri—" Floyd's Grave," where Lewis and Clarke buried Serjeant Floyd thirty-three years since; a cedar post and sign over the grave.

377. View on Upper Missouri—Sioux encamped, dressing buffalo-meat, and robes.

378. View on Upper Missouri—" The Tower," 1100 miles above St. Louis.

379. View on upper Missouri—Distant view of the Mandan Village, 1800 miles above St. Louis.

380. View on Upper Missouri—Picturesque Clay Bluff, 1700 miles above St. Louis.

381. View on Upper Missouri—" Belle Vue "—Indian Agency of Major Dougherty, 870 miles above St. Louis.

382. View on Upper Missouri —Beautiful Clay Bluffs, 1900 miles above St. Louis.

383. View on Upper Missouri—Minatarree Village, earth-covered lodges, on Knife River, 1810 miles above St. Louis. Bàtiste, Bogard, and myself ferried across the river by an Indian woman, in a skin canoe, and Indians bathing in the stream.

384. View on Upper Missouri—Fort Pierre, Mouth of Teton River—Fur Company's trading-post, 1200 miles above St. Louis, with 600 lodges of Sioux Indians encamped about it, in skin lodges.

385. View on Upper Missouri—Nishnabottana Bluffs, 1070 miles above St. Louis.

386. View on Upper Missouri—Riccaree Village, with earth-covered lodges, 1600 miles above St. Louis.

387. View on Upper Missouri—South side of " Buffalo Island," showing the beautiful buffalo-bush, with its blue leaves, and bending down with fruit.

388. View on Upper Missouri—Mouth of Yellow Stone—Fur Company's Fort, their principal post, 2000 miles above St. Louis, and a large party of Knisteneux encamped about it.

389. View on Upper Missouri—the " Iron Bluff," 1200 miles above St. Louis, a beautiful subject for a landscape.

390. View on Upper Missouri—View in the " Big Bend," 1900 miles above St. Louis; showing the manner in which the conical bluffs on that river are formed; table-lands iu distance, rising several hundred feet above the summit level of the prairie.

391. View on Upper Missouri—View in the Big Bend—magnificent clay bluffs, with high table-land in the distance.

392. View on Upper Missouri—Back view of the Mandan Village, showing their mode of depositing their dead, on scaffolds, enveloped in skins, and of preserving and feeding the skulls; 1800 miles above St. Louis. Women feeding the skulls of their relatives with dishes of meat.

393. View on Upper Missouri—Prairie Buffs, 1100 miles above St. Louis.

394. View on Upper Missouri—" The Three Domes," 15 miles above Mandans. A singular group of clay bluffs, like immense domes, with skylights.

395. View on Upper Missouri—the " Square Hills," 1200 miles above St. Louis.

396. View on Upper Missiouri—River Bluffs and White Wolves n the foreground.

397. View on Upper Missouri—Beautiful Prairie Bluffs, above the Puncahs, 1050 miles above St. Louis.

398. View on Upper Missouri—Look from Floyd's Grave, 1300 miles above St. Louis.

399. View on Upper Missouri—River Bluffs, 1320 miles above St. Louis.

400. View on Upper Missouri—Buffalo herds crossing the river. Bàtiste, Bogard, and I, passing them in our bark canoe, with some danger to our lives. A buffalo scene in their *running season*.

401. View on Upper Missouri—Clay Bluffs, 20 miles above the Mandans.

402. View on Upper Missouri—Nishnabottana Bluffs.

403. View on Upper Missouri—Indians encamping at sunset.

SPORTING SCENES.

404. Buffalo Bull, grazing on the prairie in his native state.

405. Buffalo Cow, grazing on the prairie in her native state.

406. Wounded Buffalo, strewing his blood over the prairies.

407. Dying Buffalo, shot with an arrow, sinking down on his haunches.

408. Buffalo Chase—single death ; an Indian just drawing his arrow to its head.

409. Buffalo Chase—surround ; where I saw 300 killed in a few minutes by the Minatarrees, with arrows and lances only.

410. Buffalo Chase—numerous group ; chasing with bows and lances.

411. Buffalo Chase—numerous group ; chasing with bows and lances.

412. Buffalo Chase—Cow and Calf ; the bull protecting by attacking the assailants.

413. Buffalo Chase—Bulls making battle with men and horses.

414. Buffalo Hunt under the wolf-skin mask.

415. Buffalo Chase, Mouth of Yellow Stone ; animals dying on the ground passed over ; and my man Bàtiste swamped in crossing a creek.

416. Buffalo Chase in snow drift, with snow shoes.
417. Buffalo Chase in snow drift, with snow shoes; killing them for their robes, in great numbers.
418. Attack of the Bear (Grisly); Indians attacking with lances on horseback.
419. Antelope Shooting—decoyed up.
420. Sioux taking Musk-rats, near the St. Peter's; killing them with spears. Women and dogs encamped.
421. Bàtiste and I, running Buffalo; Mouth of Yellow Stone; a frog's leap.
422. "My turn now;" Bàtiste and I, and a Buffalo Bull, Upper Missouri.
423. Dying Bull in a snow drift.
424. Buffalo Bulls fighting, in *running season*, Upper Missouri.
425. Buffalo Bulls in their "*wallow;*" origin of the "*fairie circles*" on the prairie.
426. Grouse shooting—on the Missouri prairies.

AMUSEMENTS AND CUSTOMS.

427. Ball-play Dance, Choctaw.—Men and women dance around their respective stakes, at intervals, during the night preceding the play—four conjurors sit all night and smoke to the Great Spirit, at the point where the ball is to be started—and stakeholders guard the goods staked.
428. Ball-play of the Choctaws—*ball up*—one party painted white; each has two sticks with a web at their ends, in which they catch the ball and throw it—they all have tails of horse-hair or quills attached to their girdles or belts.

Each party has a limit or bye, beyond which it is their object to force the ball, which, if done, counts them one for game.

429. Ball-play—same as 428, excepting that the ball is *down*, which changes the scene.
430. Ball-play of the women, Prairie du Chien.—Calicoes and other presents are placed on a pole by the men—the women choose sides and play for them, to the great amusement of the men.

In this play there are two balls attached to the ends of a string eighteen inches in length: the women have a stick in each hand, on which they catch the string and throw it.

431. Game of " *Tchung-kee*" of the Mandans, the principal and most valued game of that tribe.

A beautiful athletic exercise, and one on which they often bet and risk all their personal goods and chattels.

432. Horse-Racing, Mandan, on a Race-Course back of the Village, in use on every fair-day.

433. Foot-Race, Mandans, on the same ground, and as often run.

434. Canoe-Race—Chippeways in Bark Canoes, near the Sault de St. Mary's ; an Indian *Regatta*, a thrilling scene.

435. Archery of the Mandans.

The strife is to prove who can get the greatest number of arrows flying in the air at a time, before the first one reaches the ground. The most of these are *portraits* closely studied from nature. I have seen some of them get eight arrows in the air at one time.

436. Dance of the Chiefs, Sioux.

A very unusual thing, as the dancing is generally left to the young men ; given to me expressly as a compliment by the chiefs, that I might make a painting of it.

437. Dog Dance, Sioux.

The dog's liver and heart are taken raw and bleeding, and placed upon a crotch ; and, being cut into slips, each man dances up to it, bites off and swallows a piece of it, boasting, at the same time, that he has thus swallowed a piece of the heart of his enemy, whom he has slain in battle.

438. Scalp Dance, Sioux—Women in the centre, holding the scalps on poles, and warriors dancing around, brandishing their war-weapons in the most frightful manner, and yelping as loud as they can scream.

439. Begging Dance, Sacs and Foxes, danced for the purpose of getting presents from the spectators.

440. Buffalo Dance, Mandans, with the mask of the buffalo on.

Danced to make buffalo come, when they are like to starve for want of food. Song to the Great Spirit, imploring him to send them buffalo, and they will cook the best of it for him.

441. Ball-play Dance, Choctaws.

442. Dance to the Berdash, Sac and Fox.

An unaccountable and ludicrous custom amongst the Sacs and Foxes, which admits not of an entire explanation.

443. Beggars' Dance, (Sioux,) for presents.

444. Dance to the Medicine Bag of the Brave, Sacs and Foxes.

Warriors returned from battle, with scalps, dance in front of the widow's lodge, whose husband has been killed. They sing to his medicine-bag, which is hung on a bush, and throw presents to the widow.

445. Braves' Dance, Boasting, &c., Sioux.

446. Green Corn Dance, Minnatarree—Sacrificing the first kettle to the Great Spirit.

Four medicine men, whose bodies are painted with white clay, dance around the kettle until the corn is well boiled; and they then burn it to cinders, as an offering to the Great Spirit. The fire is then destroyed, and *new fire* created by rubbing two sticks together, with which the corn for their own feast is cooked.

447. **Bear Dance, Sioux**—Preparing for a Bear Hunt—Song to the Great Spirit, praying for success.

448. **Discovery Dance, Sacs and Foxes**—A Pantomime; pretending to discover game, or an enemy.

A very picturesque and pleasing dance.

449. **Eagle Dance, Choctaw**—Holding the eagle's tail in the hand, and bodies painted white.

Given in honour of that valiant bird.

450. **Slave Dance, Sacs and Foxes.**

A society of young men, who volunteer to be slaves for two years, and elect their chief or master; they are then exempt from slavish duties during the remainder of their lives, and are allowed to go on war-parties.

451. **Snow-shoe Dance, Ojibbeway**—danced at the first fall of snow, with snow shoes on the feet.

Song of thanks to the Great Spirit.

452. **Brave's Dance, Ojibbeway**—bragging and boasting.

453. **Pipe Dance, Assineboins.**

Each dancer is "*smoked*" by the chief, who sits smoking his pipe, and then *pulled* up into the dance.

454. **Straw Dance, Sioux.**

Children made to dance with burning straws tied to their bodies, to make them tough and brave.

455. **Sham Fight, Mandan Boys**—School of practice every morning at sunrise, back of the village—instructed in it by the chiefs and braves.

456. **Sham Scalp Dance, by the Mandan Boys**—danced in the village when they come in, in honour of a sham victory.

457. **War Dance of the Sioux.**

Each warrior, in turn, jumps through the fire, and then advances shouting and boasting, and taking his oath, as he "strikes the *reddened post*."

458. **Foot War Party in Council, Mandan.**

Stopping to rest and take a smoke; chief with a war-eagle head-dress on; their shields and weapons lying on the ground behind them.

459. **Camanchee War Party**—the Chief discovering the enemy and urging on his men, at sunrise.

460. **Religious Ceremony**; a Sioux, with splints through his flesh, and his body hanging to a pole, with his medicine-bag in his hand, looks at the sun from its rising to its setting.

A voluntary cruel self-torture, which entitles him to great respect for the remainder of his life, as a *medicine* or *mystery* man.

461. Dragoons on the March, and a band of Buffalo breaking through their ranks, in Texas, 1835.

462. Prairie Dog Village.

Myriads of these curious little animals sometimes are found in one village, which will extend several miles. The animals are about twice the size of a rat, and not unlike it in appearance and many of their habits. They dig holes in the ground, and the dirt which is thrown up makes a little mound, on which they sit and bark when danger approaches. They feed upon the grass, which is their only food.

463. "Smoking Horses," a curious custom of the Sacs and Foxes.

Foxes, going to war, come to the Sacs, to beg for horses; they sit in a circle and smoke, and the young men ride around them, and cut their shoulders with their whips until the blood runs, then dismount and present a horse.

464. Mandans attacking a party of Riccarees, whom they had driven into a ravine, near the Mandan village, where they killed the whole number.

465. Chippeways making the portage around the Falls of St. Anthony, with two hundred bark canoes, in 1835.

466. Camanchees moving, and Dog Fight—dogs as well as horses drag the lodge-poles with packs upon them.

These fights generally begin with the dogs, and end in desperate battles amongst the squaws, to the great amusement of the men.

467. White Wolves attacking a Buffalo Bull.

468. Ditto, ditto—a parley.

469. *My horse " Charley " and I,* at sunrise, near the Neosho, on an extensive prairie, encamping on the grass; my saddle for a pillow, two buffalo-skins for my bed, my gun in my arms; a coffee-pot and tin cup, a fire made of buffalo-dung, and Charley (a Camanchee clay-bank mustang) picketed near me.

With him alone I crossed the prairie from Fort Gibson, on the Arkansas, to St. Louis, 550 miles.

470. *Sioux worshipping at the Red Boulders.* A large boulder and two small ones, bearing some resemblance to a buffalo cow and two calves, painted red by the Indians, and regarded by them with superstitious reverence, near the "Coteau des Prairies."

471. *Camanchee Warrior lancing an Osage,* at full speed.

472. *Camanchees giving the Arrows* to the *Medicine Rock.*

A curious superstition of the Camanchees: going to war, they have no faith in their success, unless they pass a celebrated painted rock, where they appease the spirit of war (who resides there), by riding by it at full gallop, and sacrificing their best arrow by throwing it against the side of the ledge.

473. *"Bàtiste, Bogard, and I," approaching Buffalo*, on the Missouri.

474. *Wi-jun-jon (an Assinneboin Chief), going to and returning from Washington.*

This man was taken to that city in 1832, in a beautiful Indian dress, by Major Sanford, the Indian agent, and returned to his country the next spring, in a Colonel's uniform. He lectured a while to his people on the customs of the whites, when he was denounced by them for telling lies, which he had learned of the whites, and was, by his own people, put to death at the mouth of the Yellow Stone.

475. *"Butte de Mort,"* Upper Missouri, a great burial-place of the Sioux, called by the French *"Butte de Mort,"* Hill of Death.

Regarded by the Indians with great dread and superstition. There are several thousand buffalo and human skulls, perfectly bleached and curiously arranged about it.

476. *"Rain-making,"* amongst the Mandans, a very curious custom. Medicine-men performing their mysteries inside of the lodge, and young men volunteer to stand upon the lodge from sunrise until sundown, in turn, commanding it to rain.

Each one has to hazard the disgrace which attaches (when he descends at sundown) to a fruitless attempt; and he who succeeds acquires a lasting reputation as a *Mystery or Medicine man. They never fail to make it rain!* as this ceremony continues from day to day until rain comes.

477. *"Smoking the Shield."* A young warrior, making his shield, invites his friends to a carouse and a feast, who dance around his shield as it is smoking and hardening over a fire built in the ground.

478. *"The Thunder's Nest"* (Nid du Tonnerre), and a party of Indians cautiously approaching it, Coteau des Prairies.

Tradition of the Sioux is that in this little bunch of bushes the thunders are hatched out by quite a small bird, about as large (say their *Medicine-men*, who profess to have seen it) as the end of a man's thumb. She sits on her eggs, and they hatch out in claps of thunder. No one approaches within several rods of the place.

479. *Sac and Fox Indians sailing in canoes*, by holding up their blankets.

480. *Grand Tournament of the Camanchees*, and a Sham Fight in a large encampment, on the borders of Texas.

481. *Bogard, Bàtiste, and I, travelling* through a Missouri bottom, grass ten feet high.

482. *Band of Sioux*, moving.

483. *Bogard, Bàtiste, and I*, descending the Missouri River.

484. *Bogard, Bàtiste, and I*, eating our breakfast on a pile of drift wood, Upper Missouri.

485. *Medicine Buffalo* of the Sioux, the figure of a buffalo cut out of the turf on the prairie, and visited by the Indians going on a buffalo-hunt.

486. *Bogard, Bàtiste, and I*, chasing a herd of buffalo in high grass, on a Missouri bottom.

487. Feats of Horsemanship.

Camanchees throwing themselves on the side of their horses, while at full speed, to evade their enemies' arrows—a most wonderful feat.

488. Camanchee War Party meeting the Dragoons ; and one of their bravest men advancing to shake hands with Colonel Dodge, with a piece of white buffalo-skin on the point of his lance.   On the Mexican frontier, 1835.

489. An Indian Wedding, Assinneboin—young man making presents to the father of the girl.

490. Crow at his Toilette, oiling his long hair with bear's grease.

491. Crow Lodge, of twenty-five buffalo-skins, beautifully ornamented.

This spendid lodge, with all its poles and furniture, was brought from the foot of the Rocky Mountains.

492. Pawnee Lodge, thatched with prairie grass, in form of a straw beehive.

493. Camanchee Lodge, of buffalo-skins.

494. Dog Feast, Sioux ; a religious feast.

Given to Mr. Sanford (Indian agent), Mr. Chouteau, Mr. M'Kenzie, and myself, in a Sioux village, 1400 miles above St. Louis, 1833. The only food was dog's meat, and this is the highest honour they can confer on a stranger.

495. An Indian Council, Sioux—Chiefs in profound deliberation.

496. Camanchee War Party, mounted on wild horses, armed with shields, bows, and lances.

497. Scalping, Sioux ; showing the mode of taking the scalp.

498. Scalping, Mandans—" Conqueror conquered."

From a story of the Mandans—took place in front of the Mandan village.

499. Wild Horses at Play, Texas, of all colours, like a kennel of hounds.

500. Throwing the Laso, with a noose, which falls over the horse's neck.

501. Breaking down the Wild Horse, with hobbles on his fore feet, and the laso around his under jaw.

502. *A Bird's-Eye View* of the *Mandan* Village, 1800 miles above St. Louis, on the west bank of the Missouri River.

The lodges are covered with earth, and so compactly fixed by long use, that men, women, and children recline and play upon their tops in pleasant weather.

These lodges vary in size from forty to fifty feet in diameter, and are all of a circular form. The village is protected in front by the river, with a bank forty feet high, and on the back part by a piquet of timber set firmly in the ground. Back of the village, on the prairie, are seen the scaffolds on which their dead bodies are laid to decay, being wrapped in several skins of buffalo, and tightly bandaged.

In the middle of the village is an open area of 150 feet in diameter, in which their public games and festivals are held. In the centre of that is their "Big Canoe," a curb made of planks, which is an object of religious veneration. Over the Medicine (or mystery) Lodge are seen hanging on the tops of poles several sacrifices to the Great Spirit of blue and black cloths, which have been bought at great prices, and there left to hang and decay.

503. The *Interior of a Mandan Lodge*, showing the manner in which it is constructed of poles, and covered with dirt. The Chief is seen smoking his pipe, and his family grouped around him.

At the head of each warrior's bed is seen a post with his ornaments hanging on it, and also his *buffalo-mask*, which every man *keeps to dance* the buffalo-dance. Some of these lodges contain thirty or forty persons, and the beds are seen extending around the side of the lodge, all with *sacking bottoms*, made of a buffalo-skin, and the frames of the bed covered with dressed skins.

*** Reader, the hospitable and friendly Mandans, who were about 2000 in number when I was amongst them and painted these pictures, have recently been destroyed by the small-pox. It is a melancholy fact, that only thirty-one were left of the number, and these have been destroyed by their enemy, so that their tribe is extinct, and they hold nowhere an existence on earth.

Nearly twenty of their portraits can be seen on the walls, and several other paintings of their games and amusements.

MANDAN RELIGIOUS CEREMONIES.

CERTIFICATE.

We hereby certify that we witnessed, in company with Mr. Catlin, in the Mandan village, the ceremonies represented in the four paintings to which this certificate refers, and that he has therein faithfully represented those scenes as we saw them transacted, without any addition or exaggeration.

J. KIP, Agent Amer. Fur Company.
L. CRAWFORD, Clerk.
ABRAHAM BOGARD.

Mandan Village, July 20th, 1833.

504. Interior View of the *Medicine* (or *Mystery*) Lodge of Mandans, during the first three days of an *Annual Ceremony*.

This ceremony continues four days and nights in succession, in commemoration of the subsiding of the *flood*; and also for the purpose of conducting all the young men, as they arrive at manhood, through an ordeal of *voluntary torture*, which, when endured, entitles them to the respect of the chiefs, and also to the privileges of going on war-parties, and gaining reputation in war. The floor and sides of the lodge are ornamented with green willow-boughs. The young men who are to do penance, by being tortured, are seen lying around the sides of the lodge, their bodies covered with clay of different colours, and their respective shields and weapons hanging over their heads. In the middle of the lodge lies the old *Medicine-man*, who has charge of the lodge: he cries to the Great Spirit all the time, and watches these young men, who are here to fast and thirst for four days and nights, preparatory to the torture. Behind him, on the floor, is seen a scalping-knife and a bunch of splints, which are to be passed through the flesh; and over their heads are seen also the cords let down from the top of the lodge, with which they are to be hung up by the flesh.

On the ground, and in front of the picture, are four sacks (containing several gallons each of water), made of the skin of the buffalo's neck, in form of a large tortoise, lying on its back. These are objects of veneration, and have the appearance of great antiquity.

By the side of them are two *she-she-quoi*, or rattles, which are used, as well as the others, as a part of the music for the dance in the next picture.

505. This picture, which is a continuation of the ceremonies, is a representation of the Buffalo Dance, which they call *Bel-lohck-nah-pick* (the Bull Dance).

To the strict observance of which they attribute the coming of Buffalo to supply them with food during the season. This scene is exceedingly grotesque, and takes place several times in each day outside the lodge, and around the curb, or "Big Canoe," whilst the young men still remain in the lodge, as seen in the other picture. For this dance, however, the four sacks of water are brought out and beat upon, and the old *medicine-man* comes out and leans against the "Big Canoe" with his medicine-pipe in his hand, and cries. The principal actors in this scene are eight men dancing the Buffalo Dance, with the skins of buffalo on them, and a bunch of green willows on their backs. There are many other figures, whose offices are very curious and interesting, but which must be left for my *Lectures* or *Notes* to describe. The black figure on the left they call *O-kee-hee-de* (the Evil Spirit), who enters the village from the prairie, alarming the women, who cry for assistance, and are relieved by the old *medicine-man;* and the Evil Spirit is at length disarmed of his lance, which is broken by the women, and he is driven by them in disgrace out of the village. The whole nation are present on this occasion as spectators and actors in these strange scenes.

506. Represents what they call Pohk-hong (the Cutting Scene). It shows the inside of the Medicine Lodge, the same as is seen in the first picture (505).

This is on the fourth day of the ceremonies, in the afternoon. A number of the young men are seen reclining and fasting, as in the first picture; others of them have been operated upon by the torturers, and taken out of the lodge; and others yet are seen in the midst of those horrid cruelties. One is seen smiling whilst the knife and the splints are passing through his flesh. One is seen hanging by the splints run through the flesh on his shoulders, and drawn up by men on the top of the lodge. Another is seen hung up by the pectoral muscles, with four buffalo-skulls attached to splints through the flesh on his arms and legs; and each is turned round by another, with a pole, until he faints, and then he is let down. One is seen as he is lowered to the ground; and another, who has been let down and got strength enough to crawl to the front part of the lodge, where he is offering to the Great Spirit the little finger of the left hand, by laying it on a buffalo-skull, where another chops it off with a hatchet. In the right of the picture are all the chiefs and dignitaries of the tribe looking on.

507. Represents what they call the "Last Race."

After they have all been tortured in the lodge in the above manner, they are led out of it with the weights, buffalo-skulls, &c. hanging to their flesh. Around the "Big Canoe" is a circle of young men formed, who hold a wreath of willow-boughs between them, and run round with all possible violence, yelling as loud as they can.

The young fellows who have been tortured are then led forward, and each one has two athletic and fresh young men (their bodies singularly painted), who step up to him, one on each side, and take him by a leathern strap, tied round the wrist, and run round, outside of the other circle, with all possible speed, forcing him forward till he faints, and then drag him with his face in the dirt until the weights are all disengaged from him, by tearing the flesh out, when they drop him, and he lies (to all appearance a *corpse*) until the Great Spirit gives him strength to rise and walk home to his lodge.

In this scene also the *medicine-man* leans against the "Big Canoe" and cries, and all the nation are spectators. Many pages would be required to give to the world a just description of these strange scenes; and they require to be described minutely in all their parts in order to be fully appreciated and understood. (A full account of these in my *Notes and Letters.*)

NINE OJIBBEWAYS,

WHO VISITED LONDON IN 1845.

508. *Ah-quee-we-zaints*, the Boy Chief; a venerable man of 72 years.

509. *Pat-au-a-quot-a-wee-be*, the Driving Cloud; a war-chief.

510. *Wee-nish-ka-wee-be*, the Flying Gull; a medicine-man.

511. *Sah-mah*, Tobacco.

512. *Gish-ee-gosh-e-gee*, the Moonlight Night.

513. *Not-een-a-akm*, the Strong Wind.

514. *Wos-see-ab-e-neuh-qua*; a woman.

515. *Nib-nab-ee-qua*; a young girl.

516. *Ne-bet-neuh-quat*; a woman.

FOURTEEN IOWAYS,

WHO VISITED LONDON AND PARIS IN 1845 AND 1846.

517. *Mew-hew-she-kaw*, the White Cloud; first Chief of the nation.
518. *Neu-mon-ya*, the Walking Rain; War-chief.
519. *Se-non-ti-yah*, the Blistered Feet; a medicine-man.
520. *Wash-ka-mon-ya*, the Fast Dancer; a warrior.
521. *Shon-ta-yi-ga*, the Little Wolf; a famous warrior.
522. *No-ho-mun-ya*, One who gives no Attention.
523. *Wa-ton-ye*, the Foremost Man.
524. *Wa-ta-wee-buck-a-na*, the Commanding General.

WOMEN.

525. *Ru-ton-ye-wee-ma*, the Strutting Pigeon; wife of White Cloud.
526. *Ru-ton-wee-me*, Pigeon on the Wing.
527. *O-kee-wee-me*, Female Bear that walks on the Back of another.
528. *Koon-za-ya-me*, Female War Eagle.
529. *Ta-pa-ta-me*, Wisdom; girl.
530. *Corsair;* a pappoose.

TWELVE OJIBBEWAYS,

WHO VISITED LONDON AND PARIS IN 1845 AND 1846.

531. *Maun-gua-daus*, a Great Hero; Chief, 41 years old.
532. *Say-say-gon*, the Hail Storm; 31 years old.
533. *Kee-che-us-sin*, the Strong Rock; 27 years old.
534. *Mush-ee-mong*, King of the Loons; 25 years old.
535. *Au-nim-much-kwa-um*, the Tempest Bird; 20 years old.
536. *A-wun-ne-wa-be*, the Bird of Thunder; 19 years old.
537. *Wa-bud-dick*, the Elk; 18 years old.
538. *Ud-je-jock*, the Pelican; 10 years old.
539. *Noo-din-no-kay*, the Furious Storm; 4 years old.
540. *Min-nis-sin-noo*, a Brave Warrior; 3 years old.

541. *Uh-wus-sig-gee-zigh-gook-kway*, the Woman of the Upper World ; 38 years old.

542. Pappoose, born in Salle Valentino, Paris.

---

543. *Death of the White Buffalo.* A feat of the Mandan Chiefs.

544. *A Sioux War Council.* The Chief Waneton speaking, and asking of the head Chief a war-party to go against the Sacs and Foxes.

545. *Battle between the Sioux and Sacs and Foxes.* The Sioux Chief killed and scalped on his horse's back. An historical fact.

546. *The Death of Ha-wan-je-tah*, the One Horn ; head Chief of the Sioux.

> Having been the accidental cause of the death of his only son, he threw himself in the way of a buffalo-bull. (See Catlin's *Notes*, vol. ii., for a full account.)

547. *The Long Speech.*

> It is an invariable rule amongst Indians, that while any one speaks in council no one can rise. *See-non-ty-a* (the Blistered Feet), a great *medicine-man*, made his favourite boast, that when he once rose in an Ioway council of war it happened unfortunately for the council that "he began to speak just as it began to snow."

548. *Battle of the Buffalo Bulls.*

549. *Buffaloes crossing a Ravine in a snow-drift.*

550. *Buffaloes crossing the Missouri on the ice.*

551. *Grisly Bears attacking a Buffalo Bull.*

552. *Indians spearing Salmon at Night by Torchlight.*

553. *Deer-hunting by Moonlight.*

554. *Deer-hunting by Torchlight, in bark canoes.*

555. *War Party attacked in their Camp at Night.*

INDIAN CURIOSITIES AND MANUFACTURES.

Amongst this most extensive and valuable collection of them in existence, a few of the most remarkable are

A CROW LODGE, OR WIGWAM.

A very splendid thing, brought from the foot of the Rocky Mountains, twenty-five feet in height, made of buffalo-skins, garnished and painted.   The poles (thirty in number) of pine, cut in the Rocky Mountains, have been long in use, were purchased with the lodge, and brought the whole distance.   This *wigwam* stands in   the   middle   of   the   gallery, and   will   shelter   eighty   or   more persons.

Indian Cradles, for carrying their pappooses.   *Lances, Calumets* or *Pipes of Peace, Ordinary Pipes, Tomahawks, Scalping Knives*, and *Scalps.*

A very full and valuable collection of *Men and Women's Dresses* from the different tribes, garnished and fringed with scalp-locks from their enemies' heads, *Bows, Quivers, Spears, Shields, War-Eagle and Raven Head-dresses, Necklaces, Mocassins, Belts, Pouches, War-Clubs, Robes, Mantles, Tobacco-Sacks, Wampums, Whistles, Rattles, Drums, Indian Saddles, Masks for their Mystery Dances, &c. &c.*

Amongst the immense collection of Indian curiosities, &c., too numerous to be described in the catalogue, there are Skulls from different tribes, of very great interest; and particularly several from the *Flat-heads*, showing perfectly the character of this unaccountable custom, and also the Flat-head cradles, illustrating the process by which these artificial distortions are produced.

Indian Cloths, Robes, &c., manufactured by the Indians from the mountain sheep's wool, and from wild dogs' hair, beautifully spun, coloured, and woven.

END OF VOL. I.

London : Printed by WILLIAM CLOWES and SONS, Stamford Street.

The borrower must return this item on or before the last date stamped below. If another user places a recall for this item, the borrower will be notified of the need for an earlier return.

*Non-receipt of overdue notices does **not** exempt the borrower from overdue fines.*

Please handle with care.
Thank you for helping to preserve library collections at Harvard.

CPSIA information can be obtained
at www.ICGtesting.com
Printed in the USA
BVHW080321130819
555626BV00013BB/2884/P